Constitutional History of Serbia

Balkan Studies Library

VOLUME 30

Constitutional History of Serbia

by

Dragoljub Popović

BRILL | Ferdinand Schöningh

Cover illustrations: The first page of the Serbian Constitution of 1838. Karlovci Gymnasium, Wikimedia Commons/Public Domain. "The Takovski Uprising" by Paja Jovanovic, 1898. National Museum in Belgrade, Wikimedia Commons/Public Domain.

Bibliographic information published by the Deutsche Nationalbibliothek

The Deutsche Nationalbibliothek lists this publication in the Deutsche Nationalbibliografie; detailed bibliographic data available online: http://dnb.d-nb.de

www.schoeningh.de

Cover design: Celine van Hoek, Leiden
Production: Brill Deutschland GmbH, Paderborn

ISSN 1877-6272
ISBN 978-3-506-79102-3 (hardback)
ISBN 978-3-657-79102-6 (e-book)

Table of Contents

Acknowledgements

I owe my sincere gratitude to Professor Zoran Milutinović, the editor, as well as to two unknown reviewers, for their comments and suggestions, which considerably improved the original manuscript of this book.

Dragoljub Popović

Foreword

More than eighty years have elapsed since the constitutional history of Serbia was the topic of one comprehensive volume in Serbian language. As evidenced by the title of his book, Jaša Prodanović used the approach consisting of researching constitutional developments in the light of political events.[1] His method of displaying the subject was purely chronological. Prodanović's book on the constitutional history of Serbia in one volume remained an exception, for the sake of two reasons. Firstly, because of the enormous intellectual influence of the work of Slobodan Jovanović, and secondly due to the university curricula.

Between the two world wars, Slobodan Jovanović, the greatest Serbian legal scholar of all time, wrote a constitutional history of Serbia in a series of volumes, but his books went far beyond that topic. Jovanović's work is unique and goes far beyond the framework of constitutional history as a discipline. Several books of his Completed Works published in 1990 concerned different historical periods, containing an overwhelming amount of information which marvellously merged constitutional history with topics concerning political, economic and social issues.[2] Jovanović had a brilliant style which made him a champion of Serbian scholarship and academic writing. He nevertheless did not produce a work on the constitutional history of Serbia in one comprehensive volume.

Constitutional history has never been an independent and separate subject in the university curricula of Serbian and former Yugoslav law schools. It has been treated within the framework of the discipline called History of State and Law, or more recently Legal History. It therefore was a part of courses that were wider in scope and not solely focused on constitutional developments.

Constitutional history also found a place in university courses on positive constitutional law. The authors of scholarly manuals included certain passages on constitutional history within these. However, they only partly dealt with national constitutional history, preferring to cover constitutional developments in comparative law.

---

1 J. Prodanović, *Ustavni razvitak i ustavne borbe u Srbiji* [Constitutional developments and constitutional struggles in Serbia], Belgrade 1936.

2 Cf. S. Jovanović, *Sabrana dela 3* [Collected works 3], Belgrade 1990, which consists of two books devoted to the respective periods of 1842–58 and 1859–68, followed by *Sabrana dela 4–7*, which treat the period between 1869 and 1903.

Despite the unfavourable treatment of constitutional history in university curricula, Serbian academics from various universities have published numerous studies on different topics in the constitutional history of Serbia. For their valuable contributions they deserve to be mentioned, taking into account those belonging to the generation of the author of this volume, and those younger than this: M. Stefanovski, O. Popović-Obradović, Z. Mirković, Lj. Krkljuš, S. Šarkić, S. Stojčić, D. Nikolić, N. Ranđelović and M. Pavlović.

Turning to the publications in English on Serbian constitutional history, the situation seems comparable, at least as regards treating the subject in a single volume. The leading publication is more than forty years old. It is a small, elegantly presented book by Alex Dragnich, a Vanderbilt scholar, who displayed the constitutional history of Serbia *en grandes lignes*, as a process of striving for parliamentary government.[3] Dragnich's book contained less than 140 pages. As for the method, it was very much like Prodanović's, which was written in Serbian. Dragnich described his approach as 'largely chronological', but nevertheless stated that the main theme of his book was 'the struggle for democracy, and particularly the drive to secure parliamentary government'.[4] What appears to be lacking in the works of both Prodanović and Dragnich is an approach that encompasses a thorough study of constitutionalism as a concept.

Many new endeavours have occurred, and new publications come to light, in the last couple of years. This was in great part owing to a project conducted within the scope of the research of the Max Planck Institute for European Legal History in Frankfurt am Main. Professors Stolleis and Simon were in charge of a huge project concerning the whole region of South-East Europe. Professor Simon was the editor in chief of the second volume of the book encompassing the legal and constitutional developments of Serbia.[5] Serbian contributors were, in order of appearance in the volume, D. Popović, S. Šarkić, U. Stanković, Z. Mirković, S. Avramović, D. Nikolić and Ž. Bujuklić.

Some other valuable recent contributions to the study of the constitutional history of Serbia deserve to be mentioned. M. Stefanovski published a book in Serbian, researching the emergence of the 1869 Constitution.[6] On the other

3 A. Dragnich, *The Development of Parliamentary Government in Serbia*, New York 1978.

4 A. Dragnich, *The Development*, 9.

5 Th. Simon (ed.), *Konflikt und Koexistenz. Die Rechtsordnungen Südosteuropas im 19. und 20. Jahrhundert, Band II* [Conflict and coexistence: The legal systems of Southeast Europe in the 19th and 20th centuries, Volume II], Frankfurt am Main 2017. Most of the contributions were in English; some, however, were in German.

6 M. Stefanovski, *Postanak Namesničkog ustava* [The emergence of the Regency Constitution], Belgrade 2016.

hand, T. Marinković largely treated historical topics in his book on Serbian constitutional law published in English.[7]

Owing to the publications mentioned, one might say that the state of scholarly research has become ripe for a new synthesis. There is the need for a fresh approach to the constitutional history of Serbia which is both chronological and subject oriented, one that makes an effort to study the evolution of constitutionalism as well as narrating events chronologically. At the same time, publishing on the constitutional history of Serbia in English reaches out to a wider range of academics and offers the possibility of discussion on a broader basis.

This book is a case study of the constitutional developments of a small nation, which like many others has adopted foreign cultural concepts and political institutions. It consists of three parts. Part One deals with mainstream developments, taking into account events and the evolution of institutions. Part Two displays the evolution of two fundamental concepts – human rights and the rule of law. A chapter on teaching constitutional law in Serbia, indispensable for a proper understanding of Serbian constitutional history, concludes that part. Part Three deals with mutual relations between Serbia and Yugoslavia, from the standpoint of constitutional developments. It was necessary to do this to complete the case study of a country that had been an independent state and then a part of Yugoslavia, before returning to the form of nation-state.

7 T. Marinković, 'Serbia', in: *International Encyclopedia of Laws: Constitutional Law*, Alphen aan den Rijn 2019.

PART ONE

Developments

CHAPTER 1

Origins of the Modern Nation

1.1 Nation Building

It is not easy to determine the beginning of Serbian nation building. The issue has at least two aspects, because the process of nation building can be perceived in its political and cultural dimensions. The former has been most frequently mentioned, primarily because of its simplicity in approach, which is based on establishing political facts. According to that criterion the nation building started with the armed rebellion against the Ottomans in the Pashalik of Belgrade, which is today in central Serbia, in the year 1804. The events are known as the First Serbian Uprising; this lasted until 1813, when the Serbian insurgents were defeated by the Ottoman troops.

The cultural aspect of the process of nation building is, however, older than the political one, and its importance matches the political aspect. It dates back to the second half of the eighteenth century, and its starting point cannot be precisely established. It was in the epoch of rationalism that the Serbs, living without their own nation-state and under different monarchies, slowly launched the process of self-identification, so as to perceive themselves as a nation among nations.

The emergence of the self-identification process in modern times can be found in the works on history, and also in literature. To sketch an image of the intellectual evolution, one can refer to the historical works of Pavle Julinac and Jovan Rajić. It was in Venice in 1765 that Julinac (1730–85) published his *Short Introduction to the History of Slavo-Serbian People*, the first modern history of the Serbs. In 1794–95 Rajić (1726–1801) published his work of a broader scope in Vienna and Moscow, entitled *The History of Various Slavic Peoples, particularly the Bulgarians, Croats and Serbs*. As for the literary works, Dositej Obradović (1739–1811) is considered to be the founder of modern Serbian literature. He contributed to the self-identification of the Serbian people by the introduction of vernacular elements into the literary idiom.[1] The milestone publication in that respect was his autobiographical work, which appeared in Leipzig in 1783,

1 Cf. the attitude of the most prominent literary critic at the turn of 19th and 20th centuries on the issue. J. Skerlić, 'Dositej Obradović', an essay reproduced in D. Obradović, *Izabrana dela* [Selected works], Belgrade 2005, 28.

 | DOI:10.30965/9783657791026_002

under the title *The Life and Adventures of Dimitrije Obradović Who as a Monk Was Given the Name Dositej*.

It therefore seems justified to place the beginning of the Serbian nation building in the last quarter of the eighteenth century.[2] The political aspect of the process was to some extent the aftermath of the intellectual endeavours performed on the path towards modern national self-identification which had preceded it. The fruits of political action were nevertheless decisive, because after the defeat of the Serbian insurgents in 1813 the Second Serbian Uprising followed in 1815, which ended in a ceasefire and a compromise with the Ottoman armed forces. On the grounds of the compromise a specific form of Serbian home-rule was introduced in the pashalic of Belgrade, which indeed was the germ of today's Serbia. The Serbs were subsequently granted autonomy by the imperial acts of the Ottoman Porte in the 1830s; those acts created a vassal Principality of Serbia, under the Sultan's sovereign power.

The nation building as a cultural process continued into the first half of the 19th century both in the Serbian principality and in the neighbouring regions of the Habsburg monarchy inhabited by the Serbs. The Serbs living in the Habsburg monarchy formed a middle class of merchants and small entrepreneurs and were better educated than their ethnic brethren living in the autonomous principality. Nevertheless, the latter as a defined political unit took a lead role in political matters and became pivotal in further developments.

The situation as described creates a problem in determining the period in which the nation building was accomplished. The delimitation of the period should primarily concern social developments in the vassal Principality of Serbia, because of its outstanding historical role. One could assess that the rounding up of the process of nation building occurred when a whole network of national institutions was set up in the principality. Those institutions do not encompass exclusively political ones, but also economic and cultural, such as the national post service, the university, the codification of law, the foundation of a learned society and the like. These were all achieved towards the beginning of the second half of the nineteenth century, which leads to the conclusion that Serbian nation building should be considered as completed in the 1850s.[3] Nevertheless some scholars were inclined to extend the period of Serbian nation building into the second half of the nineteenth century. Alex

---

2 Cf. S. Marković, 'Patterns of National Identity Development among the Balkan Orthodox Christians during the Nineteenth Century', *Balcanica* XLIV (2013), 216, who finds the 'nucleus of the Serbian nation' in the years between 1783 and 1803.

3 On the achievements in respective sectors cf. D. Jevtić, 'Novi vek – Srbija', in: D. Jevtić and D. Popović, *Narodna pravna istorija* [People's legal history], Belgrade 2012, 123–47.

Dragnich was one such scholar; he distinguished between the nation building period and the period of constitutionalism, which made him extend the nation building until the second half of the 1860s.[4]

In summary there were three landmarks in the formation of the Serbian nation during the first half of the nineteenth century. The first was the uprising of 1804 against the Ottoman rule in the pashalic of Belgrade, which is today in the central part of Serbia. The second was the outcome of the uprising, which resulted in the institution of home-rule in 1815 and later on of autonomy for the Serbs, granted by the Ottoman Porte. The third landmark came decades later. It was the instauration of the oligarchs' regime in a country that was a vassal state, dependent on the Sultan. The oligarchs came to power in 1842.

1.2 Events

The First Serbian Uprising

Towards the end of the eighteenth century the Serbs living in the Pashalik of Belgrade slowly started overcoming the backwardness of their society. The territory of the pashalic was at the northern frontier of the Ottoman Empire. In the course of centuries many Serbs had migrated to the neighbouring Habsburg Empire to escape the Ottoman rule, so that the Serbs lived on both sides of the frontier. The Serbs inhabiting the pashalic of Belgrade were mostly peasants, living in large families (*zadruga*). Their social life was governed by the patriarchal institutions of a rural society. Nevertheless, there were signs of economic growth at the turn of the century. The agricultural production in the pashalic of Belgrade was increasing, and the Serbs, for the most part owners of small plots of land, launched themselves into trade of agricultural products. The main article of export was livestock, destined for the market in the Habsburg monarchy. Fruit and cereals were also exported to the same destination.[5]

Economic progress was, however, hindered due to political circumstances, provoked by the regime installed in the pashalic. Notably, Turkish feudal lords called *dahis* (or *dahije* in Serbian) refused to obey the Sultan, and in order to collect and enjoy their feudal revenue they imposed a regime of terror. They murdered the lawful governor of Belgrade in 1801 and ruled on their own.[6] The

---

4 Cf. A. Dragnich, *The Development*, 11–48.

5 For the Serbian society on the eve of the First Serbian Uprising, cf. V. Stojančević, 'Srpski narod pred prvi ustanak' [Serbian people before the first uprising], in: *Istorija srpskog naroda V – 1* [History of the Serbian people, vol. 1], Belgrade 1981, 17–24.

6 ibid. 27–28.

feudal duties heavily burdened Serbian peasants in a country of half a million people in which there were practically no cities, except for the suburbs of Turkish fortresses, only partly inhabited by the Serbs. The terror reached its peak at the beginning of 1804, when the dahis committed a massacre of more than one hundred prominent Serbs who were local leaders. In Serbian leaders of this type were called *knez*, which is a word that also means prince, but they were not noblemen, for there was no nobility in the country. A knez simply enjoyed undisputed authority within a local community, based on the confidence of his neighbours in a village or region.

The massacre of January 1804, which is known in Serbian as *seča knezova* (slaughter of knezes), led to revolt and an uprising broke out in February of the same year. This was the First Serbian Uprising mentioned above, whose leader was Karađorđe Petrović (1768–1817). He was a livestock trader who had volunteered in the Serbian militia (in German *Freikorps*), fighting on the Austrian side in the Austro-Turkish War of 1787–88.[7] Karađorđe obtained his position of leader spontaneously, by acclamation of the people who had gathered in order to start the rebellion. He was proclaimed to be *vožd*. The word is an ancient form of the word *vođa*, which means leader in Serbian. Karađorđe at first took the title of commander, which was subsequently altered to leader.[8]

Initially the aim of Serbian insurgents was to put an end to the terror. They asked the Sultan and the Imperial Porte for protection. In the course of time, however, after constantly fighting Ottoman troops and owing to their successful warfare, the insurgents rephrased their tasks and put forward the idea of ending the subjugation to the Ottoman rule. Notably, the concept of nation-state did not exist at the beginning of the 19th century. Therefore the primordial idea of the insurgents was to live under the rule of a Christian monarch. The idea led to a dilemma: should the Serbs try to become subjects of the Russian or the Austrian Emperor? The former was Orthodox, like the Serbs, but his realm was far away; the latter was a Roman Catholic, and his empire was just across the river, neighbouring Serbia. When the Serbian Uprising broke out, the Habsburgs, who had been masters of Serbia from 1717 to 1739, indeed had plans to incorporate Serbia into the Habsburg monarchy, as a simple province without any special feature of its status. The Serbs were not particularly sympathetic to such projects, and preferred the Russian protection.[9]

7 S. Šarkić, 'The Beginning of Serbian Constitutionality', in: Th. Simon (ed.), *Konflikt und Koexistenz*, 234.

8 Cf. M. Pavlović, *Srpska pravna historija* [Serbian legal history], Kragujevac 2005, 222.

9 Cf. D. Popović, 'The Dawn of Human Rights in Serbian Legal Thought', in: Th. Simon (ed.), *Konflikt und Koexistenz*, 194–95.

Put simply, the attitude of the Serbs towards the problem of becoming subjects of a Christian monarch was based on the assumption that the Russians, being 'fraternal, Slavic and Orthodox' would help them.[10] The insurgents sent a deputation to Russia to ask for help. The Russian government, for its part, sent envoys to Serbia. One of the envoys was an Italian who had previously served in the French army, before joining the Russian military corps, in which he had the rank of colonel. His name was Philippo Paulucci (1779–1849). On his arrival in Serbia he got in touch with the insurgent leaders and managed to convince them to sign a document, which was drafted in a strange mixture of Russian and Church Slavonic languages. The document of July 1807 has been named the Paulucci Convention. It consisted of thirteen provisions, of which the first was the most important.[11] In the first provision of the document the Serbian people expressed the desire to live under the protection of the Russian Tsar, as well as to obtain from him a governor to rule the country and a constitution. *Konstitucija* was the word used in the strange mixture of languages in which the document was drafted. This was a relatively clear idea of annexing Serbia to Russia. However, for those researching the attitude of the leaders of the First Serbian Uprising towards the issue of the future status of Serbia, the destiny of this convention appears to be decisive.

The Russian envoy did not sign the convention, whereas three of the Serbian leaders put their signatures on it. Following the custom of that time, the signatories were expected to use their seals as well. Two of them did so, but Karađorđe, the vožd, made an exception. He declared he had lost his seal.[12] This little episode reveals something profound. It was clear that the leader of the national revolution, which the uprising indeed was, failed to rub stamp the idea of integrating Serbia into a Christian Empire. The germ of th ation-state was already present in his mind.

As of December 1806, the insurgents were in control of the Belg e fortress. The formation of the Serbian government structure was already prog-ress, and the government institutions had moved to Belgrade. The c in of the Serbian institutions of government lay in Karađorđe holding the der's position and commanding the insurgent troops with much popular s port. The next stage of the process came in 1805 with the formation of gove ient,

10 S. Šarkić, 'The Beginning', 236.

11 On the events that led to negotiations between Paulucci and the Serbian leade s well as for the text of the Convention, cf. S. Šarkić, 'The Beginning', 238–41.

12 V. Karadžić, *Istorijski spisi* [Historical writings], Belgrade 1985, 21–23; S. Šark 'The Beginning', 241–42.

or Government Council (*praviteljstvujušči sovjet* in old-style Serbian; no longer used today). This was the first body of central government in Serbia.

Despite the fact that at the very beginning of the insurrection against the Turks the insurgents had chosen one leader, recognising his command and leadership, the Serbs were fighting in their respective regions of the country under the command of local leaders. In other words, there was no sufficient coordination between the leaders. Moreover, some of the local leaders showed tendencies to proceed independently in many ways. Vuk Karadžić (1787–1864), the famous language reformer, linguist and historian, who witnessed the events, left a lengthy document on the history of Serbian government institutions during the First Uprising. His text has the title *Praviteljstvujušči Sovjet Serbski za vremena Kara-Đorđijeva ili Otimanje ondašnjijeh velikaša oko vlasti* (The Serbian Government Council of Karađorđe's time or the power struggle of the magnates).[13] Early in the evolution of the First Serbian Uprising the insurgent leaders had already become aware of the fact that it was necessary to create a government structure. As already mentioned, they faced the challenge by founding the Government Council (*Praviteljstvujušči sovjet*).

Vuk Karadžić reports that the Government Council was founded in the summer of 1805, at the Assembly of Notables. He mentioned the names of the members of the newly founded body. The first among them was Matija Nenadović, an Orthodox priest highly involved in the insurgency against the Turks. Božidar Grujović was mentioned as secretary of the Council's chancery. Nenadović, who became the Council President, i.e. the first prime minister of modern Serbia, had been the head of the delegation of Serbian insurgents sent to Russia to ask for help. On his way to St Petersburg he met Grujović, a young Serbian lawyer from Austria, who had just been appointed professor of law in the University of Kharkov. Grujović joined the insurgents sent to Russia to ask for help and came to Serbia with them. Apart from these, five more members were subsequently appointed to sit in the Government Council, coming from various parts of Serbia. The Government Council resided in two Orthodox monasteries, before moving to the city of Smederevo, where it organised the chancery. Eventually the Government Council moved to Belgrade, after the liberation of the city. Once in Belgrade this body was enlarged, and at the request of the Council itself twelve new members were appointed from different parts of the country.[14] Before it settled in Belgrade, the Government Council was reshuffled and its new President became Mladen Milovanović, Karađorđe's close friend. He remained in office until 1809. By the end of his term of office

13 V. Karadžić, *Istorijski spisi*, 9–69.
14 ibid. 12–15.

the question of organisation of power in Serbia had already been put on the agenda. Its essence concerned the installation of a monarchy in Serbia.[15]

At the beginning of the First Serbian Uprising Karađorđe was elected supreme military commander, but he showed the intention of becoming a monarch and moreover making that position hereditary in his family. Such an intention was vehemently opposed by some of the magnates, whose opposition gained the support of Russian diplomats.[16] There were almost permanent tensions between Karađorđe on the one side and the magnates on the other. It was Karađorđe himself who launched the idea of settling the issue of relations between the vožd and the magnates on grounds of principle. The idea materialised in constitutional acts of November 1808 and January 1811. Stojan Novaković, historian, university professor, diplomat and politician, reproduced these acts in his book on the constitutional history of Serbia during the First Serbian Uprising.[17] Both constitutional acts were peculiar from a legal standpoint, and their substance clearly reflected the circumstances in which they were adopted.

The constitutional act of 1808 was adopted in the Government Council session. It encompassed two commitments. One was the pledge of loyalty and obedience of all commanders and the entire population of the country, through which Karađorđe and his legitimate descendants were each recognised as first and supreme leader. The other was Karađorđe's commitment to safeguard the people and to recognise the Government Council as the country's supreme court.[18]

The constitutional act of 1811 was adopted in a session of the Assembly of Notables in the presence of more than sixty persons.[19] It was more elaborately written than the one of the previous constitutional act. However, the form remained the same. The act consisted of the exchange of oaths between Karađorđe and the notables. Neither of the constitutional acts passed in Serbia in times of the First Uprising could qualify as a constitution in the proper meaning of the term. They were hardly operative, short lasting, and above all they neither laid down foundations of the institutions of government, nor regulated their status and relations. The constitutional acts of 1808 and

15 S. Šarkić, 'The Beginning', 262–64.

16 ibid. 261–62.

17 S. Novaković, *Ustavno pitanje i zakoni Karađorđeva vremena* [The constitutional question and the laws of Karadjordje's time], Belgrade 1907, 47–48 and 90–93 for the texts. See also D. Janković, *Srpska država Prvog ustanka* [The Serbian state of the First Uprising], Belgrade 1984, 149–73.

18 S. Šarkić, 'The Beginning', 265.

19 ibid. 272.

1811 nevertheless evidence the emergence of two phenomena – the monarchy and the oligarchy. Those two were in conflict, but neither managed to prevail decisively, because of the sequence of events. The Serbs failed to resist a new attack. The Ottoman imperial power defeated the Serbian insurgent troops in 1813.[20] Serbia once again found itself under the Ottoman rule.

Home-rule and Autonomy

After the defeat in 1813, Serbian military commanders split into two groups. Some of them went into exile in the neighbouring Habsburg Empire. Indeed, this was the case for the leader of the First Serbian Uprising – Karađorđe Petrović. Karađorđe left the country, while some of his brothers in arms remained in Serbia, despite the fear of Turkish terror and revenge. Peace, however, could not be properly restored in the country. Between September and December 1814 a rebellion took place, which the Ottoman Porte managed to suppress with an armed hand. Some months later, another insurrection started in April 1815; it was given the name of the Second Serbian Uprising. The commander in chief of the Turkish troops then opted for a compromise instead of an armed confrontation with the insurgents. He made a deal with the leader of the Second Serbian Uprising, Miloš Obrenović (1780–1860). The deal, which was never put in writing, provided for a specific kind of ethnic power-sharing in Serbia. Miloš was to rule over the Serbs, whereas the Turkish pasha, who remained resident in the Belgrade fortress, was to rule over the Turks across the whole land.[21] That is how a home-rule of the Serbs was introduced, and it had as a consequence the streamlining of Serbian policies into diplomatic endeavours aimed at granting the status of autonomy to Serbia by the Ottoman Porte.

At the beginning of his rule Miloš's policy focused on two goals, both of which concerned constitutional issues. One of them was the status of Serbia: Miloš strove for a new Serbian autonomy that would be placed on solid ground, i.e. granted by the Ottoman Porte. Such a strongly founded status for the country was to replace the precarious arrangement that the Serbian leader had previously had to make with the Ottoman pasha. The other goal consisted of Miloš's efforts to achieve recognition of his personal status as a ruler of Serbia. For that, he needed the formal recognition of his compatriots, but also an act of the Ottoman Porte. The two goals were intertwined and provided grounds

---

20 Vuk Karadžić reports, although without being certain about the figures, that there were some 80,000 Turks against 15,000 Serbs in the decisive operations near the Drina river. Cf V. Karadžić, *Istorijski spisi*, 281.

21 ibid. 127.

for manipulation. Miloš was in the position to identify his personal interest with that of the emerging Serbian nation.

Miloš Obrenović was an illiterate peasant. He was skillful in contacts with people in the sense that his discourse was simple, which made him spontaneous. Therefore he did not create distance from the masses of peasants he was usually addressing. At the same time, he was the leader of his country, which was on the path towards emancipation from foreign rule. One of the terms Miloš put forward for defending the national cause was that he should be treated as a proper ruler, both inside and outside of Serbia. Soon after the beginning of his rule, the Serbian people recognised him as a ruler. In a session of assembly in November 1817 an act was adopted which proclaimed Miloš Obrenović to be *verhovni knez i pravitelj* (Supreme Prince and Ruler) of the people. Under the same act the people pledged loyalty to the Prince, stating that they were to faithfully obey the Prince's commands issued in pursuing benefit to the fatherland. Miloš was thus recognised as a Prince. The assembly that adopted the act could be considered the National Assembly (*Narodno-serbski sabor*), at least in name, although Dragnich rightly observes that Miloš 'picked and controlled' the members of the assembly.[22] By virtue of the act, however, his ruling power became legal and legitimate from the internal, Serbian standpoint.[23]

Despite the fact that when communicating with the masses Miloš did not make himself different from his interlocutors, he wanted by all means to be placed before any other of his compatriots. Little by little, irrespective of his peasant background, he started manifesting features of a monarch, placing himself above the people. As time went on, his self-confidence and vanity were on the rise. Vuk Karadžić witnessed the phenomenon. He left a long description of Miloš's rule under the title *Tajni spisi o knezu Milošu Obrenoviću – Osobita građa za srpsku istoriju našega vremena* (Secret documents on Prince Miloš Obrenović – historical material for contemporary Serbian history).[24] Vuk reports that in the beginning Miloš was satisfied with the title of *knez*. After a while he wanted to distinguish himself from other officials who had the same title, e.g. a village knez. Miloš therefore introduced the older version of the same word and began to use the title of *knjaz*. It so happened, however, that someone explained to the Serbian Prince that in Russian language there was no difference between the two forms of the same word, so that for the

22 A. Dragnich, *The Development*, 18.

23 M. Stefanovski, *Srednjovekovna shvatanja uzorne vladavine* [Medieval conceptions of exemplary rule], Belgrade 2018, 198–99. The author included a chapter on the period of home-rule in Serbia, considering it an aftermath of the medieval times, which were her main subject of interest.

24 V. Karadžić, *Istorijski spisi*, 159–209.

Russians each Serbian *knez* was indeed *knjaz*. Since the distinguishing thus failed, Prince Miloš ordered, to satisfy his vanity, that any other official traditionally called *knez* should change their title to *kapetan* (captain). In the same way the Prince reserved for himself and his brothers and sons the right to be addressed as *gospodar* (master), while any other was entitled to be addressed as *gospodin* (gentleman).[25]

On the one hand, the Prince made efforts to distinguish himself from the ordinary people, while on the other the status of Serbia was not legally recognised by the Ottoman Porte. The Prince, although proclaimed by the people, still lacked recognition from the Sultan, who was the sovereign of Serbia. To resolve that issue, Miloš launched wide-ranging diplomatic efforts. Towards the end of the 1820s these entered into the final stage and eventually proved fruitful in December 1830 when the Sultan issued an act recognising autonomy to Serbia. The act is known among the Serbs, including in the academic writing, as the *1830 Hatt-i Serif*. The *Hatt-i Seriff* was a Turkish expression for the form of the act, which was sealed in gold. In modern Serbian the word has become a separate noun, written *hatišerif*, and pronounced accordingly.

The 1830 Hatt-i Serif was the act of recognition of Serbian autonomy under the Sultan's sovereign power. Serbia became an autonomous territory with its own, independent internal government. The Turks still living in Serbia were ordered by the Sultan to leave the country and sell their property. The Ottoman Porte was to remove troops from Serbia, except for garrisons in six Serbian cities, including Belgrade, which were to remain in fortresses. The Serbian Prince was allowed to keep a regiment of his own armed force, to preserve order in the country. The Serbs were allowed to organise their own postal and public health services, educational institutions and the like. Alongside the 1830 Hatt-i Serif the Sultan administered another act known as the *berat*, by virtue of which Miloš was recognised as the hereditary Prince of Serbia. His male ascendants were to come to power by their own right.[26]

The 1830 Hatt-i Serif was communicated to the Serbian people in a solemn way. It was proclaimed and read in public, first in Turkish and then in Serbian. Aware of the fact that the Turks might express dissatisfaction with the provisions of the act granting autonomy to Serbia, Miloš chose a place away from the Belgrade fortress to read the act in public and celebrate its entering into force. Nowadays this location is in central Belgrade, near St Mark's Church. The whole atmosphere was solemn and cheerful at the same time. An anecdote

---

25 ibid. 181.

26 For the texts of the 1830 Hatišerif and the berat, cf. M. Gavrilović, *Miloš Obrenović, knj. III* [Miloš Obrenović, vol. III], Belgrade 1908, 604–09.

says that on the occasion Prince Miloš declared, 'Brethren, we have become a nation.'

The Question of Constitution

The 1830 Hatt-i Serif provided for Serbian government institutions in its paragraphs 2 and 15, which were in contradiction. In paragraph 2 it was stipulated that Miloš Obrenović obtained the title of Prince, which was to be preserved in his family. The Prince was to govern 'in cooperation with an assembly composed of notables of the country'. The word used to denote the body was *skupština* in Serbian. The text of paragraph 15, however, referred to the same body but used the word 'council' (*sovjet* in the old-style Serbian). It read: 'So long as the above-mentioned members of the council do not commit any offence against my Sublime Porte ... they shall remain in office'.[27]

Behind the dilemma created by the text stood a discrepancy of the attitudes of the Russian diplomacy on the one side and the Serbian Prince on the other. The Russians were pushing the Ottoman Porte to settle the matter of autonomy for Serbia. At the same time, they wanted to impose limits on the princely power in Serbia, and favoured the introduction of a council composed of notables for this purpose. Miloš opposed such a design, for he preferred the assembly as a body he would cooperate with. His skills in communicating with masses of peasants put him in the position to pursue populist policies by streamlining the work of assemblies. The text of the 1830 Hatt-i Serif remained unclear in this respect, but the Serbian Prince and his entourage turned to a broader issue based on the wording of the act introducing Serbian autonomy. The 1830 Hatt-i Serif granted 'the independent internal government' (*nezavisimo vnutrenje pravlenije* in old-style Serbian). The Serbs interpreted the notion of independent internal government in the sense that the vassal principality of Serbia was entitled to adopt a constitution. That is how the constitutional question came to the agenda.

Already in 1831 two documents were drafted in Serbia regarding the constitution. To date, their authors remain unknown. Although never published, they nevertheless attracted the attention of academics. The two drafts have not played a prominent role in the constitutional history of Serbia, but they evidence several characteristic traits of the situation in Serbia right after obtaining autonomous status.

---

27 On paragraphs 2 and 15 of the 1830 Hatišerif, cf. D. Popović, *Prapočetak srpskoga parlamentarizma – klice i preuranjen plod* [The very beginning of Serbian parliamentarism – sprouts and premature fruit], Belgrade 1996, 18–20. Unless otherwise indicated all translations are mine – DP.

First and foremost, the drafts of 1831 display the opinion of the Serbian Prince and his close collaborators that the vassal principality of Serbia was entitled to adopt a constitution. In respect of the term by which to designate such an act, there was some hesitation. One of the drafts had the name *Plan konštitucije* (Plan of constitution), whereas the other was named *Ustav* (the word which equals the term 'constitution' in modern Serbian). The third important feature of the drafts concerns the organisation of power in Serbia as envisaged in those documents. In that respect the two drafts were different. The one called *Ustav* included some provisions on the separation of powers. However, in both drafts the body that was to cooperate with the Prince in legislation was small: eight senators in one draft and nine councillors in the other. In one of the drafts the Prince was empowered to put forward three candidates for each place in the Senate before the assembly, which was to elect one of them to sit. In the other the councillors of the Popular Council were to be elected by the people, but the Prince had the authority to approve the election. It remains a mystery who the authors of the drafts were, because there were no learned lawyers in the country at the time when they emerged. However, the preponderance of the Prince in the organisation of power in both drafts offers clear evidence for the conclusion that the drafts of 1831 originated in the Prince's entourage.[28]

Prince Miloš was in a specific position in terms of the 1830 Hatišerif. Serbia was recognised as a hereditary principality of which Miloš was the Prince, but he was nevertheless supposed to rule the country with the coopertation of a certain body, which the Sultan's act designated ambiguously. The Serbian Prince was illiterate and had no knowledge of political institutions, but he was used to communicating with Ottoman officials, which made him distrustful and cunning. Being by no means ready to give up pulling the strings of power in the country, he wanted to rule with ministers that he could appoint and remove at will; alternatively, if there should be a body to cooperate with, that body was the assembly. Miloš was a fairly good orator who knew how to steer the proceedings of assemblies. Today we would say he was a populist.

Vuk Karadžić made a remark on Miloš's intentions, referring to the provisions of the 1830 Hatt-i Serif in his famous letter to the Serbian Prince, sent in 1832 from exile. His remark was that Miloš had wished the text of the act granting autonomy to provide that the Prince was to rule with the people's assemblies. According to Vuk that would enable the Prince to cheat on both the people and the assemblies. That was, however, impossible, due to the fact that there was no provision for the people's assembly in the 1830 Hatt-i Serif, where only an assembly of notables was mentioned. Moreover, the assembly

---

28 For the 1831 draft constitutions in detail, cf. D. Popović, *Prapočetak*, 20–34.

of paragraph 2 of the act was renamed as 'council' in its paragraph 15. Whether with an assembly of notables or with a council, Miloš was constrained to rule in cooperation with a body that would be small in number. That created the idea, understandable in light of the Prince's illiteracy and ignorance of political theory, that he would confuse a council in the sense of a Senate with a council of ministers, or cabinet. Therefore Vuk put in the comments of his letter that the Prince 'together with his secretaires has been constantly dreaming to create a cabinet of ministers instead of a Senate'.[29]

Vuk Karadžić was well informed, and his prediction proved to be right. As of 1834, the Serbian Prince started shaping the country's institutions in the sense that Vuk's letter had announced in mid-1832. As of March 1834, Prince Miloš started appointing ministers for the first time. Until then, he had been accustomed to rule with reliance on the help of his private secretaries, who were his personal servants. At first there was no procedure by which a minister should be appointed. It was enough for the Prince to address someone as *popečitelj*, which is the old-style Serbian word for minister, and the person in question would be appointed. The ministers by no means formed a council to deliberate political issues. The Prince's attitude towards them remained the same as the one he had previously had towards secretaries in his private service. In spite of all that, the appointing of ministers was a step forward, through which the first features of modern government were introduced. Between March and June 1834 Miloš appointed five ministers, thus completing the cabinet.[30]

Between 1 and 14 of June 1834 a French diplomat was on a mission to Serbia. His name was Bois-le-Comte, and he was reporting to his minister in Paris on the situation in Serbia. The reports contained remarks concerning constitutional questions.[31] The Serbian Prince ordered his collaborators to consult with the visitor on constitutional issues. We do not know today what documents were presented to the French diplomat. We learn from Bois-le-Comte's comments communicated to the minister in Paris that the draft presented to him was based on the confusion of powers. Bois-le-Comte reported that out of the existing council, which was the highest court as well, the Serbian Prince was inclined to create the upper house of a legislative body in which six ministers

29 V. Karadžić, *Istorijski spisi*, 234. For Vuk's letter to the Prince of 1832 see Part Two, Chapters 4 and 7.

30 D. Popović, *Prapočetak*, 53.

31 S. Novaković, 'Srbija u 1834 – pisma grofa Boa-le-Konta to De Rinji, ministru inostranih dela u Parizu o tadašnjem stanju u Srbiji' [Serbia in 1834 – Letters from Count Bois-le-Comte De Rigny, Minister of Foreign Affairs in Paris about the situation in Serbia at that time], *Spomenik SKA* XXIV, Belgrade 1894.

would also sit.[32] The French diplomat criticised the draft he was presented with from the standpoint of a learned European. He perceived the concepts displayed by the Serbs as if they were intending to introduce a two-house system of legislative body. He was probably mistaken when he alleged that the assembly would have enormous power in Serbia, according to the drafted documents he had seen. On the other hand, he was right to remark that political and administrative powers were vested in the same body as well as regarding the immovability of ministers, which was also provided for.[33]

There was a lot of confusion in circles surrounding the Serbian Prince as regards constitutional matters. Without any positions among the collaborators trained in law, the Prince was trying to introduce modern political institutions, as he understood them, with the intention of continuing his own unhampered governance of the country. Those who were not satisfied with the Prince's autocratic rule were in favour of limiting his powers. Both sides wanted a constitution to be adopted: the Prince to affirm his power, and the opponents to put limits to it. In such an atmosphere, the stage was set for the adoption of the First Serbian Constitution in February 1835.

The 1835 Constitution

In the first half of the 1830s the constitutional question was on the agenda. Prince Miloš perceived constitution as an act that would enhance his power in the sense of legitimacy and also contribute to the dignity of the country. His ideas were not about limiting power, introducing guarantees of civic and human rights or anything of the like. Some among his collaborators, however, understood the concept of constitution in its proper sense. This was also the case for those who were not satisfied with the Prince's rule. Miloš was impeding free trade by favouring his own commercial partners, for he was engaged in trade himself. He had also appropriated plots of land left by the Muslim population that had moved out of Serbia in ways which were not always lawful. Some of the rich landowners and merchants were dissatisfied, and this added value to the question of adopting a constitution for Serbia.

It was in January 1835 that Miloš's wife (the Princess) and his son Mihailo were visiting a family in Kruševac, where they stayed for a couple of days. During the stay it was revealed to the Princess and the young Prince that there was dissatisfaction in the country, as well as that a rebellion against Miloš was in preparation. Soon afterwards, in the second half of the same month a rebellion broke out in Jagodina, the city in the Morava valley. Its leader was

32 ibid. 44–45.
33 ibid. 45.

Mileta Radojković, and as such the whole set of events came to be known in history as Mileta's rebellion (*Miletina buna*). The insurgents set their troops on march to Kragujevac, where the state treasury was, aiming to get hold of it. However, the Prince disposed of the troops that remained faithful to him. Both the insurgents and the troops loyal to the Prince were in the city of Kragujevac, without entering into an armed conflict. Miloš who was in Požarevac all this time, sent his secretary Dimitrije Davidović to negotiate with the rebels. An agreement was brokered and the two sides withdrew the troops, thus putting an end to the conflict. The only outcome of the rebellion was to set the date for the next meeting of the popular assembly. That body met in Kragujevac in February 1835 on the day of *Sretenje* (Candlemas) and on the second day of its work adopted the First Serbian Constitution, which is therefore known in Serbian as *Sretenjski ustav* (Candlemas constitution).[34]

There were different sorts of assemblies in Serbia in the time of the national revolution. If an assembly embraced representatives from all parts of the country, it could be considered national, bearing in mind that there were no proper elections at that time. Men were sent to sit in the assembly in an informal way; they simply required the confidence of their neighbours to be able to represent them.

Miloš convoked the assembly on Sretenje, i.e. mid-February 1835 in Kragujevac. The number of representatives cannot be properly established in the sources, but one historian's cautious estimation is of around 2,400.[35] The assembly was convoked with the aim of adopting a constitution for Serbia and remained in session for three days. The sessions were held in the open air in front of a grandstand erected for that purpose. The whole event was solemn and serene, and the text of the constitution was read before the assembly in session. Its author was one of the Prince's secretaries, Dimitrije Davidović (1789–1838), a Serb from Austria who had no background in law. The assembly approved the text that was read by acclamation. There was neither a debate nor any sort of vote. Once the reading of the text was finished, the Prince and the members of the assembly pronounced the oath, invoking the Holy Trinity, to observe the constitution and remain faithful to it.[36] In light of the facts just presented, it appears that Slobodan Jovanović was perfectly right in his judgment about the

34 On Mileta's rebellion and the events, cf. D. Popović, *Prapočetak*, 73–80; for the texts of all Serbian constitutions in times of monarchy, cf. M. Jovičić (ed.), *Ustavi Kneževine i Kraljevine Srbije 1835–1903* [Constitutions of the Principality and Kingdom of Serbia 1835–1903], Belgrade 1988.

35 R. Ljušić, *Kneževina Srbija (1830–1839)* [The Principality of Serbia (1830–1839)], Belgrade 1986, 137.

36 D. Popović, *Prapočetak*, 81–82.

First Serbian Constitution. The 1835 Constitution was granted to the people by the Prince. Jovanović put it rightly: 'The Candelmas Constitution was in fact granted by the Prince without participation of the assembly; the latter was convoked only to take notice of it.'[37] The contents of the 1835 Constitution go hand in hand with Jovanović's conclusion on the form of its adoption. It was a constitutional settlement that favoured the ruling Prince.

The text of the 1835 Constitution consisted of 142 articles, grouped in fourteen sections. The language was elegant, although some expressions were vague, probably due to the fact that the author of the draft, Dimitrije Davidović, was not a lawyer. It was remarked in academia that Davidović was influenced by the French declarations on human rights, as well as by the school of natural law.[38] Notably, the contents of the Constitution covered both the organisation of power and provisions on human rights. In form it could match contemporary constitutions in Europe.

Article 5 of the 1835 Constitution read as follows: "Serbian authorities are three: legislative, executive and judicial". Although the provision seems to have taken the concept of separation of powers as its inspiration and starting point, such an impression fades away in the presence of Article 6 of the Constitution. That provision did not mention the judicial power at all. It provided that two constitutional factors jointly held both the legislative and executive authority in the country. Those two factors, or constitutional organs, were the Prince and the State Council. The article provided on the composition of the State Council. It consisted of six ministers, whose portfolios were enumerated, and of an undetermined number of state councillors (*iz neopredjeljenog čisla državni Sovjetnika*, in old-style Serbian).

The National Assembly found a place in the 1835 Constitution in the provisions of Section VIII of the text, in articles 82 to 91. The National Assembly was composed of one hundred representatives. A special act was to provide for the elections. The main item regarding the role of the National Assembly was contained in Article 86 of the Constitution. It provided that no tax can be introduced or imposed without the approval of the National Assembly. This provision was repeated in Article 91, which closed the Section, stating that the National Assembly was the only authority empowered to levy taxes. Notably, although there were some other items on the competence of the National

37 S. Jovanović, *Ustavno pravo* [Constitutional law], Belgrade 1907, 1.

38 On the influences, cf. D. Popović, 'Dimitrije Davidović – od narodne k pojedinačnoj slobodi' [Dimitrije Davidović – from national to individual freedom], in: J. Trkulja and D. Popović (eds), *Liberalna misao u Srbiji – prilozi istoriji liberalizma od kraja XVIII do sredine XX veka*, Belgrade 2001, 34.

Assembly provided outside Section VIII of the Constitution text, it was clear that it was not envisaged that the National Assembly would participate in legislation. Its role was limited to approving the imposition of taxes.

The preponderance of the Prince's power within the system of government was secured through several provisions. Thus, by virtue of Article 66 of the Constitution, the Prince was empowered to appoint and dismiss ministers. There was a *caveat* for a minister dismissed: Article 66 provided *in fine* that such a minister would become a councillor, i.e. a member of the State Council. This reminds us of the ideas we have already met among the people surrounding Prince Miloš in the first half of the 1830s. The French diplomat in his visit to Serbia reported to his minister on the confusing ideas of his hosts. Remarkably, the Prince was empowered to appoint all authorities and all Serbian public servants, as provided for in Article 16 of the Constitution, which included the members of the State Council. The same applied to the President of the State Council, according to Article 59 of the Constitution.

However, the decisive issue is about the preponderance in the power game, envisaged in the Constitution articles. The Prince could remove ministers at will, which meant that he would prevail in the executive power, but he was also to proceed in legislation together with the State Council. Could the Prince pursue policies of his own in legislation as well? For that purpose the Prince had two levers: the veto and the responsibility of the members of State Council.

There was a lot of discussion among scholars in respect of the Prince's veto power contained in Article 14 of the 1835 Constitution. There were authors who expressed the view that the Prince's veto was suspensive. Others hesitated, while others still were of the opinion that the text provided for an absolute veto.[39] It is extremely difficult today to reach firm conclusions about a text that never applied in practice, especially in light of the fact that its author had no formal training in law whatsoever. The text of Article 14 of the Constitution was clear in its first sentence, stating that the Prince was empowered to veto a bill twice. The problem came with the second sentence of the same article. It referred to the situation in which the Prince might find himself faced with a bill presented for approval for a third time. The text read that the State Council was under obligation to provide reasons if sending a bill to the Prince for a third time. The reasoning was to demonstrate that the bill was neither detrimental to the people, nor unconstitutional (*ne idu na pagubu naroda ili protivu ustava državnoga*, in old-style Serbian). Should the Prince find the reasons

39 For an outline of the discussion, cf. D. Popović, *Prapočetak*, 89–91. The author of this book is among those who interpret the text of the article in the sense of an absolute veto.

sufficient, he was to approve the bill; however, should that not be the case, the Prince was still allowed to withhold approval.

The Prince would have probably been able to avoid rather sophisticated and – from a lawyer's standpoint – vague and problematic provisions on the veto power. The Constitution provided more efficient ways for him to reach a position superior to any other constitutional factor and pursue his own will and policies. The confusion of ideas reigning in the Prince's entourage as regards constitutional matters found expression in the concept that the members of the State Council were to be accountable for their work. Thus, according to Article 55 of the Constitution, the State Council as a whole could accuse any of its members on the grounds of committing an offence against either the Sultan or the Prince, or against the interest of the Serbian people. In the case of such an accusation the State Council would bring the accused before the Prince, who would be competent to try the offender. This does not even call for comments. It suffices to remark that the Prince would be entitled to try the case of someone who offended against the Prince himself.

Article 74 of the Constitution continued along the same lines. Although it was provided in Article 73 that a member of the State Council could not be held liable for his opinion expressed in the legislative procedure, Article 74 provided for the situation in which exactly that might occur (*ako bi se međutim dogodilo* [if, however, that happens]). In that case the member of the State Council was entitled to ask that body for protection or step down from office. Moreover, Article 90 of the Constitution provided for the power of the National Assembly to accuse the State Council (*tužiti se Knjazu na državni Sovjet*), in case the State Council had acted unconstitutionally. This should be interpreted in the light of what has been noted above in this chapter: Prince Miloš was a populist who was capable of streamlining the work of the assemblies.[40]

The 1835 Constitution was not a democratic one; it was granted by the Prince and its provisions were not intended to limit the Prince's power. Indeed, it provided for the Prince's supremacy.[41] However, there was a significant element of progress in its provisions if we consider the situation in the Principality of Serbia in the mid-1830s. Dimitrije Davidović, who drafted the text, although not a lawyer, was a convinced patriot and liberal. He undertook efforts to introduce constitutional monarchy in Serbia, albeit in a form containing mild and gentle limits to the Prince's power. Davidović's noble idea seems to have been

40 ibid. 91–92 for the levers of the Prince's power and preponderance.

41 Cf. T. Marinković, 'Serbia', 26. For the opposite opinion, in favour of the State Council's supremacy, cf. J. Prodanović, *Ustavni razvitak*, 61.

one of letting the Prince pursue his own policies but acting within the framework of procedures provided for by the Constitution.

The 1835 Constitution had a poor destiny. Confronted with the dissatisfaction of foreign powers, as well as of the Ottoman Porte, then sovereign of Serbia, Prince Miloš had already suspended the Constitution adopted in mid-February by the beginning of March, and eventually repealed it on 11 April 1835. The adoption of the First Serbian Constitution did not remain an episode, but on the contrary left traces and consequences on future developments. Notably, after the revocation of the 1835 Constitution the Serbian constitutional question remained open. It was transformed into a constitutional crisis to which various actors, such as the Serbian Prince, foreign powers and the Ottoman Porte, searched for a solution.

It was in April 1835 that Prince Miloš formed a drafting committee with the task of revising the text of the constitution that had been repealed. The work of the committee resulted in a draft constitution that was sent to Constantinople, where it ended up in the complicated channels of Turkish bureaucracy and international diplomatic activities.[42] Another draft of a constitutional revision was prepared by one of the Prince's secretaries, Stefan Radičević, a Serb from Austria who, like the author of the text of the 1835 Constitution, had no training in law. He was the one who had read in person the text of the 1835 Constitution at the session of the National Assembly. Radičević's draft was discussed in the circle of the Prince's secretaries and some other persons at the beginning of May 1835. The trouble with the draft consisted in the fact that it was more liberal than the 1835 Constitution, which made the Prince turn against the draft's author and even insult him during the debate.[43] The Russian diplomacy also played a role in the constitutional crisis in Serbia. In July 1835 a Russian diplomat was committed on a mission to Serbia in order to influence and streamline the work on revising the 1835 Constitution. He approved some of the drafts whose production was in progress.[44] That was all in vain. Towards the end of 1835 it became clear that the Serbs were unable to resolve the question of adopting a constitution for their country without the intervention of the Sublime Porte and the powerful international factors whose diplomatic representatives were active in Constantinople. The question of passing a constitution for Serbia became an object of international attention and deliberation. Diplomatic endeavours continued for several years.

---

42 R. Ljušić, *Kneževina Srbija*, 151–53.

43 D. Popović, *Prapočetak*, 106–14.

44 ibid. 114–16.

The 1838 Constitution

Russian diplomacy put pressure on Prince Miloš to settle the issue of the constitution. Towards the end of 1836 and in 1837, the pressure increased so that the Serbian Prince appointed a new drafting committee for that purpose. The Russians did not find its work sufficiently expedient, which resulted in appointing a new committee with the same task in February 1838. Meanwhile a learned Serb from the Habsburg monarchy, who had a PhD in Law from the University of Vienna, came to Serbia in 1837. He was committed by the Prince to prepare a civil code for Serbia. His name was Jovan Hadžić (1799–1869), and his background was as a member of the Serbian gentry living in Austria. Hadžić became involved in constitutional matters and prepared a draft constitution. A member of the rich Serbian middle class in Austria, composed of merchants, landowners and learned men, Hadžić was not fond of the illiterate Prince with his peasant background. This drafter envisaged limitations of the Prince's power, so that the Prince found the draft constitution inadequate.[45]

The work aimed at drafting a constitution for Serbia was transferred to Constantinople. Aware of the ongoing negotiations between diplomats and Turkish authorities on the issue, Prince Miloš sent a deputation of three persons to take part in the process of drafting a text of constitution for Serbia.[46] The key person of the deputation was Avram Petronijević (1791–1852), a businessman and skillful diplomat who was close to the Prince, but was nevertheless sympathetic to the Prince's opponents as well. He had taken part in Mileta's rebellion against the Prince at the beginning of 1835. Petronijević played a double role to some extent. Receiving instructions from the Prince on the one hand, he was close to the Russian diplomats and Ottoman authorities on the other. His actions contributed considerably to the final shaping of the text of the 1838 Constitution.[47]

In December 1838 the Sultan granted constitution to Serbia. One issue was then entrenched – Serbia would not dispose of its constituent power under the 1830 Hatišerif, which posed the foundations of its autonomy. The constituent power was vested in the Sultan.[48] Because of the fact that the 1838 Constitution was granted to Serbia by the Ottoman Porte, it became known as the 'Turkish Constitution' for Serbia. This name has remained in common use to date, and also applies in academic writing.

45 On Hadžić's draft constitution, cf. J. Prodanović, *Ustavni razvitak*, 72–79.

46 On negotiations in Constantinople, cf. ibid. 80–85.

47 Lj. Kandić, 'Ustav of 1838. godine – "Turski ustav"' [The constitution of 1838: 'the Turkish constitution'], in: M. Jovičić, *Ustavi*, 62–63. For more details, cf. R. Ljušić, *Kneževina Srbija* [Principality of Serbia], 165–83.

48 S. Jovanović, *Ustavno pravo*, Belgrade 1907, 16.

The 1838 Constitution took the form of a letter, containing the text with constitution provisions. It does not follow the model of any contemporary constitutions because it has no sections or subsections, but only paragraphs, which seem somehow scattered at first glance. There was a system, however, for out of sixty-six paragraphs, the first forty-four were devoted to three constitutional factors. Notably, paragraphs 1–5 regulated the powers of the Prince. Paragraphs 6–29 regulated the position and powers of the Council, and paragraphs 30–44 were devoted to the judiciary. The rest of the Constitution text provided broadly speaking on human rights, although due to the specific order of provisions in the Constitution some of those concerning human rights found their place before paragraph 44; this was the case of paragraph 27 of the Constitution, for example. The 1838 Constitution thus provided for two main areas of constitutional law: organisation of power and human rights. However, its text was inferior from a language standpoint when compared to the 1835 Constitution.

Two principal constitutional factors in the 1838 Constitution were the Prince and the Council. The latter had no attribute; it was just called Council, or *Sovjet* in the old-style Serbian. By virtue of paragraph 1 of the Constitution, the Prince was granted his title, to be hereditary in his family. Miloš Obrenović was addressed in the short preamble of the text as the Prince of Serbian People. Paragraph 3 provided that the Prince was vested with executive power. For that purpose the Prince was empowered by paragraph 4 of the Constitution to appoint three ministers (*popečitelji*) who were to form the central government of the country. Their positions were enumerated in the paragraph: they were interior, finance and justice ministers. However, in addition to the three ministers provided for in paragraph 4, paragraph 5 provided for another official. The paragraph was styled in a peculiar way and in a language that is no more in use in modern Serbian. Its essence was to provide for a special Prince's Representative, who was to hold the portfolio of foreign affairs and indeed act as the prime minister.[49]

The Constitution text then passed to the issue of regulating the other constitutional factor, namely the Council. The diction of the text remained the same as in the first five paragraphs. The Sultan ordered the Prince to form a Council of seventeen members. The crucial feature as regards the Council's powers within the framework of the political settlement introduced by the 1838 Constitution consisted in the fact that the Council was competent to legislate in cooperation with the Prince.

49 ibid. 302.

The Constitution provided that seventeen members, aged at least thirty-five, were to sit in the Council, as well as detailing their appointment and responsibility. The core power of the Council was to legislate in cooperation with the Prince; it could introduce bills and present them to the Prince. The Council took decisions by majority vote of its members, as provided for by paragraphs 11, 13 and 14 of the Constitution.

The Prince was empowered by virtue of paragraph 8 to appoint members of the Council, as well as its President. The whole set of provisions mentioned so far might give the impression of the Prince's supremacy or at least of his preponderance within the framework of organisation of power in the constitutional settlement. That impression is altered in the presence of paragraph 17 of the Constitution, which read: 'Those 17 Members of the Council shall remain in office, unless it is proven before my Sublime Porte that they committed some offence, or transgressed the laws and regulations of the country.' This paragraph was the most important for the whole construction of political settlement under the 1838 Constitution. Paragraphs 8 and 17 of the Constitution, read in conjunction, made clear that the Prince was empowered to appoint the members of the Council, but he could not destitute them. That power was retained by the Sultan himself. To borrow the expression from Dragnich, the position of the Council was such that it 'could defy the Prince with impunity so long as it had the confidence of the Port'.[50]

The position of the Council in the entire constitutional settlement was completed by another act. It was the *Ustrojenije Sovjeta* (Organisation of Council Act) of April 1839. The provisions of the Act went beyond the Constitution provisions, for it was provided that the Prince could appoint ministers, choosing them only from among the members of the Council. If a minister were removed, he would still hold his seat in the Council. Moreover, the Organisation of Council Act provided that the Prince could appoint to sit in the Council only a person who would enjoy the support of its sitting members.[51] This limited the Prince's power to a considerable extent, while the powers of the Council were indeed enlarged by the Act, beyond the Constitution text.[52]

The 1838 Constitution provided for the justice system in Serbia. The main provision in this respect was in paragraph 30 of the Constitution. It provided for a three-tier justice system. At the village level there was a justice of peace, which was called *primiritelni sud*. It was composed of three justices of peace

50 A. Dragnich, *The Development*, 20.

51 S. Jovanović, *Ustavobranitelji i njihova vlada, Sabrana dela 3* [The defenders of the constitution and their government, Collected works 3], Belgrade 1990, 122.

52 Cf. D. Jevtić, 'Novi vek – Srbija', 130.

elected by the population, and its competence was limited to minor criminal and civil matters. Apart from that, paragraph 30 provided for courts of first instance, which were to sit in each of the seventeen districts of Serbia. By virtue of paragraph 35 the courts of first instance, called *sudovi okružija* (district courts), were competent to try all civil and criminal cases, as well as misdemeanour and commercial cases. On top of that, paragraph 30 of the Constitution provided for a unique *Apelacioni sud* (Court of Appeals) with a seat in the capital city. The district courts were composed of a President and three judges, whereas the Court of Appeals had a President and four sitting judges. The Constitution text also provided in short for the most important elements of the courts' procedure, as well as for the independence of judges; the latter in paragraph 42 of the Constitution.

The last paragraph of the 1838 Constitution ordered the Serbian Prince in a general manner to maintain the rule of law, by observing the rights of the inhabitants of Serbia. The Sultan expressed his order in the old-style Serbian language as follows: 'Ja Ti nalažem k tomu, da uvažavaš stanje, čest, čin i službe svakog; da bdiš najpače o tom, da točke i uslovija ustavna gore izložena budu izvršivana u celosti i za svagda' (I hereby order Thee to respect the status, honour, rank and dignity of everyone, as well as to take care that the abovementioned paragraphs and conditions of this Constitution be executed in full and forever).

Oligarchs in Power

Prince Miloš was not satisfied with the constitutional settlement of 1838. He intended to seek support from the assembly, the institution whose work he was able to streamline and dominate. However, the assembly was not envisaged among the institutions of the 1838 Constitution. The Prince therefore issued a decree in March 1839 providing that the National Assembly was preserved in Serbia as a customary institution. The decree was issued on the basis of the Prince's agreement with the Ottoman Porte and Russia.[53] The abovementioned Organisation of Council Act of April 1839 was in a way aimed to counterbalance the Prince's decree of March the same year. The struggle for power was underway between Miloš and his opponents. The latter were rich people with interests in trade and possession of land. They were members of the Council and relied on the provisions of the 1838 Constitution, fervently defending these. Some of them became known while fighting against the Ottomans in the uprisings, leading the people from their respective regions of the country. That is what brought them the reputation which provided the

53 S. Jovanović, *Ustavno pravo*, Belgrade 1907, 1.

foundation for their opposition to the Prince.[54] The whole group of persons opposed to the Prince towards the end of the 1830s was given the name of *ustavobranitelji* (constitution defenders) because of their adamant stance in favour of the provisions of the 1838 Constitution. Their design was to limit the Prince's power to such an extent that it would turn Serbia into oligarchy.

Miloš Obrenović, with his patriarchal background, his inclination towards autocracy and arbitrary rule and his intention to become a proper monarch in the vassal principality of Serbia, could not comply with the limitations of his power introduced by the 1838 Constitution. He abdicated in June 1839 and left the country. He was succeeded by his son, Mihailo Obrenović (1823–68) who remained on the throne for several years only. Like his father before him, Mihailo could not find a mode of understanding with the influential group of constitution defenders. They made him step down from the throne in September 1842. Although a new Prince was brought to the throne, the form of government substantially became an oligarchy. The new Prince enthroned by the oligarchs, acting as defenders of the constitution, was Aleksandar Karađorđević (1806–85), the son of the leader of the First Serbian Uprising. Karađorđe, the leader of the uprising and the vožd between 1804 and 1813, had been murdered on his return to Serbia from exile in 1817, following an order of Prince Miloš. Aleksandar Karađorđević was army officer and was appointed as Prince Mihailo's *officier adjoint*.

To enthrone a new Prince, the constitution defenders had to go beyond constitutional rules and provisions. Even after Miloš's abdication, the only legitimate Prince of Serbia had to be a member of the Obrenović family. Paragraph 1 of the 1838 Constitution was clear on that point: 'the dignity of the Prince is given to Thee in person and to Thy family' were the Sultan's words addressed to Miloš. Searching for legitimacy after Mihailo's abdication, in a situation in which there was no one eligible of Miloš's posterity, the constitution defenders turned to the same lever that Miloš was planning to use against them. They convoked the National Assembly. It was legal, owing to the above-mentioned Miloš's decree of March 1839. The National Assembly ratified the choice made by the influential oligarchs. Aleksandar Karađorđević was definitively proclaimed Prince of Serbia in June 1843. The Ottoman Porte approved the act of the Serbian National Assembly.[55]

The new Prince was brought to the throne by those who were in the position to hold power. They were not numerous in the beginning; they were oligarchs. As already mentioned above, the core of that group were rich people

54 S. Jovanović, *Ustavobranitelji*, 129–30.

55 A. Dragnich, *The Development*, 124.

with the background in the national revolution, in which many of them were the leaders. However, little by little as time went on the group was subject to transformations. It was enlarged, so as to almost represent a strata of society, but those who were new to that strata belonged to the newly formed Serbian bureaucracy. This transformation contributed to the weakening of the Council in political matters, for the Council remained the body from which the oligarchs' policies were carried on.[56]

In the beginning, the oligarchs were more educated than their main enemy, Miloš Obrenović, but like him they also had a patriarchal background. In spite of such a background, however, they were in favour of modernisation of the Serbian society. The state of affairs in Serbia both in respect of economic and social developments made a real and proper modernisation hardly imaginable. Because of their patriarchal background, the oligarchs were indeed mostly conservative. Their policies were aimed at modernisation of the Serbian society in the way they understood the notion of modern institutions. In brief, the essential item of their policies was to introduce the peaceful enjoyment of property for everyone, which was to be achieved by adopting laws and enforcing them by administrating justice via the courts. This was in contrast with the autocratic mode of governance which Prince Miloš had followed. Conservatives aiming to modernise the country, they could fulfil their task only partially, and stopped wherever a move seemed too liberal in their view. The critical point was the one of political rights. The oligarchs were in favour of introducing civil rights, above all the protection of property, but they were vehemently opposed to political rights and the political participation of the people in matters of government. That is why the reforms they introduced were assessed, to borrow the expression from Dragnich, to be a rudimentary modernisation. The oligarchs organised the postal service of the country. They improved the education system and founded the *Licej*, which was the forerunner of the first Serbian university. At the same time, the oligarchs sent young men to attend foreign universities and receive their degrees abroad.[57]

The oligarchs' most important contribution to the constitutional developments consisted in their endeavours aimed at construction of the State. The oligarchs organised the public service, improving the position of public servants and increasing their numbers. The public servants were in a poor position in the previous system of Miloš's patriarchal autocracy, because the Serbian Prince had treated them almost as domestic servants. Having a post in the public service in the oligarchs' regime became a career. A whole class of

56 S. Jovanović, *Ustavobranitelji*, 130–31.

57 A. Dragnich, *The Development*, 23–28.

modestly educated bureaucrats emerged in Serbia, which was to be a cause, in the course of time, of the dissatisfaction of the country's inhabitants. The public servants were one of the pillars of the oligarchs' government, and became a particular class of the Serbian society.[58]

The organisation of the judiciary was also a controversial process with mediocre results. The 1838 Constitution laid the foundations of the organisation of the Serbian judiciary. Their implementation met obstacles in practice, mainly because of the lack of learned lawyers in the country. The facts put forward by Slobodan Jovanović are illustrative in that respect. In 1844 the civil code was adopted. In that same year, three district court Presidents out of seventeen were illiterate; ten others could only make a signature and only one had formative training in law. Seven years later, in 1851, the situation in the Serbian judiciary was not much better. There was only one illiterate district court President, but no lawyer whatsoever among them. In 1853, when the Civil Procedure Code was adopted, the courts' personnel in Serbia consisted of 242 persons, among which there were forty-nine lawyers, but nevertheless still sixteen illiterate judges.[59]

The functioning of the oligarchs' government was marked by tensions between the two principal constitutional factors – the Prince and the Council. Owing to the slow transformation of the power holders from a small group of influential rich people into a sort of bureaucratic class which lacked proper contact with people at large, the Prince managed to counterbalance the oligarchs. It was not an easy task for the Prince, because he did not have a proper constitutional background as a solid foundation for his position. He was elected by the National Assembly: Serbia was indeed an elective monarchy. The Prince's title was not envisaged to pass on to his descendants, and his family didn't form a dynasty.

The Council and the Prince were opposed on many particular issues, but in general they both tended to put the entire government of the country under exclusive control, each to the detriment of the other constitutional factor. According to the 1838 Constitution the Prince was empowered to appoint ministers (paragraph 4) but the Council had the power of budgetary review of their activity (paragraph 15), which provided grounds for both factors to influence ministerial action. Frequent ministerial crisis broke out on various occasions. Throughout the period of oligarchy, which lasted for sixteen years between 1842 and 1858, there were eleven cabinets, or central governments, as they were called. However, they were led by no more than six first ministers,

58 S. Jovanović, *Ustavobranitelji*, 51–52.
59 ibid. 37–38.

or Prince's Representatives, as their title then was. Three cabinets had Avram Petronijević as the leader, three others were headed by Aleksa Simić. Stefan Marković formed two cabinets, and Ilija Garašanin, Aleksa Janković and Stevan Magazinović led one cabinet each.[60] The political life of Serbia was relatively turbulent, despite the pre-modern environment in which political struggles took place. There were no political parties in the country, and the participation of the people in matters of government was excluded in principle. However, in times of national crisis and at the end of the oligarchs' regime interventions of the people in political matters were significant.

The national revolutions in Europe of 1848 produced a specific echo in Serbia, the outcome of which consisted in convoking the National Assembly. The Prince and the Council were unanimous on the issue of summoning the national representation. The election rules were enacted and the National Assembly met in Kragujevac in July 1848. As its work began on St Peter's Day, it has been known as *Petrovska skupština.* Although it was envisaged that 250 taxpayers would elect one member of the National Assembly, there were also members sitting of their own right, such as district governors, bishops, the metropolitan bishop and the like. Moreover, peasants from all over the country attended the sessions, which were held in the open air, despite the fact that they were not elected representatives. Slobodan Jovanović remarked that the 1848 National Assembly resembled a village fair more than an assembly.[61] The immediate reason for convoking the assembly was the events in the neighbouring Habsburg monarchy where the Hungarian rebellion was underway. Since many Serbs lived in Austria and were subjects of the Habsburg crown, the Imperial Court of Vienna made an appeal to them to fight the Hungarian insurgents, which the Serbs accepted. Therefore the main item on the agenda was how to help their Serbian brethren living in Austria in their fight, but the National Assembly, once in session, went beyond that issue. Its members expressed the view that the National Assembly should sit once a year. The Prince and the Council agreed to this in principle, and the Council undertook to appoint a committee to draft relevant legislation. However, the National Assembly did not meet in the ten years that followed its session in 1848. When it met again it overturned the oligarchy and put an end to that form of government.

60 cf. D. Mrđenović, *Ustavi i vlade Kneževine Srbije, Kraljevine Srbije, Kraljevine SHS i Kraljevine Jugoslavije (1835–1941)* [Constitutions and governments of the Principality of Serbia, the Kingdom of Serbia, the Kingdom of Serbs, Croats and Slovenes and the Kingdom of Yugoslavia], Belgrade 1988, 61–65.

61 S. Jovanović, *Ustavobranitelji*, 204.

The next session of the National Assembly occurred on St Andrew's Day 1858, so that it was given the name of *Svetoandrejska skupština*. Its prelude was a complicated struggle for power between the Prince on the one side, and some influential members of the Council on the other. The latter considered various ways of getting rid of the Prince, including conspiracy to kill him. When all other means failed they decided to convoke the National Assembly. A law was enacted for that purpose in November 1858 providing for the election of 376 representatives and sixty-three sitting in their own right, e.g. the clergymen.[62] The National Assembly was convoked to hold sessions in Belgrade in mid-December 1858.

The composition of the National Assembly was peculiar. There were no political parties or proper political affiliations, but nevetheless several groups were discernible. The Prince's supporters in the National Assembly were confronted by those who wanted to overturn the Prince. Among the latter there were followers of the two influential members of the Council who initiated the idea of convoking the National Assembly. They were supported by an immensely rich businessman, Miša Anastasijević, who was elected to represent the voters of Belgrade and became appointed to chair the sessions of the National Assembly. Another group was animated by the young Serbian liberals, mostly educated in foreign universities, who had brought genuine liberal ideas on their return to Serbia. They were nationalists as well as being liberals.[63] The liberal young lions who will show up in the National Assembly sessions were at first indifferent towards the idea of overturning the Prince, but they got in touch with the third group opposed to the Prince: the supporters of the Obrenović dynasty. Two dynasty members were in exile – Miloš and his son Mihailo. They had followers in the country, and a number of representatives of the National Assembly were in favour of the idea of restoring the dynasty to the throne of Serbia. The liberals, however, in this case preferred the son to the father. Miloš was a ruler of the old patriarchal style, completely unfit for a liberal image. On the contrary, the younger Prince in exile, Mihailo, was educated and, having spent more than fifteen years in Europe, gave the impression of a modern ruler. Despite fundamental differences in many aspects, the liberals formed a block with the supporters of the Obrenović family.[64] The National Assembly, whose sessions started on St Andrew's Day 1858, arrived at two major decisions. The first consisted of the adoption of new legislation on

62 A. Dragnich, *The Development*, 32–33.

63 On the emergence of Serbian liberals, cf. S. Jovanović, *Ustavobranitelji*, 206–07.

64 ibid. 216–19.

the National Assembly itself and the second was the decision to overturn the Prince.

The liberals first put forward their bill on the National Assembly, which was adopted after a week of discussion. The new legislation provided for considerable powers of the National Assembly. The core of those lay in the financial area. The National Assembly was empowered to approve raising taxes. It was also competent in the procedure of adopting some of the most important legislation, e.g. concerning the Prince, the Council and the cabinet ministers, despite the fact that it didn't have full legislative power.[65] Liberal ideas dominated the new legislation. Once the liberals were satisfied, the National Assembly turned to the issue concerning the Prince's position on the throne. The sequence of events led to the solution of that problem.

The whole drama of overturning the Prince happened in three days. Its first stage was the attack on the Prince at the session of the National Assembly, where it was suggested that the Prince should step down from the throne. To resist the attack, and once the representatives' session was over, the Prince convoked the Council in the evening. Sitting in the Council he realised that he had lost the support of that body too. The Council was in agreement with the National Assembly, and the councillors solicited the Prince to resign. The Prince then decided to leave his palace and escaped to the Belgrade fortress, which still hosted a Turkish army garrison, where the Prince sought protection of the Turkish paša. The Serbian throne thus became vacant at the end of the first day of the drama.

The second day was critical. The National Assembly held sessions in private, but the people gathered in front of the building where the session was in course, shouting slogans in favour of the Obrenović dynasty. At one point the secretary of the National Assembly – a prominent liberal called Jevrem Grujić – stepped onto the balcony to read in public the decisions of the National Assembly. They were the following: the Prince was ousted, the Obrenović dynasty was restored and the National Assembly itself was to take over the government's authority in Serbia for the moment. The Serbian army and police were put under the interim command of Stevča Mihailović, a representative, and one of the Obrenović followers.

Finally, on the third day feverish debates took place, in which pistols were shown, because the representatives were not forbidden to carry them during sessions. The arms were not used, however. The National Assembly appointed three regents who were to govern the country until the arrival of the newly elected former Prince – Miloš Obrenović. One of the regents was Mihailović,

65 For the substance of the act in brief, cf. S. Jovanović, *Ustavno pravo*, Belgrade 1907, 21.

and another was Ilija Garašanin, one of the influential councillors who initiated the idea of convoking the National Assembly. The third regent was Jeftimije Ugričić, a person with much less influence in political matters than the other two.[66]

The two major decisions taken at *Svetoandrejska skupština* were in contrast. A liberal act on the National Assembly was accompanied by the restoration to the throne of a Prince who used to rule in the 1830s in a patriarchal way, exercising arbitrary power. The main outcome of the events was, however, the end of oligarchy as the form of government in Serbia.

1.3 Institutions

The Approach

One who wishes to research and present the developments of institutions of government as a slow process of transformation inevitably has to face a methodological problem. The institutions as they emerged and were shaped in the course of Serbian constitutional history, and especially in its formation period, had their names and forms stemming from pre-modern times. Those were adapted during the evolution of Serbian society, so as to obtain modern forms and names. A researcher should therefore approach the historical reality in its genuine setting, while using terms that would be able to provide a link to the understanding of the past.[67] Bearing that in mind, this part of the chapter will focus on several topics: head of state, assemblies, council, executive power and judiciary.

Head of State

Head of state as an institution emerged from pre-modern concepts. When the First Serbian Uprising against the Ottoman power broke out in 1804, it was necessary for coordination purposes to put someone in charge of commanding the insurgents. That is why a leader was chosen, who was given the informal title of vožd. The title was accepted by the masses of insurgents, as well as the person – Karađorđe – who was generally recognised as the leader. The

66 On the whole set of events *in extenso*, cf. S. Jovanović, *Ustavobranitelji*, 237–59.

67 On the emergence of Serbian public institutions in brief, cf. Z. Mirković, *Srpska pravna istorija* [Serbian legal history], Belgrade 2017, 114–16.

leader showed a tendency to decide on his own on matters of warfare and governance, which created a problem that was resolved by giving oaths in parallel. The leader promised to obey the interests of the people and the position of his collaborators, while they in turn took an oath of allegiance to him. The leader had been elected at the very beginning by acclamation, so that the oaths only confirmed what once had been decided in an informal gathering of the people.

Despite the efforts made at constructing a government in the modern sense of the term between 1804 and 1813, the whole fragile system crashed with the defeat in the battlefield. However, it was natural at the beginning of the Second Serbian Uprising in 1815 to again appoint someone by acclamation to command the troops and lead the people. The memory of 1804 was still present, and the mode of election was repeated. Another person was elected in an informal gathering of the people. However, the title of vožd was not used in 1815. The leader, Miloš Obrenović, got the title of knez, which applied to the leaders of local communities at different levels in times of peace. By all means it was to denote outstanding persons of undisputed authority in their respective communities. The next step was made in 1817 when the leader was elected by an assembly to be the knez of Serbia. The word knez is usually translated by the word Prince in English. It did not refer to any sort of nobility for the simple reason that there was no such social class in Serbia.

Miloš Obrenović, the Prince of Serbia as of 1817 by the will of the people as expressed at the assembly, accentuated his higher position in respect of the masses and at the same time endeavoured in times of home-rule to obtain recognition from the sovereign, i.e. the Ottoman Porte. He was successful in 1830, when the Sultan granted him the title and position of the hereditary Prince of Serbia. Miloš was the Sultan's vassal, which was a position preferable to being the leader of an emerging nation, even if domestically recognised to be the ruler of the country. After subsequent developments, Miloš and his son and successor, Mihailo, were forced to step down from the throne, a fact that provoked a constitutional dilemma which the sovereign power resolved in a practical way and regardless of the constitution rules of the year 1838. The Serbs chose themselves a new Prince who did not belong to the Obrenović family. This was in contradiction with paragraph 1 of the 1838 Constitution, but the Ottoman Porte accepted the change on the Serbian throne. The constitutional position of Prince Aleksandar Karađorđević was different when compared to the two previous rulers belonging to the Obrenović family. He was elected as a Prince whose election was only approved by the sovereign. It was therefore still doubtful towards the end of the 1850s whether Serbia was indeed a hereditary principality.

Assemblies

At the beginning of the 19th century popular assembly was an institution of Serbian society rooted in tradition and customary law. People would gather in small groups in order to decide on matters of common interest. What was called a *skupština* (assembly) existed at the level of a village. Across a broader territory was the *knežina*, consisisting of several villages, which was a part of *nahija*, i.e. a district in the Ottoman Empire. There was a Serbian notable in each village, with the title of knez. His principal duty was to care for the collection of taxes that the villagers owed to the Turkish authorities. At the level of knežina the respective notable with the same duty had the title of *obor-knez*. The territorial unit in the administrative organisation of the Ottoman Empire, which encompassed a territory broader than the knežina, was the nahija. In the time of home-rule Serbia preserved the administrative division inherited from the Ottoman Empire. As of 1819, there were twelve nahijas. In each of them there was a Serbian knez.

Since the Serbs were used to attending assemblies at different levels of territorial organisation, the assemblies continued to exist in the period of home-rule. Their composition was not set up strictly, so that they were usually assemblies of the notables and the people. There were no rules on the procedure of the assemblies, and their sessions took place in the open. People would attend those meetings carrying arms and discuss matters in an informal way. The *skupštine* (assemblies) were therefore dominated by those who were in the position to either influence the public or advance personal attitudes in a more authoritative way than the others. There was no proper voting, and decisions were taken in a traditional, informal mode. On many occasions the assemblies at various levels expressed the wishes of the people who attended them, and put proposals to the power holders at the national level of government, which was slowly emerging.

With the emergence of the country's central government, the question of an assembly at the national level came onto the agenda. It was raised and treated within the context of pre-modern political life in Serbia in the time of home-rule. The mindset of an average Serb adapted easily to participation in the assembly because they were already held at a sub-national level and it did not take too much effort to attend. This is one of the reasons why the idea of *participation*, of whatever kind, or the possibility of influencing decisions, was present, but not the idea of *representation* in the modern sense. The latter, however, appeared in connection with the council (a topic to which we shall return later in this chapter). With an assembly at the national level the concept of representation was inevitable, and it slowly emerged in practice. Prince

Miloš used to summon assemblies, and in his respective letters to local authorities he would announce place and date of the assembly, and ask the local knez to come with a certain number of people from his area. Those were appointed by local authorities rather than local people, but were nevertheless supposed to represent the population of their region. There were the beginnings of the concept of representation in this mode of proceeding. The appointees indeed represented the people from their territory, although they were not elected by the people.

The irregularity of sessions was a characteristic feature of the assemblies, especially at the beginning of the home-rule period. Before that, i.e. between 1804 and 1815, fifteen assembly sessions were held. Afterwards, there were further three sessions up to 1817. Following this there was a pause of seven years, but then between 1824 and 1829 there were ten assembly sessions, i.e. more than one per year. In the 1830s twelve sessions were held. The sessions tended to become regular, but that trend was interrupted under the oligarchs. Between 1842 and 1858 only five assembly sessions were held.[68]

The notion of assembly found room in political negotiations on the status of Serbia, attracting the attention of foreign diplomats. The question was whether an assembly or a council was to limit Prince Miloš's arbitrary rule. Miloš opposed the Russian idea of introducing a council of notables for that purpose and favoured the concept of assembly instead, for he was capable of manipulating the work of assemblies in his populist way. As we have seen above, the 1830 Hatt-i Serif that introduced the autonomy of Serbia remained unclear at that point.

Speaking in proper terms of constitutional law, the first sufficiently comprehensive concept of National Assembly appeared in the 1835 Constitution. A National Assembly was envisaged that, despite lacking full legislative powers, would have the power to approve raising of taxes in the country. The 1838 Constitution remained silent on the National Assembly, but as we have realised above, Prince Miloš managed to preserve it as an institution of customary law. Assemblies that were held under the 1838 Constitution were few but significant. In 1842 the National Assembly elected a new Prince and in 1843 it confirmed the election. In 1848 it was decided in principle that the National Assembly sessions were to take place regularly, once a year. Eventually in 1858 the oligarchs' regime was overturned by the decisions of the National Assembly. The latter thus came close to the modern concept of a representative state organ, but it nevertheless lacked stability in the sense of holding regular sessions. Besides,

68 www.parlament.gov.rs/narodna-skupština/skupština 1804–2014.

it was founded neither in the provisions of the constitution nor in any fixed legislation – only that passed *ad hoc* for the special occasion. The National Assembly in the time of the oligarchs was convoked exclusively in times of crisis when the destiny of the nation appeared to be at stake and also when Serbia stood before fateful decisions, such as electing the Prince.

Council

The council is one of the most controversial government institutions in the constitutional history of Serbia, as far as the period of nation building is concerned. The idea that a group of persons limited in number should proceed together with the leader of an emerging nation state in conducting the business of government had appeared already towards the beginning of the First Serbian Uprising. The first council, called *praviteljstvujušči sovjet*, was founded as early as 1805. Several ideas were mixed at its formation, e.g. helping the leader by cooperation in the sphere of governance, limiting the leader by way of co-decision and even representation of the people and the regions of the country. In practice, the council functioned primarily like a government or *popečitelji* (cabinet of ministers).

The situation changed in times of home-rule. Prince Miloš was strongly opposed to the idea of a council, i.e. a body of influential persons that was small in number and could rival him in the exercise of power.[69] Once the autonomy was introduced, the question remained open because of the ambiguity of the language and the expressions used in the Sultan's act of 1830. An assembly of notables was mentioned in one paragraph, and the council in another. The institution of council found its place in the earliest draft constitution made in Serbia at the beginning of the 1830s by unknown authors. The mixture of ideas was present in the drafts. Their authors envisaged a small body that would cooperate with the Prince, but the members of that body were to hold both legislative and executive powers and act as ministers. The concept of separation of powers did not play a role. In the earliest constitution of 1835 the council was envisaged in a similar way. That body was to share both legislative and executive powers with the Prince. Basically the same model was maintained in the 1838 Constitution. The Prince and the council of seventeen members shared both powers mentioned. The difference between two constitutions consisted in the provisions on the relations of the Prince and the council. In the 1835 Constitution, as we have demonstrated above, the Prince was superior, whereas in the 1838 Constitution he could rule only in agreement

69 cf. J. Prodanović, *Ustavni razvitak*, 34–35.

with the Council. Its members were not responsible to the Prince, and he could not remove them from office.

Notably, under the rules of the 1838 Constitution the features of confusion of powers were present in the sense that the officials holding executive power, i.e. *popečitelji* (ministers), sat in the council. Moreover, the ministers could be chosen exclusively among the council members.

Executive Power

Executive power in the ideas of those who are not trained in law is hardly discernible from any other power. Its essence consists of issuing orders to others, which the addressees must follow. An anecdote says that at the very beginning of the First Serbian Uprising, when he was elected leader, Karađorđe asked the people who had just elected him, 'Will you obey my orders?' The confusion of powers as a concept prevailed among the Serbs at the beginning of the 19th century, and it remained dominant throughout the fifty years that followed in a country where learned lawyers were few.

However, despite the fact that the doctrine of separation of powers was unknown, or at least had no impact in practice, it became clear that there should be some specialisation among the power holders in the sense that some of them had to face practical challenges in an efficient way. Situations occurred that required an immediate response, and those who were to provide such a response were ministers, or in the old-style Serbian *popečitelji*, i.e. persons holding executive power. Of course, the head of state himself – the *vožd* in the First Serbian Uprising, the *knjaz* under the home-rule and beyond – was also empowered to act in any situation imaginable. The ministers were only to help him within their scope of competence. Neither the head of state nor the ministers were at first perceived as persons who would be deprived of competence in the framework of the administration of justice. It was, however, easier to separate the executive from the judiciary than to draw a line between executive and legislative powers. Indeed, until the end of the 1850s the executive and the legislative were not separated in Serbia. The legislators sat in the council of seventeen members together with the ministers of central government. Notably, only some of the legislators were ministers. The confusion of powers reigned, despite the noble wording of Article 5 of the 1835 Constitution, which read 'Serbian authorities are three: legislative, executive and judicial'. The drafter of the text put forward the idea of separation of powers, which was impossible to carry out in practice. The article just quoted remained a *lettre morte*. If that was the case as regards separation of legislation and the executive, it was nevertheless different insofar as judiciary was concerned.

Judiciary

There was an early effort to separate the judiciary from the other two branches of government. Vuk Karadžić relates that towards the end of 1807, while the *praviteljstvujušči sovjet* was still in Smederevo, that body sent an order to the regional authorities to organise a court of law in each and every *nahija*. It was to be composed of three judges and a scribe, the latter to serve as a sort of registrar. Notably, Vuk Karadžić explained that although it had been stated in the order that the judges should be elected by the people, they were indeed appointed by the regional authorities.[70] In his historical writings he also touched on the idea of forming a high court in Belgrade which would be presided over by the justice minister, but that idea was not carried out until 1813, when the Serbian rule came to an end.[71]

In times of home-rule the Serbian government lasted longer and the foundation of institutions became inevitable. The justice continued to be rendered by the Prince himself, as well as by local authorities, but courts were slowly organised. Vuk Karadžić himself was for a while appointed President of the Belgrade court. The whole activity aimed at organising the judiciary in the country was performed without systematic ideas and clear concepts. It was the 1838 Constitution that put the Serbian judiciary on solid ground. It incorporated some of the existing institutions, which were known to the people. For example, *primiritelni sudovi* (justices of peace) were to sit in every village and be composed of judges elected by the people. The district courts and a Court of Appeals were to be composed of appointed judges trained in law, but we have seen above that such an organisation of courts was hardly feasible.

During the oligarchs' rule there were some reforms of the judiciary, and they mostly concerned the highest level of the administration of justice. The Supreme Court was founded in 1846. However, the Prince was still in a position to quash any judgment of the Supreme Court at will. Slobodan Jovanović expressed himself nobly on that issue, stating that the Prince preserved the power of cassation.[72] He was deprived of that power in 1855, and in 1858 the Supreme Court was organised after the French model of a Court of Cassation. The Serbian judiciary had managed to catch up with modern ideas, at least in terms of the organisation of its courts.

***

70 V. Karadžić, *Istorijski spisi*, 17.

71 ibid. 42.

72 S. Jovanović, *Ustavobranitelji*, 36.

In an overall review of government institutions in Serbia in times of nation building, a conclusion can stand that the country was slowly overcoming its pre-modern structure. Efforts aimed at modernisation were successful in many aspects. However, a completely modern state structure was not introduced. Some of the pillars of the modern organisation of power were still lacking at the end of the 1850s. Among those were the concepts of separation of powers and people's representation, as understood in the modern sense of the terms.

CHAPTER 2

Constitutional Monarchy

2.1 Restoration and Constitution

By decision of the National Assembly, Miloš Obrenović was invited to return to the throne in Serbia. At first glance, it was a restoration, and everything seemed to be in compliance with the constitution rules. However, the reality was slightly different. Neither was it a proper restoration, nor was the compliance with the constitution secured. The whole story of Miloš's return to power in 1859 should be considered in light of the fact that Serbia was a vassal country, a dominion of the Ottoman Porte. The vassal principality enjoyed the constitution given by the sovereign. Notably, a Sultan's special envoy was present at the sessions of the National Assembly of Serbia, which opened in December 1858, on St Andrew's Day.[1] The Sultan's envoy did not influence the work of the national representation, but from a constitutional standpoint his presence was a symbol of the Ottoman sovereign power over the vassal principality.

Miloš was in Bucharest at the moment he received the news on the decision of the National Assembly.[2] He was cautious and acted prudently. There was a regency in Serbia, appointed by the National Assembly, to which Miloš tacitly agreed, without making any move at first. He waited for a message from the Ottoman Porte stating the sovereign's position on the issue of his return to Serbia. The Prince in exile was fully aware of the fact that he was unable to return to power in the vassal principality without the sovereign's approval. Once he had received a message that was in favour of his return to the Serbian throne, Miloš took action. Still in exile, he removed the regents and appointed his faithful follower, Stevča Mihailović, to hold power as his only representative in Serbia.[3]

1 The old, unreformed calendar was followed then, but this date is indicated according to the new calendar.

2 On the proceedings of the National Assembly of 1858, opened on St Andrew's Day, in detail, cf. Ž. Živanović, *Politička istorija Srbije u drugoj polovini devetnaestog veka, knjiga prva* [Political history of Serbia in the second half of the nineteenth century, book one], Belgrade 1923, 32–48.

3 S. Jovanović, *Druga vlada Miloša i Mihaila, Sabrana dela 3* [The second government of Miloš and Mihailo, Collected works 3], Belgrade 1990, 277. The first edition of the volume appeared in 1923.

 | DOI:10.30965/9783657791026_003

However, when some time later the Ottoman Porte issued a formal act, a *berat* of 1859 recognising him as the Prince of Serbia, Miloš found the act detrimental to the interests of his family. The act confirming the Prince's title and dignity was different from the one of 1830 on the same subject. Miloš was recognised as Prince of Serbia, but the Obrenović dynasty was not restored. His descendants were not mentioned in the Sultan's act. The explanation for such a decision being supplied by the Ottoman Porte was based on purely practical grounds. Miloš had one son, Mihailo, whom the Sultan declared himself ready to recognise as Miloš's successor. Mihailo did not have legitimate children, and that was the reason which provided grounds for the Sultan's decision. Miloš was restored to the throne and his son was to succeed him; however, the restoration was incomplete because the Sultan's act did not provide for an Obrenović dynasty.[4] Serbia at that time brought to mind an elective, rather than a hereditary, monarchy.

The fact that the restoration was incomplete made Miloš try to re-establish the hereditary principle and the line of succession to the throne in his family, in order to secure the dynasty. In the communication with Ottoman officials he invoked arguments in his favour, namely the election to the princely dignity at the assembly of 1817, the Sultan's berat of 1830 and the decisions of the National Assembly of 1858. By doing so, Miloš might appear as a legitimist, faithful to constitutional rules. That was by no means the case, if we consider his fundamental attitude towards the validity of the 1838 Constitution.

On his return to Serbia Miloš had a conversation with the Sultan's special envoy to the Serbian National Assembly. The Serbian Prince openly declared he could not govern the country under the 1838 Constitution. He was in favour of amending the constitution, or rather abolishing it as a whole. When the Turkish official asked him what he was planning to do while the 1838 Constitution was still in force, the Serbian Prince responded quite simply that he was not going to observe its provisions.[5] Miloš's reasoning was very simple: he had stepped down from the throne because he could not rule under the 1838 Constitution, and in 1858 the National Assembly had then invited him to return to the throne, which in his view meant the abolition of the 1838 Constitution that was in force.[6] The style of governance Miloš introduced on his return was in compliance with this rudimentary constitutional doctrine, consisting of his oversimplified attitude towards the validity of the Constitution. The Prince started and kept on appointing and destituting ministers at will. He proceeded

4 ibid. 317.
5 ibid. 308.
6 ibid. 285.

to purge the administration and renewed his populist policies, favouring the peasants to some extent by liberating them from part of their debts. From the standpoint of institutions, Miloš's main foothold was the National Assembly, which was susceptible to manipulation.

Miloš Obrenović passed away in September 1860. His second rule in Serbia lasted less than two years, however it was not merely an episode. Although short, it was not unimportant. Out of two major constitutional issues that were on the agenda, the incomplete restoration didn't produce significant consequences for further developments. On the contrary, the question of the validity of the 1838 Constitution remained unresolved and was present in the political life of the country throughout the next decade.

2.2 Constitutional Settlement of 1861

Origins

Mihailo Obrenović succeeded his father on the throne and became the Prince of Serbia. He also had a problem with the 1838 Constitution, and had once stepped down from the throne unable to rule in compliance with its provisions. Despite having this feature in common, Mihailo was different from his father. Having spent more than fifteen years in exile, he was formed in different circumstances and had different life experiences from his father. He was educated, spoke German and French fluently, had married a Hungarian Princess and had proper European manners, attitudes and appearance. When he ascended the throne, he promised the rule of law. His proclamation read: 'Let each and everyone know that while Prince Mihailo is in power, the law is the supreme will in Serbia.'[7] Mihailo's major political ideas were to unite the country and overcome the divisions between various political factions, in order to prepare for the achievement of his ultimate goal: the war on Turkey he planned to declare one fine day, in order to liberate the Serbs still living under the Ottoman rule. Mihailo also aimed to modernise Serbia along the lines of his somewhat conservative ideas, which were of European inspiration. In a speech given on the occasion of the opening of Mihailo's monument in Belgrade city centre, Stojan Novaković (1842–1915), historian, diplomat and politician summarised Mihailo's noble intentions. He declared that the Prince's endeavours were aimed at developing Serbian schools, traffic, industry, and also Europeanising the country.[8] A French journalist and historian, A. Ubicini, who

---

7 ibid. 349.
8 S. Novaković, *Beseda* [The Speech], Belgrade 1882, 7.

was Mihailo's contemporary, gave a review of the Prince's policies concerning political matters, describing them as tending to introduce what he labelled as regular or legal government.[9] The noble ideas of European inspiration, which guided the Serbian Prince in his reign, were nevertheless in discrepancy with his achievements.

Prince Mihailo's attitude towards the Ottoman Empire and the task of national liberation made him uneasy about asking the Sultan to grant Serbia a new constitution. At the same time, it was clear that the constituent power was vested in the Sultan, who was the sovereign of Serbia. To avoid addressing the Ottoman Porte on the issue and to proceed to carrying out his ideas of modernisation, Mihailo made a compromise. He did not pass a constitution, but a set of laws were enacted which fundamentally altered the constitutional settlement in Serbia. The new settlement emerged soon after he ascended the throne.

Several laws were adopted in 1861 and 1862 that provided the framework of the constitutional settlement, which the Prince inspired. The most important among them were the *Ustrojenije državnog sovjeta* (Organisation of State Council Act) of 17 August 1861 and the *Zakon o Narodnoj skupštitni* (National Assembly Act) of the same date. The former was completed by the *Ustrojenije centralne državne uprave* (Organisation of Central Government Act) of 10 March 1862. The acts of 1861 were adopted at the session of the National Assembly, which opened in August 1861 on the Feast of the Transfiguration. That is why it has been known in Serbian language as *Preobraženska skupština*. The acts are usually called Mihailo's organic laws in the scholarship. However, because of the fundamental alteration of the constitutional settlement that they brought, some went so far as to claim that the organic laws were indeed a new constitution. It was suggested to name it the Transfiguration Constitution, in parallel with the Candlemas Constitution of 1835.[10]

Among scholars Mihailo has been portrayed as a despot. Slobodan Jovanović was of the opinion that Serbia under Mihailo's rule resembled the German bureaucratic despotic monarchies of the eighteenth century, or even tsarist Russia.[11] The latter comparison can, however, hardly stand. The former was followed by Alex Dragnich, who, despite admitting that the Prince wanted to strengthen legality, labelled Mihailo's system of government as enlightened

---

9 A. Ubicini, *Constitution de la Principauté de Serbie*, Paris 1871, 23.

10 cf. M. Pavlović, *Preobraženski ustav – prvi srpski ustav* [The Transfiguration Constitution – The first Serbian constitution], Kragujevac 1997.

11 S. Jovanović, *Druga vlada*, 412.

despotism.[12] It is true that the Prince could not achieve the ideal announced in the proclamation of 1860. His understanding of the rule of law stopped at the concept of legality, i.e. implementing enacted laws regardless of their substance.[13] However, the form of government in Serbia in the times of Prince Mihailo was a constitutional monarchy. Despite the Prince's conservatism and disapproval of modern constitutional concepts, he introduced that form of government in Serbia. It is a paradox of history that a constitutional monarchy was introduced in contradiction to the provisions of the formally valid 1838 Constitution.

Role Models

Slobodan Jovanović points out that the sources of Prince Mihailo's inspiration were probably German. A book that treated the topic of organisation of administration, i.e. public service, which appeared right before Mihailo's accession to the throne was significant in that respect. The author of the book was one of Mihailo's most faithful followers, Miloje Lešjanin. Lešjanin was a lawyer, educated at German universities. He had also studied in Paris and spent some time in England.[14] His book was published in Vienna in 1859. To borrow the expression from Slobodan Jovanović, the book meticulously followed contemporary German scholarship.[15] Lešjanin's ideal was an efficient and well-organised public service which performed in the public interest. The title of the book pointed to its author's major ideas as regards administration of a state and the organisation of public service: *Državna služba i državne sluge* (Public service and public servants).[16] The volume made an enormous impression on the public at large. There were even rumours that Prince Mihailo himself was the real author of the book. If that question remains open, it is certain that the topic of the volume was treated in line with Mihailo's views on the subject.[17] Prince Mihailo received his education in Germany and was under the impact of German academic and social attitudes, which aligned well with the Prince's European albeit conservative ideas. The constitutional settlement he introduced in Serbia transformed the country into a constitutional monarchy modelled after a German pattern.

---

12 A. Dragnich, *The Development*, 40.

13 cf. Part Two, Chapter 7.

14 For Lešjanin's biography, cf. M. Đ. Milićević, *Pomenik*, Belgrade 1888, 298–99.

15 Thus S. Jovanović, *Druga vlada*, 367.

16 M. Lešjanin, *Državna služba i državne sluge*, Vienna 1859.

17 D. Popović, 'Begriff des Rechtsstaates nach den Auffassungen der Serbischen Rechtsprofessoren im XIX. Jahrhundert' [Concept of the rule of law according to the views of the Serbian law professors in the 19th century], *Rechtstheorie* 24 (1993), 21.

A brief review to compare contemporary German constitutions can provide guidance for the assessment of the 1861 constitutional settlement in Serbia, before we turn to the institutions of the latter. Two examples taken at random display the same image of the model considered from the standpoint of the state structure. The Constitution of Würtemberg of 1819 provided for two state bodies, apart from the King, as constitutional factors;[18] these were the Assembly of Estates and the Privy Council. The composition of the latter was regulated in paragraph 55 of the Constitution. It consisted of ministers who held respective portfolios and other members appointed by the King. By virtue of paragraph 57, the King was empowered to appoint and dismiss the members of the Privy Council at will. The King was under obligation, as provided by paragraph 127 of the Constitution, to convoke the Assembly of Estates once in three years.

The institutions provided for by the Constitution of Kurfürstentum Hessen of 1831 were fairly comparable to those of Würtemberg. The constitutional factors were the same. The Prince (Kurfürst) was under obligation to convoke the Assembly of Estates once in three years, as provided for in paragraph 80 of the Constitution. The highest State authority in Hessen had a different name from the one in Würtemberg, but both had similar compositions. Paragraph 106 of the Constitution provided that the Prince had the authority to immediately exercise his reigning powers.

Eventually paragraph 4 of the Constitution of Würtemberg had a provision that paralleled paragraph 10 of the Constitution of Kurfürstentum Hessen. The provisions, slightly different in wording, had tripartite structures. The first element in each was to pronounce that the monarch was the head of state (*Haupt des Staates* in Würtemberg, *Oberhaupt des Staates* in Hessen). The second element had the same wording. Its purpose was to provide that all state powers were vested in the monarch ('vereingt in sich alle Rechte der Staatsgewalt'). The third and final element of the two norms was to provide that the head of state, i.e. the monarch, had to exercise the powers conferred to him in compliance with the constitution.[19] This will provide grounds for comparison with the Serbian constitutional settlement of 1861 in terms of the organisation of power.

18 For the relevant texts of the constitutions of German monarchies, cf. https://www.jura.uni-wuerzburg.de.

19 In the text from Hessen, 'und übt sie auf verfassungsmässige Weise aus'; in the text from Würtemberg, 'und übt sie unter den durch die Verfassung festgesetzten Bestimmungen aus'.

Institutions

The organisation of power in Serbia under the 1861 constitutional settlement was comparable to the one in German monarchies in the first half of the nineteenth century. There were three constitutional factors: the monarch, a council and an organ of national representation. As for national representation, there was a fundamental difference between the German monarchies, on one side, and the Serbian system on the other. The representative organ in German lands was an Assembly of Estates. There was no stratification in Serbian society, and no aristocracy, so that the national representation in Serbia was a one-chamber National Assembly elected by the people. In brief, according to the National Assembly Act of 1861, there was one representative elected by 2,000 taxpayers. The National Assembly did not have a permanent seat; instead, the Prince was empowered to convoke it to a city of his choice. Out of the three meetings of the National Assembly under the rule of Prince Mihailo, two were held in Kragujevac and one in Belgrade. The Prince had the right to appoint the speaker of the National Assembly, as well as to dismiss him. The National Assembly was not vested with legislative power. The latter was reserved for the State Council and the Prince; however, the representatives could put forward suggestions for the legislative factors to adopt a law. The ministers had to be present at the National Assembly sessions and had to report to this body regarding the public spending made by their respective ministries in the three-year period that intervened between two sessions of the National Assembly.[20] The striking similarity with German monarchies, as far as the National Assembly is concerned, was this regular three-year period between sessions.

The State Council was competent to legislate together with the Prince. Paragraph 17 of the Organisation of State Council Act of 1861 empowered the Prince to appoint and dismiss councillors. However, some requirements were envisaged for holding that post. A councillor had to be at least thirty-five years old, and to have spent at least ten years in public service. The councillors were thus put in the position of public servants, although of the highest rank. At the same time, they were to legislate aiding the Prince in this respect. Slobodan Jovanović's comment on the position of the State Council within the constitutional settlement of 1861 was short and incisive. His remark was that 'the Prince meant everything, while the State Council meant nothing'.[21] That was true. However, a parallel appears if the Serbian provisions of Prince

---

20 On the National Assembly, cf. S. Jovanović, *Druga vlada*, 377–79; A. Dragnich, *The Development*, 40–41.

21 S. Jovanović, *Druga vlada*, 360.

Mihailo's legislation in this respect are compared to the Constitution of Würtemberg. Paragraph 54 of the latter reads, 'The Privy Council forms the highest exclusively advisory authority immediately subject to the King and his sovereign decision'.[22] In the Kingdom of Würtemberg the King who had granted the Constitution in 1819, William I, was in power until 1864, opposing liberal ideas to the end of his reign. He was most likely one of those whom the Serbian Prince was trying to follow in matters of government.

The mighty Council of the previous regime, which relied on the rules of the 1838 Constitution, was transformed by the legislation of 1861 into an almost administrative body, or, to borrow the expression from Dragnich, 'into an ordinary bureaucratic instrument' of the Prince.[23] Moreover, that body was to legislate with the Prince, who, according to paragraph 5 of the Organisation of State Council Act of 1861, disposed of absolute veto power. In brief, it was Mihailo's personal regime.

The *Ustrojenije centralne državne uprave* (Organisation of Central Government Act) of 10 March 1862 completed the image. A novelty appeared in that act in respect of terms: the word *popečitelj* was no more in use; the term *ministar* (minister) was employed instead. Another novelty was the number of ministerial portfolios. There were four under the 1838 Constitution, but their number increased to seven in 1862. For the first time, the ministers formed a proper council or cabinet which deliberated political issues. There was also leadership in cabinet: one of the ministers acted as the prime minister along with holding a portfolio, either of foreign or home affairs. The ministers were accountable to the Prince who appointed and dismissed them at will.[24] Once again, this resembles the rather conservative constitutional settlements existing in some German kingdoms at the time, which we have discussed above. The political settlement of 1861, as completed by the legislation of 1862, was by no means liberal. It was indeed specific in several aspects.

A Constitutional Monarchy without a Constitution

With Prince Mihailo on the throne, Serbia came to the doorstep of the form of government that is usually known as constitutional monarchy. Its form of government indeed corresponded with that pattern. In response to any remark that Serbia during Mihailo's reign did not have a proper constitution, one could answer firstly that a constitutional monarchy can rely on an unwritten

22 Der Geheime Rath bildet die oberste, unmittelbar unter dem Könige, stehende und seiner Hauptbestimmung nach bloss berathende Staatsbehörde.

23 A. Dragnich, *The Development*, 41.

24 S. Jovanović, *Druga vlada*, 365–66.

constitution. Secondly, Mihailo's legislation of 1861 was a sort of constitution, albeit not codified and incomplete because it lacked the constitutional guarantees of fundamental rights. Therefore, the whole analysis of the political settlement in Serbia between 1861 and 1868 is limited to the issue of organisation of power. In this respect, Serbia followed the model of what German academics call earlier forms of constitutional monarchy.[25] Serbia was backward, and followed the pattern of the form of government which had developed mostly in the monarchies of southern Germany decades before it was received in Serbia. In essence, it consisted in the requirement that the monarch exercise his powers in compliance with the rules posed in advance by the constitution.

Serbian constitutional history had already known an attempt to introduce constitutional monarchy, in 1835. The noble intentions of Dimitrije Davidović, who drafted the 1835 Constitution went in that direction. He made efforts to persuade Mihailo's father, Miloš, to accept such a system of government, in which his personal will would be carried out, but in a way that encompassed legal procedures provided for by the constitution. Miloš agreed, but since the constitution never properly entered into force, we do not know today whether he would have been able to refrain from his characteristic arbitrariness and act as a constitutional monarch. Any conclusions that find grounds in Miloš's general conduct and his attitude towards the constitution during his short rule in 1859/60 speak against such a possibility. The 1835 Constitution had been designed for him, just as Mihailo went on to tailor the 1861 constitutional settlement to meet his own requirements, but it is indeed unlikely that Miloš could have sustained any such constraint.

Miloš and Mihailo were different personalities, but they had at least two features in common. Firstly, they were skillful in diplomatic communications. Miloš managed to get the status of Serbia settled by the Sultan and to confine the Ottoman garrisons to the fortresses in 1830. Mihailo was successful in negotiating an agreement with the Ottoman Porte to put an end to any sort of Ottoman presence in Serbia. In 1867 the Turkish garrisons left for good. Secondly, both the father and the son were conservative, although their attitudes in matters of government were not similar. Miloš was an illiterate peasant of authoritarian mindset, while his son was an educated European gentleman. This does not mean, however, that the son was less conservative than the father. Not all conservatisim is the same. Miloš was patriarchal, accustomed to communicating and negotiating with the Ottomans. Mihailo was European-oriented in

25 On the phenomenon, cf. C. F. Menger, *Deutsche Verfassungsgeschichte der Neuzeit, 7. Auflage* [German constitutional history of modern times, 7th edition], Heidelberg 1990, 122–23.

politics, noble in manners, but by no means liberal: his perception of constitutional monarchy did not embrace civil liberties. In February or March 1868, nevertheless, just several months before his own assassination, he committed Radivoje Milojković, chief justice of the Court of Appeals, to draft a new constitution.[26] The fact speaks in favour of the thesis that Prince Mihailo was on the cusp of building a constitutional monarchy in Serbia, although his ideas were never put into writing in one single document.

2.3 The 1869 Constitution

Emergence

Prince Mihailo was assassinated in June 1868, in the picnic area of Topčider, near Belgrade. Although the motives of the plot that led to the assassination of the Prince have never been properly ascertained, it is most likely that they were rather personal and not politically founded.[27] A provisional regency was established in all haste the same night, the army was put on alert and the regency announced that the Grand National Assembly would be convened. A provision of the National Assembly Act of 1861 empowered the Grand National Assembly, whose membership was four times larger than that of the regular National Assembly, to elect a new Prince in the case of a vacancy.[28] The issue of vacancy on the throne had nevertheless been resolved before the Grand National Assembly met. The day after the assassination, the war minister, Milivoje Blaznavac, made the army swear allegiance to Mihailo's relative, Milan Obrenović (1854–1901), who was the grandson of Miloš's brother. Milan was fourteen years old and lived in Paris; Prince Mihailo had taken care of his education. Once in session, the Grand National Assembly only had to ratify the election of the new Prince to the throne of Serbia and elect a permanent regency. The regents were Blaznavac, Ristić and Gavrilović. They continued in Mihailo's footsteps as regards constitution making.

On 20 June 1868, the same day on which the Grand National Assembly met, the regency issued a proclamation which laid down the foundations of its policies, as well as those of the political regime that was emerging.[29] Notably, the regents remained faithful to the wording of Prince Mihailo's proclamation of 1860, issued on his accession to the throne. Their proclamation repeated

26 J. Prodanović, *Ustavni razvitak*, 150.
27 Ž. Živanović, *Politička istorija Srbije*, 201.
28 A. Dragnich, *The Development*, 48.
29 On the proclamation, cf. Ž. Živanović, *Politička istorija Srbije*, 215–16.

the stance that the law was the supreme will in Serbia. They went further in promising the continuation of Prince Mihailo's endeavour to raise the strength of the people. It was stated in that context that the country's political institutions were burdened with deficiencies, which the late Prince had planned to improve. On one hand, it was natural to seek legitimacy in the late Prince's acts and intentions; on the other, the regents made it clear that they would continue the work of drafting a new constitution for Serbia.

The regents appointed a huge committee of more than seventy members entrusted with the task of producing text for the new constitution. However, the work of the committee did not materialise in a draft constitution.[30] Debates in the committee sessions went along the lines of the 1868 draft constitution. The outstanding features of that draft were a two-house body of national representation, provisions on its competence and ministerial responsibility.

As to the national representation body, the 1868 draft constitution envisaged a two-house legislative body whose lower house would be elected, whereas its upper house was to be divided into three parts. The first group of upper house members consisted of those entitled to sit of their own right, e.g. the metropolitan bishop and other bishops, the Prince's heir when he attained majority, but also all the members of the Council of State.[31] The second group of members were those elected by their respective corporations, e.g. three justices of the Court of Cassation elected by their peers, or two university professors elected in the same way. Eventually the Prince would be entitled to appoint to the upper house a certain number of members from among district governors, judges of first instance courts, army officers and priests. Such a composition has recently been considered in academia as an outcome of foreign influences coming from comparative constitutional law.[32]

The competence of the national representation body also stood under the impact of comparative law. This was evident in provisions reserving the legislative initiative for the government, as well as in providing for the preponderance of the lower house in legislation, and especially in adopting the budget. Mirjana Stefanovski analysed the comparative law aspect of the issue in detail.[33] Eventually, the ministerial responsibility was also provided for in the 1868 draft constitution, where it was construed as a sort of criminal responsibility that could be put in motion by the houses of the national representative

30 J. Prodanović, *Ustavni razvitak*, 177; M. Stefanovski, *Postanak Namesničkog ustava* [*The Genesis of the Regency Constitution*], Belgrade 2016, 46.

31 M. Stefanovski, *Postanak*, 19–20.

32 ibid. 20–23.

33 ibid. 23–28.

body. However, it did not correspond with the parliamentary concept of the motion of censure.[34]

When the regents convened the Grand National Assembly they submitted their own draft constitution, due to the fact that there was no document forthcoming from the committee they had appointed and entrusted with the task of preparing a new Constitution text. In the recent scholarship, Mirjana Stefanovski made an effort to meticulously analyse the texts, and concluded that the draft submitted to the Grand National Assembly by the regents was indeed a revised 1868 draft constitution.[35] The Grand National Assembly was convened in Kragujevac and opened by the regents' address on 12 June 1869. Having deliberated the draft, it adopted the Constitution on 29 June.[36] The 1869 Constitution has been known ever since under the name of the Regency Constitution. At the moment of its adoption in the Grand National Assembly, Serbia was still a vassal state under the Sultan's sovereign power. However, owing to the diplomatic success of 1867, when the Turkish garrisons left Serbia, the country was heading for full independence. The Ottoman Porte found no issue in the fact that a constitution was adopted without any intervention of the sovereign power.

Institutions

The most important government institutions of the 1869 Constitution were the Prince, the National Assembly and the cabinet of ministers. The principality of Serbia was by virtue of Article 1 of the Constitution 'a hereditary constitutional monarchy with the national representation'. The Prince was, according to Article 3, the head of state, vested with all state powers that he had to exercise in compliance with the constitution. It was stipulated in Article 4 of the Constitution that the Prince was vested with the legislative power together with the National Assembly. Article 6 provided that the executive power was vested in the Prince. The Prince's dignity was hereditary in the Obrenović family, and the Prince had to be Orthodox Christian.

Right after the provisions concerning the monarch, and in line with constitutions that were in force in Europe in the second half of the 19th century, articles 22 to 40 of the 1869 Constitution contained provisions on the rights and duties of Serbian citizens. Along with civil rights, political rights were guaranteed, such as, for instance, freedom of religion (Article 31), freedom of expression (32), right to a remedy (33) or right of petition (34). We have seen

34 ibid. 28–31.

35 ibid. 44–62.

36 J. Prodanović, *Ustavni razvitak*, 179–85.

above that political rights found a place neither in the 1835 Constitution, nor in the 1838 one. For the first time, provisions on political rights were in the Constitution text. Times had changed in Serbia before the 1869 Constitution was adopted. There were liberal ideas among the intelligentsia, which showed up at the National Assembly of St Andrew's Day of 1858. The political settlement under the rule of Prince Mihailo was targeted with criticism by the liberals. The Prince was inclined to introduce changes despite his basically conservative political attitudes. The provisions on fundamental rights in the 1869 Constitution were of liberal inspiration, albeit rather general in character, and some of them referred to special legislation that was to be enacted. This was the case, for example, of Article 32 *in fine*, which provided that the freedom of the press was to be regulated by a special law. Those provisions, as well as the 1869 Constitution as a whole, were for the great part drafted according to contemporary European standards. Although they could not properly match liberal-democratic concepts of Europe in their time, they nevertheless created conditions for the development of constitutionalism in Serbia.[37]

In respect of the national representative body, the drafters of the 1869 Constitution deviated from their original source of inspiration – the draft that Prince Mihailo committed to in 1868. The latter envisaged a two-house legislative body, while the regents eventually opted for a one-chamber National Assembly. The discussions among political actors in the late 1860s provoked a large debate in academia. This was recently summarised by M. Stefanovski.[38] Her main conclusion on the subject was that the composition of the National Assembly in the 1869 Constitution originated in the regents' intention to introduce preponderance of the cabinet of ministers over the national representative body.[39]

The composition of the one-chamber National Assembly in the 1869 Constitution was peculiar. Article 42 of the Constitution provided that the national representation could be either the Grand National Assembly, or the regular National Assembly. The Grand National Assembly was four times bigger, as regards the number of deputies, than the regular. Article 89 of the Constitution provided that its members were elected by the people. That was only partly the case with the regular National Assembly, whose members were national representatives elected by the people and appointed by the Prince. This points to the primordial concept, which envisaged a two-house national representation that was transformed into a single-chamber body, consisting,

37 cf. T. Marinković, 'Serbia', 30.
38 cf. M. Stefanovski, *Postanak*, 125–41.
39 ibid. 135.

however, of two types of representatives sitting together. According to Article 45 of the Constitution, a quarter of the deputies of the regular National Assembly were appointed by the Prince, and three quarters were elected by the people. The right to vote was restricted, and the same applied to eligibility for the National Assembly. Only men who were taxpayers enjoyed the right to vote and were eligible. Since the tax requirement was not excessive, Dragnich estimated the electoral system to be close to 'universal manhood suffrage'.[40]

The competence of the National Assembly introduced a novelty. Article 54 of the Constitution provided for the legislative power of the national representative body for the first time in Serbian constitutional history. However, it was stipulated in the same provision that the National Assembly could put on the agenda only those matters that had been communicated to it by the Prince. This meant reserving the legislative initiative for the government; the Prince was practically the chief executive, since he appointed those who held the respective power.

The expression 'executive power' did not find a place in the 1869 Constitution. Its Article 99 provided that the council of ministers was at the top of the public service. The same provision stated that the Prince was empowered to appoint and dismiss ministers as well as the President of the council of ministers, i.e. the prime minister. Notably, Article 100 of the Constitution, which followed, provided that the ministers were responsible for their acts before the Prince and the National Assembly. The same article provided for ministerial countersignature of the Prince's acts.

The germ of parliamentary government was there, despite the fact that in articles 101 to 104 that followed, the ministerial responsibility was shaped as the one for criminal offences. The National Assembly was competent to accuse a minister, who would then be put on trial before a special tribunal. The latter was to be organised according to a future statute on the subject, which was referred to in Article 104 of the Constitution.

The 1869 Constitution also provided for the *Državni savet* (Council of State). The name of this body in Serbian language was the same as for the State organ, which existed under the 1861 constitutional settlement. In this book the body instituted in 1861 was called *State Council*, which literally corresponds to the Serbian expression, in order to underline the difference of competence between the two bodies of the same name. Notably, the State Council of 1861 had the power to legislate together with the Prince, which was no more the case with the Council of State of the 1869 Constitution. By virtue of Article 90

40 A. Dragnich, *The Development*, 52; for the composition of the National Assembly, see also M. Stefanovski, *Postanak*, 131.

of the Constitution, the latter was primarily competent to draft legislation, to issue consultative opinions on legislative drafts and to decide on petitions against ministerial decisions in matters of administrative disputes.

The members of the Council of State were appointed by the Prince. The organisation and competence of that body were shaped in the 1869 Constitution after the model of the French *Conseil d'Etat* that had already found followers in comparative constitutional law.

The judiciary faced peculiar developments under the constitutional settlement of 1861, i.e. Prince Mihailo's second reign in Serbia. The court system remained unaltered for a quarter century: after an initial act was passed in 1840, it was not until 1865 that new legislation was adopted. This was the *Zakon o ustrojstvu sudova* (Organisation of Courts Act), which provided for the district courts in the first instance, the Court of Appeals in the second instance and the Court of Cassation as the court of second appeal.[41]

During Mihailo's second reign, the judiciary faced challenges and troubles. The greatest of all was the wrecking of the Supreme Court. The Prince put five judges of that court in prison, because they had been found guilty of intentionally distorting the law and wrongly judging. They were sentenced by a special tribunal, which established that the Supreme Court justices had committed those crimes by acquitting a group accused in a case of conspiracy allegedly aimed at overthrowing the dynasty due to lack of proof.[42]

The 1869 Constitution was adopted only five years after the scandalous events that shook the Serbian judiciary to its very foundations. The Constitution text contained guarantees of fair trial, although in a somewhat abstract way, leaving room for further legislation. For example, it was stipulated in Article 108 of the Constitution that the court system should encompass several tiers, but the provision stopped at enunciating the principle. The courts of different instances were not mentioned in the Constitution, as had been the case with Article 30 of the 1838 Constitution. The legislation on judiciary was completed with the *Zakon o sudijama* (Judges' Act) of 1881, which introduced guarantees of judges' independence and made their tenures secure.[43] The Judges' Act was the landmark in the history of the Serbian judiciary. It provided that only persons with legal training were eligible to hold the judge's office in Serbia. The system of appointment was such that judges of the first instance courts were appointed by the cabinet of ministers. Justices of the Court of

41 cf. D. Jevtić, 'Novi vek – Srbija', 143.

42 A. Dragnich, *The Development*, 43–44; on the conspiracy case in detail, S. Jovanović, *Druga vlada*, 432–42.

43 D. Jevtić, 'Novi vek – Srbija', 155.

Appeals and the Court of Cassation were appointed by the cabinet, but from lists presented by the sitting justices in those courts. Slobodan Jovanović brilliantly summarised the substance of the 1881 Act in a simple phrase: 'that Act introduced the independence of the judiciary, which had not existed before its adoption'.[44]

2.4 Constitution in Action

Emergence of Ministerial Responsibility

The most important developments that occurred under the 1869 Constitution were the recognition of ministerial responsibility and the formation of political parties. The latter has been subject to a relatively wide range of research among scholars, whereas the former has attracted less interest. It is one of Alex Dragnich's outstanding contributions to the study of Serbian constitutional history, to have pointed to the process of the emergence of ministerial responsibility in practice. Dragnich relied on primary sources, mostly on the minutes of the National Assembly sessions, to develop his thesis. In his view ministerial responsibility emerged in several steps in the 1870s.[45]

It was before political parties were formed in Serbia that a council of ministers, i.e. a cabinet, stepped down, confronted with the outcome of a vote in the National Assembly. The prime minister was Jovan Marinović (1821–93). He formed his cabinet in October 1873.[46] In October 1874 parliamentary elections took place and the National Assembly met in session at the beginning of November. Although there were no properly organised political parties in the country, the outcome of the elections was favourable to those who were considered to be liberals. Marinović, for his part, was rather conservative and found his cabinet's position precarious. At the beginning of its session, the National Assembly debated the draft of its address in answer to the Prince's opening speech. The prime minister introduced a proposal of the address, which was put to a vote. The National Assembly supported the cabinet's proposal by sixty-one votes to fifty-eight, with three abstentions. The prime minister was of the opinion that with such a tiny majority supportive of his cabinet in the National Assembly, he could no more govern the country, and therefore resigned. The

44 S. Jovanović, *Vlada Milana Obrenovića, knjiga druga 1878–1889* [Government of Milan Obrenović, Book two 1878–1889], Belgrade 1927, 72–73.

45 A. Dragnich, *The Development*, 53–56.

46 On the formation and work of the cabinet, cf. Ž. Živanović, *Politička istorija Srbije*, 280–94; G. Stokes, *Politics as Development: The Emergence of Political Parties in Nineteenth-century Serbia*, Durham and London 1990, 22–30.

wording of his letter to the National Assembly was remarkable. The prime minister stated that 'the majority of three votes was so weak that the cabinet cannot hope, not even for a second' to survive and remain in office.[47] The prime minister was fully aware of the fact that to remain in office it was essential to enjoy the confidence of the National Assembly. It was for the first time in the constitutional history of Serbia that a cabinet was censured and stepped down from office because it did not have the confidence of the National Assembly. It occurred even without a proper vote of no confidence in the government.

Soon after this first event that announced developments leading towards parliamentary government, the confidence vote came into practice in the National Assembly. When Marinović stepped down from office his interior minister, Aćim Čumić (1836–1901) was entrusted with the mandate to form a new cabinet.[48] Succeeding Marinović, as the new prime minister Čumić had to confront himself with a number of interpellations on various subjects that were a clear sign of the dissatisfaction of National Assembly members with the work of the cabinet. To fight this dissatisfaction, Čumić chose specific tactics. Instead of trying to provide arguments against criticism and enter into parliamentary debate, the prime minister repeatedly raised the question of confidence in the cabinet. His tactics proved successful, for he won the confidence vote each and every time. However, because of such a practice Čumić had to face the resignations of some of the cabinet ministers who disagreed with him. His cabinet worked in an atmosphere of political tensions and could not last more than two months. The prime minister resigned.

The practice of a confidence vote, introduced by Čumić as prime minister, was another step towards parliamentary government in Serbia. In light of such a practice, it was becoming clearly evident that a cabinet was unable to remain in office without the confidence of the National Assembly. The subsequent cabinets proceeded along the same line, being careful to secure parliamentary confidence.[49] Ministerial responsibility in the form of accountability of the cabinet as a whole before the national representation body became a part of the Serbian political and constitutional settlement in the second half of the 1870s. Under the constitutional monarchy, Serbia was heading for parliamentary government. The formation of political parties led the country in the same direction.

---

47 A. Dragnich, *The Development*, 55; G. Stokes, *Politics as Development*, 39; Ž. Živanović, *Politička istorija Srbije*, 299.

48 On Čumić cabinet, cf. Ž. Živanović, *Politička istorija Srbije*, 299–309.

49 A. Dragnich, *The Development*, 55–56.

Formation of Political Parties

Political parties in the modern sense of the term were formed in Serbia from the 1870s onwards. They were properly shaped in respect of organisation and programmes in the 1880s, and their activities very much animated Serbian political life. Three parties were formed in Serbia in the 19th century: liberals, progressives and radicals. Liberals were the first to come to the political scene. Liberal ideas came to Serbia from abroad, brought by the Serbian students who had studied in Western Europe, especially in Paris. There was an eruption of liberal ideas at the Assembly of St Andrew's Day of 1858. However, that assembly ended up with the restoration of the Obrenović dynasty to the Serbian throne.

The liberals were in favour of annual meetings of the National Assembly, and also of freedom of the press and of improving education in Serbia. In foreign policy they were nationalists, trying to achieve liberation of the Serbs still living under the Ottoman rule at that time. The latter made them close to Prince Mihailo's attitudes, while the former created a distance from his regime. The provisions of the 1869 Constitution met the requirements of the liberals only in part. Throughout the 1870s the liberals were not properly organised as a political party. In spite of that, a prominent member of the liberal circle, a diplomat with a PhD from Heidelberg University, had been close to Prince Mihailo and after his death became a regent and an outstanding politician of the new regime. This was Jovan Ristić (1831–99), who had headed the cabinet under the rule of Prince Mihailo for a while. The 1869 Constitution was indeed his achievement. In the new political settlement Ristić was a regent for Prince Milan Obrenović, so he strongly inspired the drafting of the constitution, although it did not quite fit his political ideas.

Under the 1869 Constitution, Ristić was the outstanding prime minister in the 1870s. He was at the forefront of determining the line of Serbian foreign policy, which proved to be successful. In 1875 an international crisis occurred in the Balkans, triggered by the insurrection of the Serbian population in Bosnia and Herzegovina against the Ottoman rule. The next stage of the crisis was the Russo-Turkish War of 1877–78, which Serbia joined on the Russian side. To end the whole crisis, a congress of great powers was convened in Berlin. Its outcome was the Treaty of Berlin, which determined the territories and the status of states in the Balkans. The Treaty of Berlin of 1878 recognised Serbia as an independent state, which rounded up the process of emancipation of the new, modern nation in terms of international law. Moreover, Serbia increased its territory, since it acquired by virtue of the same treaty four districts in the south-east. Ristić represented Serbia at the congress, seeking support mostly from Austria-Hungary, the great power which was then given an international mandate to restore peace in Bosnia and Herzegovina.[50]

It was at the beginning of the 1880s that the liberals organised as a modern political party. The party attracted support in the social strata of bureaucracy, publishing a programme in 1881 which proclaimed political freedoms in domestic policy and the liberation of Serbs living under the Ottoman rule in foreign countries.[51] During the 1870s the liberals had rivals in a political circle of conservatives. The latter altered their name, somewhat paradoxically, to 'progressives'.

The progressives came to power in 1880 as a more or less coherent group of young conservatives, and by the next year they were properly organised as a political party. Prominent intellectuals of the younger generation, such as Čumić, Mijatović, Novaković, Milutin Garašanin and Piroćanac, most of them university professors, were among its members.[52] The same social classes that were supportive of the liberals were also supporters of the progressives – public servants, bureaucrats, intelligentsia, all of them inhabiting cities in the times when cities were few and the rural population by far prevailed in the country. However, the national representation under the 1869 Constitution, which sat in one single chamber, was twofold. Besides the elected members in the National Assembly, there were also those appointed by the Prince to sit. These were called 'government MPs' and their presence provided a margin of manoeuvre for the cabinet to pursue its policies.

The progressives' policies followed Western political ideas and aimed to introduce European values and standards in Serbia. They opposed the former liberal government and introduced considerable reforms. Their major endeavour was to overcome the patriarchal social structure of the country, introduce modern institutions and establish political freedom. The above-mentioned legislation on independent judiciary was their achievement, i.e. the outcome of carrying out their programme. The same applies to the legislation on freedom of expression and freedom of association and the like. The progressives also launched important welfare projects at the cost of the budget.[53] Two circumstances were decisive for the destiny of the Progressive Party. The first consisted in the fact that it was somewhat excessively close to the monarch, and the second was the emergence and rise of the Radical Party.

---

50 On Ristić's role as regards representing Serbia at the congress in Berlin, cf. Ž. Živanović, *Politička istorija Srbije*, 369–90.

51 A. Dragnich, *The Development*, 61.

52 On progressives' leaders, cf. S. Jovanović, *Vlada Milana Obrenovića*, 121–23.

53 A. Dragnich, *The Development*, 62–63.

The People's Radical Party was the first political party in Serbia to have an organisation that spread all over the country. Besides the Steering Committee in Belgrade, the party had local committees in many cities.[54] Such a decentralised structure enabled the party to get in touch with the masses, and especially with the peasants. The radicals started as followers of the earliest socialist ideas in Serbia. Their ideological predecessor was Svetozar Marković (1846–75), who had studied in Russia and Switzerland and adopted socialist ideas. Marković criticised the liberals. He was in favour of addressing the peasant masses in Serbia, and consulting them on political matters. His general views were based on agrarian collectivism.[55] The radicals on one hand abandoned the economic aspect of Marković's ideas, because they were not well received by Serbian peasants, who preferred individual ownership of their small plots of land. On the other hand, the radicals preserved Marković's political ideas, which relied on popular sovereignty and local self-government, representing the foundations of his criticism of the 1869 Constitution. The most prominent members of the Radical Party were Milovanović, Pašić and Protić, but its true leader was Pašić.

In their political programme the radicals demanded a new constitution that would be drafted along the lines of their ideas. The radicals were the only political party in Serbia that addressed the peasants. They did so by sending skillful orators to campaign for a radical change of the constitutional and political settlement in the country. That is what led them to gain enormous support among the masses. The method used in the radicals' propaganda was largely populist. Their target group was peasants, whom they confronted with people inhabiting cities, reproaching the latter for neglecting the peasants' interests. The radicals idealised the peasantry to some extent, ensuring their political messages complied with the wishes of that social class. In a country with a tradition of popular poetry, songs and dances appeared which promoted the radicals' stances in favour of peasants' interests.[56] A verse of a political poem hinting at disobedience and resistance can be illustrative in that respect. It read:

Ustaj seljo, ustaj rode, Da se spaseš od gospode!	Rise up peasant, rise my kin, From gentlemen save your skin!

54 S. Jovanović, *Vlada Milana Obrenovića*, 112.
55 ibid. 115–17.
56 On idealising the peasantry, ideology and symbols, cf. S. Naumović, 'Ustaj seljo, ustaj rode: Simbolika seljaštva i politička komunikacija u novijoj istoriji Srbije' [Rise up, peasant, rise my kin: Symbolism of the peasantry and political communication in the recent history of Serbia], *Godišnjak za društvenu istoriju II/1 1995*, 46–49.

The radicals claimed that their party was the only one representing the people in general: not just the upper classes, but indeed the lower classes and peasantry. They were under the impact of the socialist attitudes of Svetozar Marković. Nikola Pašić (1845–1926), one of the most prominent radicals, wrote that the radicals did not want to prohibit private property, but to raise industry on the basis of associated labour instead.[57] The two other political parties were portrayed by the radicals as close to the throne. They were labelled as *dvorske stranke* (palace parties). Such propaganda was successful to a large degree.

The radicals thus became the strongest political party in Serbia. The attitude of the Radical Party towards Prince Milan was decisive for political developments in the country in the 1880s. The Prince was in favour of preserving the 1869 Constitution, considering it an adequate instrument for the development of Serbian society. The radicals were in favour of a change and clashed with the Prince. From the constitutional point of view, one of the core issues in the dispute was the scope of power of the executive, and within that framework the position of the head of state in a constitutional monarchy. The issue was by no means exclusively academic. It was indeed subject to the evolution of political events.

Monarch's Constitutional Role

Several important events took place while the progressives were in power. In 1882 Serbia was proclaimed a kingdom. Milan Obrenović became the first King in Serbian modern history. The background of the proclamation, which occurred all of a sudden in February 1882, was by no means festive. After the Treaty of Berlin, Serbia was under obligation to construct a railway line from the north to the south-east of its territory, so as to enable a connection between Central Europe and Istanbul. The government concluded a contract with foreign bankers which turned out to be detrimental to the Serbian budget and provoked dissatisfaction of the public at large and, last but not least, a debate in the National Assembly.[58] The cabinet was about to fall, and the monarch decided to save it by proclaiming a kingdom. Milan Obrenović had already secured consent for such a move from Serbia's closest neighbour, and one of the world's great powers at the time: in 1881, Austria-Hungary concluded a treaty with Serbia. It remained unknown to the public for more than a decade and therefore obtained the name 'Secret Convention'. One of its provisions envisaged Austria-Hungary's acceptance in advance of the proclamation of a new Kingdom of Serbia. Moreover, Serbia's powerful neighbour promised

57 G. Stokes, *Politics as Development*, 98.

58 See S. Jovanović, *Vlada Milana Obrenovića*, 98–100, on parliamentary debate.

diplomatic support at the international level for this transformation of the country's status. This was of enormous importance, since the world's powers followed Austria-Hungary's policy lines in affairs concerning Serbia. The latter was in the political sphere of the former, because of the Austro-Russian agreement in respect of the Balkans. The western part of the peninsula, including Serbia, was considered to be in the Austrian zone of influence, while the eastern side was left to the Russians.[59]

The proclamation of kingdom did not put an end to the political crisis in the country. Already in March 1882 the opposition deputies abandoned sessions of the National Assembly. By virtue of Article 82 of the 1869 Constitution, the national representation needed a quorum of three quarters of its members to sit lawfully. Since fifty-one radicals and two liberals left the sessions, the work of the National Assembly was blocked. The opposition required general parliamentary elections, but the progressives' cabinet decided to hold elections only in those constituencies in which the MPs who abandoned the National Assembly were elected. The idea was to fill vacated seats only.[60]

The by-elections were scheduled in mid-May, which made the King activate and act as if he were a politician. King Milan went on a tour all over the country, visiting fourteen cities in one month, strongly campaigning against the radicals and in favour of the progressive candidates. The outcome of the elections was nevertheless unfavourable for the government: forty-five radical candidates were elected. When the opposition left the National Assembly once again, the cabinet organised new by-elections at the end of May. As the result was poor for the government, which obtained only two seats, the cabinet decided to apply a special mode of counting votes. Namely, only votes that had not been given for the candidates of the party that had left the National Assembly were taken into consideration. The idea was that those deputies did not intend to sit at all, even if re-elected. With such peculiar arithmetics, some of the elected persons that obtained the seats had only two votes in their favour.[61]

Besides the irregularity of the May by-elections of 1882, the King's conduct was decisive from a constitutional standpoint. The Crown was active in political matters, and the mechanism of constitutional monarchy did not seem to function correctly, i.e. as provided for by the Constitution. The King entered into the political game, siding with one group of politicians against their political adversaries. This pattern of conduct would continue in Serbia, and

59 ibid. 56–57.

60 A. Dragnich, *The Development*, 70.

61 S. Jovanović, *Vlada Milana Obrenovića*, 139–44.

the question of the position of the Crown would persist even in times of parliamentary monarchy. However, in 1882 there was a huge amount of tension between the progressives' cabinet and the Crown on one side, and the People's Radical Party on the other. The tensions culminated in 1883 with an armed rebellion.

New parliamentary elections took place in September 1883, showing a poor outcome for the cabinet once again. The radicals won sixty-one seats in the National Assembly against thirty-four won by the progressives and eleven by the liberals. The independent candidates won in seven constituencies. The prime minister resigned, but the King did not want to entrust the most influential political party, which won the elections, to form a cabinet. He preferred, instead, a cabinet which did not enjoy the confidence of the National Assembly. A manoeuvre was made which was strongly in contrast with the spirit and the letter of the Constitution. The National Assembly session was opened by a royal decree and adjourned by another immediately afterwards. The move aimed to avoid presenting the cabinet in parliament, and its outcome was a government that was exclusively accountable to the King. Article 100 of the Constitution provided, however, that the ministers were responsible both to the monarch and the National Assembly. The King thus had an obedient cabinet, enabling him to govern the country as it pleased him and without national representation. The People's Radical Party, the winner in the elections, was not invited to the cabinet because of the King's animosity towards its members and programme.

Tensions were high all over the country, and rebellion broke out in eastern Serbia, in the Timok region. The reason for rebellion was a military issue. Serbia had a regular army, as well as a militia. That is why the people had firearms at home, given to them by the government as militia members. The progressives' government decided to switch from one model of firearms to another, and therefore required all those who possessed firearms to return these before they could receive the new model. That would practically mean the disarmament of the militia.[62] The government's decision provoked unrest and protests. The people feared they would not be given new arms once they returned those that they possessed. Clashes between armed militians and regular army troops occurred in autumn 1883. The former were defeated in a couple of weeks in a ferocious action of the government troops. The standing army restored peace during the state of emergency that was proclaimed, the insurgents were court-marshalled and the radical leaders were accused of high treason. In sum, there were more than ninety death sentences pronounced,

62 ibid. 183.

and twenty resultant executions. Several hundred people were sentenced to prison. Some of the radical leaders escaped into exile, including Nikola Pašić, who spent several years in Bulgaria, escaping a death sentence pronounced *in absentia*.[63] The radicals were thus suppressed, and new parliamentary elections were held in January 1884, bringing a majority in the National Assembly favourable to the government. The prime minister of the non-parliamentary cabinet resigned and the King entrusted a progressive leader with the formation of a new cabinet.

The new prime minister, Milutin Garašanin (1843–98), was one of the Progressive Party leaders; his cabinet followed conservative policies, restrictive as regards political freedoms. In the year following its formation, the Garašanin cabinet had to face a considerable challenge. Serbia went to war against Bulgaria in November 1885. The cause of war was the wish to maintain the Balkan equilibrium. The Treaty of Berlin had created two Bulgarian entities: the principality of Bulgaria and East Rumelia, the latter of which remained under a Turkish governor. When the two entities proclaimed unification, the Serbian King and government found in such an event a reason to claim that the international order was violated. The warfare did not prove successful for the Serbian side, but the great powers intervened to introduce first ceasefire and then peace, maintaining the *status quo*.[64]

King Milan faced another problem in the second half of the 1880s. The problem was primarily personal in appearance, but had consequences on the functioning of political institutions in Serbia. Milan Obrenović had married young, at the age of twenty-one. His spouse was Natalija Keško (1859–1941), daughter of a Russian aristocrat and Moldavian princess. She was the granddaughter of the former ruling Prince of Moldavia. The couple had a son, Aleksandar (1876–1903). The marital problems of the Serbian royal couple, which began in 1885, became evident the next year and were reflected in politics. The Queen left the country for the Crimea, taking the Crown Prince with her. On her return, a compromise was reached by the spouses in respect of the Prince's education. The cabinet was trying to avoid scandal, while the radicals in opposition sided with the queen, and eventually a divorce agreement was brokered.[65] The whole set of circumstances provoked the fall of the progressives' cabinet.

---

63 A. Dragnich, *The Development*, 71–72; on the Timok rebellion *in extenso* in English, G. Stokes, *Politics as Development*, 258–90.

64 On the war *in extenso*, cf. S. Jovanović, *Vlada Milana Obrenovića*, 243–300.

65 A. Dragnich, *The Development*, 74–75; for more detail, cf. S. Jovanović, *Vlada Milana Obrenovića*, 354–78.

Ristić returned to power in mid-1887, but would remain prime minister for just a couple of months. His cabinet was important because of its composition. Notably, the King agreed to the participation of the radicals in government. He did not want to grant pardon to Pašić and those whom he considered responsible for the rebellion of 1883, but nevertheless for reasons of political opportunity he decided to tolerate a liberal–radical cabinet. Moreover, when Ristić stepped down after only half a year in office, the King entrusted the radicals to form a cabinet. Sava Grujić (1840–1913), army officer and minister of defence in the previous cabinet, became prime minister, under the condition that the minister of foreign affairs had to be a King's appointee. Grujić's first cabinet entered office at the very beginning of 1888 and lasted only four months. It was the first Serbian government composed of radicals, whose complex relations to the king marked Serbian political and constitutional history. King Milan altered his attitude towards the radicals, remodelling his policy line in internal and to some extent also in international affairs. His new stance towards political matters included the adoption of a new constitution. It was adopted in 1888.

With the significant alteration of the King's attitude towards the most influential political party, Serbia seemed to be at a new beginning on the path leading to the introduction of parliamentary government. Notably, some claim that such a form of government is at a beginning when the monarch agrees to entrust the governance of the country to the politicians he disagrees with. That was the case for Serbia in 1888. Moreover, the King agreed to the drafting of a new constitution. Serbia was apparently at the doorstep of a parliamentary form of government.

2.5 The 1888 Constitution – A Landmark

Emergence

Appearances were misleading. King Milan regretted to some extent his decision to invite the radicals to the cabinet. He was generally dissatisfied with their policy line, and especially with different acts adopted in the National Assembly. A constitutional issue occurred in April 1888 between the monarch and the prime minister. The King refused royal assent to an act approved by the National Assembly. The prime minister stepped down, and the King entrusted a high-ranking bureaucrat to form a new cabinet composed of public servants and some progressives.[66] The episode in which the King and the prime minis-

66 S. Jovanović, *Vlada Milana Obrenovića*, 365–66; A. Dragnich, *The Development*, 76.

ter clashed was significant. The King's stance prevailed completely because the prime minister was unable to find support in the National Assembly against the King's will. His only option was to resign.

King Milan was a person inclined to mood swings. In 1888 he thought of abdication in favour of his son. While in such a mood, he embraced the idea of creating a new political climate in Serbia, which would rely on consenting to the rules of the game by the King and all three political parties. Following that line of reasoning, the King decided to enter into the process of remodelling the political settlement of the country. The Crown was nevertheless driven by circumstances. The divorce of the royal couple was not well accepted in a patriarchal country where divorces were rare, albeit allowed by the canon law of the Orthodox Church. Only two days after the divorce of the royal couple was made public, the King issued a proclamation to convene the Grand National Assembly, the body vested with constituent power by virtue of Article 89 of the Constitution. The King also appointed a committee composed of members belonging to all three political parties existing at the time, with the task of drafting a new Constitution text. The three party leaders were deputy Presidents of the committee, while the King in person chaired its sessions. Indeed, two bodies were formed – the plenary and an inner committee.[67] The debates in the committees, as well as later at the sessions of the Grand National Assembly, displayed a variety of ideas, although their mainstream was a tendency to introduce parliamentary government. Some tones of debate, however, deserve highlighting. For instance, the King rejected the radicals' proposals to introduce a provision on the sovereignty of the people into the new constitution. The same was the destiny of radical proposals on universal male suffrage. The King's role in preparing the draft was important. The King influenced the work of the constitution drafters to a considerable degree, while trying to remain neutral in respect of the parties. Eventually, the King agreed on a draft that was an outcome of a compromise between the liberals and the radicals.[68] The Grand National Assembly, elected in November, met in session in December 1888 and adopted the new constitution in the same month. The 1888 Constitution was a landmark in the constitutional history of Serbia because of its substance: it provided for parliamentary government.

---

67 S. Jovanović, *Vlada Milana Obrenovića*, 379–80; J. Prodanović, *Ustavni razvitak*, 283–84.

68 On rejecting the radicals' proposals, cf. J. Prodanović, *Ustavni razvitak*, 284, 289, 295; on the compromise, cf. S. Jovanović, *Vlada Milana Obrenovića*, 388.

Institutions

The 1888 Constitution provided that the legislative power was vested in the King and the national representation (Article 33). The executive power was vested in the King, who was to exercise that power by intermediary of his responsible ministers (Article 38), whereas the judiciary was with the courts (Article 39). The 1888 Constitution had more provisions on human rights than the previous one of 1869. The heading of the respective part of the Constitution text was changed. In 1869 the Constitution provided on 'Rights and Duties of Citizens in General', while in the 1888 Constitution the respective heading read 'Constitutional Rights of Serbian Citizens'. Constitutional guarantees of human rights were stronger in the 1888 Constitution than ever before in Serbia. Apart from a large and, to some extent, detailed catalogue of human rights provided in articles 6 to 39 of the Constitution, three general remarks should be made in respect of their constitutional guarantees. First, Article 147 proclaimed the independence of the judiciary. We have seen above that the independence of the judiciary had been provided for by the legislation; the 1888 Constitution included a constitutional guarantee of its independence. Second, articles 117 and 118 provided for a strictly constitutional rule. The monarch was not entitled to legislate in the state of emergency, as used to be the case by virtue of Article 56 of the 1869 Constitution. Third, in the previous constitutional settlement a public servant could be sued so as to be accountable for his acts in service only in the presence of permission of the minister competent for the relevant sector of the public service. The 1888 Constitution put an end to such a system by providing in Article 185 that 'every public servant is accountable for his acts done in service'.[69]

Article 33 of the Constitution conferred the legislative power to the King and national representation. The national representation organ was the National Assembly, which remained a one-chamber body. It could be either the regular assembly or the Grand National Assembly. The former was vested with the legislative power, together with the King, whereas the latter had the constituent power. The censal regime of the previous constitution was maintained, because articles 79 and 95 of the 1888 Constitution provided that only taxpayers disposed of the right to vote and were eligible.

By virtue of Article 102 of the Constitution, the National Assembly had to convene in a regular session on 1 November in the capital city, and sit for at least six weeks. The deputies of the National Assembly were allowed to enter bills, which were no longer the privilege of the cabinet, as was the case under

69 S. Jovanović *Vlada Milana Obrenovića*, 381.

the 1869 Constitution. It was stipulated *expressis verbis* in Article 34 of the 1888 Constitution.

The executive power was vested in the King. It had to be exercised through responsible ministers. The King was limited by ministerial countersignature, as provided by articles 56 and 136 of the Constitution. Both the National Assembly and the King were empowered to accuse a minister by virtue of Article 137 of the Constitution. This provision was followed by three others which shaped this pattern of responsibility after the one applying to criminal offences. Remarkably, Art. 140 of the Constitution contained a provision forbidding the King to grant pardon to a minister sentenced in a due process. This sort of ministerial responsibility was not used by parliamentarians to censure a government. We have seen above that ministerial responsibility in the parliamentary sense of the term emerged in Serbia in parliamentary practice. It was essential that a cabinet could not remain in office without the support of the National Assembly, but it was equally important that the Crown preserved its prerogative, which was going to be one of crucial constitutional issues under the 1888 Constitution.

The Council of State was preserved in the 1888 Constitution with basically the same scope of power as in the 1869 Constitution. An important novelty was that the monarch was no longer competent to appoint all the councillors. That body consisted of sixteen members. Eight of these were elected by the National Assembly from a King's list of candidates. The other half were appointed by the King, but they were chosen from the list of candidates presented to him by the National Assembly.

The judiciary was independent, the jury trial was preserved and the constitution posed the basis of the judicial system in Article 150. The system was a three-tier one, encompassing the first instance courts, the Court of Appeals and the Court of Cassation. Guarantees of a fair trial were provided for. The King was competent to appoint judges, but when making appointments he was under obligation to choose from the lists presented to him by the Court of Appeals and the Court of Cassation. For appointments of the justices in appeal and in cassation, the respective lists were presented by the Council of State and the Court of Cassation.

The auspices were good for Serbia in the presence of such a Constitution text. The parliamentary government could function under the liberal provisions of the 1888 Constitution. That constitution was the landmark on Serbia's path towards modern institutions of parliamentary government. The political parties agreed to the rules of the game, but the complete image of the Serbian political scene encompassed the Crown. King Milan was on the throne, his son and heir Aleksandar was of minor age, and the King decided to abdicate and leave the throne to his son. Unstable in his private life, the king fell in love with a lady and planned to start a new and quiet life away from political affairs. However, that was not his only intention.

King Milan accepted the 1888 Constitution, agreed to let the radicals govern the country, but he followed tactics which he thought were well founded. He was of the opinion that the people would realise the bad sides of the radical regime, suspect partisanship and in future ask him to return to the throne. Milan abdicated in February 1888, and as he was entitled by the provision of Article 70 of the Constitution to appoint regents for his son on the throne he appointed two generals, Protić and Belimarković, and a politician, Ristić, who indeed dominated the regency. Ristić was one of the regents for Milan himself, before he attained majority. By appointing the regents, King Milan wanted to preserve his influence in the political affairs of Serbia.

Implementation of the 1888 Constitution

The implementation of the 1888 Constitution lasted until 1901 and had two phases. The turning point came in April 1893. Before that date two radical cabinets succeeded one another. The main features of the radical governance were the preponderance of the national representation over the executive, decentralisation of government, improving relations with Russia and freedom of political parties' actions. The radical leader in exile, Nikola Pašić, who had been sentenced for high treason *in absentia*, was granted pardon by the regency.[70] The political settlement was functioning in line with the precepts of the parliamentary form of government. The situation changed in April 1893, when King Aleksandar, still a minor at the age of seventeen, led a coup d'état.

First Grujić and then Pašić headed the radical cabinets between February 1889 and August 1892. The Pašić cabinet stepped down on a constitutional issue. One of the regents, general Kosta Protić, passed away in June 1892. According to Article 71 of the Constitution, the National Assembly was empowered to fill the vacancy. Pašić suggested its special session for that purpose, which Ristić, the most powerful in the regency, refused, fearing that Pašić himself might be elected regent.[71] The prime minister and the dominating regent clashed on a constitutional issue. A regular National Assembly session was scheduled on 1 November each year by the letter of Article 102 of the Constitution. The king had the right to convene an extraordinary session according to Article 103. The latter provision made the regency, i.e. Ristić in person, master of the game.

70 S. Jovanović, *Vlada Aleksandra Obrenovića, knjiga prva* [The government of Aleksandar Obrenović, Book I], Belgrade 1929, 33–34; A. Dragnich, *The Development*, 81–82.

71 A. Dragnich, *The Development*, 84; S. Jovanovic, *Vlada Aleksandra Obrenovića I*, 181.

Feeling that the popularity of the radicals was weakening, he rejected the prime minister's proposal to convene an extraordinary session of the National Assembly. The prime minister then made a gambler's move and resigned in August 1892, hoping to win in the elections. Ristić invited a liberal to form a cabinet, and new parliamentary elections were held in February 1893, in which the liberals were victorious, winning sixty-nine seats out of 134.

The system introduced by the 1888 Constitution still seemed to function following the model of parliamentary government. When the radical cabinet stepped down in August 1892, Ristić declared, addressing the radicals and representing the Crown, 'Gentlemen, I have made an appeal to the people; if they vote in your favour, you can return'.[72] The Radical Party did not return to power, because of the unfavourable outcome of the elections. The liberal cabinet continued in office. However, the political situation in the country was tense. A sudden move of the young King introduced a new element that put Serbia on a path somewhat different from the one that was apparently prevailing, and leading to the parliamentary form of government.

On 1 April 1893, King Aleksandar Obrenović, seconded by the army, proclaimed he took the royal prerogatives. The King was not yet seventeen, but he proclaimed himself to be of age for the step taken. It was a coup d'état. The King's move was anti-constitutional and illegal, but at first the young monarch didn't seem ready to go too far. A new cabinet was formed, headed by a moderate radical and the King's former tutor, Lazar Dokić, a physician and professor of anatomy. The radicals thus remained in power, and apparently the whole constitutional settlement was not fundamentally disturbed. Once again, the appearances were misleading.

The prime minister passed away in December the same year, and was followed in office by another moderate radical, Sava Grujić, who had already headed the cabinet twice. His third cabinet lasted less than two months and he stepped down on a legal issue which had considerable constitutional consequences. Milan Obrenović, the former King who had left the country, returned to Serbia in January 1894. There was an act of parliament passed in 1892, which prohibited the ex-King to return to the country. The transgression of law was evident. Since the cabinet was unable to remove the former King from the country, the prime minister resigned.

Đorđe Simić, a career diplomat with brilliant references in service, and also a moderate radical, formed a new cabinet which once again only lasted two months. The King dismissed the cabinet on the grounds that the ministers were not ready to fight the radicals, i.e. the King's enemies. Little was left

72 S. Jovanović, *Vlada Aleksandra Obrenovića I*, 191.

of the concept of parliamentary government in Serbia in those days. On one hand, the National Assembly could not counterbalance the monarch's power. On the other, King Aleksandar was governing the country with cabinets that were considered to be neutral as regards party affiliations, but they were composed at the King's will and fully loyal to the monarch. However, the question of the former King was still open, and one of the neutral cabinets, which had Svetomir Nikolajević, a university professor, as prime minister, issued a decree in April 1894 that annulled the act of parliament of 1892, forbidding Milan Obrenović to dwell in Serbia. The case of validity of the government's act was brought before the Court of Cassation, which ruled in May 1894 that the decree was invalid. The reasoning of the Court of Cassation was that a law, i.e. an act of parliament, could not be revoked by a government decree.

King Aleksandar was at a crossroads; he could either comply with the ruling of the Court of Cassation, or transgress the law and step beyond the framework of legality. The King chose the latter. Only four days after the ruling of the Court of Cassation, Aleksandar led another coup d'état. The King abolished the 1888 Constitution and returned in force the Constitution of 1869. The story of the implementation of the 1888 Constitution was over, as well as the first attempt of introducing parliamentary government in Serbia.[73] Throughout the next seven years the constitutional crisis continued. It was not resolved until the end of King Aleksandar's reign, despite the fact that a new constitution came into force.

2.6 The 1901 Constitution – An Exception

Background

The rest of the reign of King Aleksandar Obrenović can hardly qualify as a constitutional monarchy. It was a personal regime of the monarch. Between January 1894 and October 1897 five cabinets held. The young King was receiving advice from his parents, who were in disagreement on everything, including political matters. The main political issue was relations between the Radical Party and the Crown. These were complex and influenced by changing circumstances. As of 1897, the two kings, Milan and Aleksandar, were in Serbia. Milan was popular with the army, and Aleksandar feared his father might attempt to regain the throne. The cabinet appointed in 1897, which managed to last for three years, was headed by Vladan Đorđević, a surgeon, who had no impact

73 D. Jevtić, 'Novi vek – Srbija', 172–74; A. Dragnich, *The Development*, 84–87; and *in extenso* S. Jovanović, *Vlada Aleksandra Obrenovića I*, 211–301.

in choosing ministers. It was a Crown cabinet. To borrow the expression from Alex Dragnich, it was 'a nonparty personal regime, firm and strict'.[74] The Queen was no more in the country when the former King and the King on the throne clashed on a personal issue which had far-reaching consequences on the constitutional history of Serbia. It was the question of Aleksandar's marriage.

Although solicited by the government to marry an Austrian noblewoman, King Aleksandar chose a lady from Belgrade twelve years his senior, a childless widow, who, as it turned out in course of time, could not give birth. The marriage, which took place in 1900, was not well accepted among the people. Aleksandar's parents were both against the marriage.[75] The queen mother lived in France and the former King, Milan, left for Austria before his son married. The former King was forbidden to return to the country once again, this time by his son. Milan passed away in February 1901 and was buried in a Serbian monastery in the territory of Austria-Hungary. Several months later, King Aleksandar decided to grant a new constitution to his subjects.

The 1901 Constitution was granted in April. From the standpoint of institutions, it represented an exception. It was the only Serbian constitution that provided for a two-house system of national representation. King Aleksandar negotiated the issue of a new constitution for Serbia both with the radicals and the progressives. Their political ideas, as well as the King's intentions, shaped major features of the text of the 1901 Constitution. On one hand, borrowing the expression from Slobodan Jovanović, the King's main intention was the 'taming of the radicals'. On the other hand, both progressives and radicals wanted to limit the royal prerogative, putting it within the framework of the constitution. The political parties nevertheless had different approaches as regards the modes of achieving the goal. The radicals wished to limit the monarch by balancing the prerogative with the power of the National Assembly that relied on the votes of the peasant masses. The progressives feared such a body and were therefore in favour of a two-house system of national representation.[76] Their idea went, to some extent, hand in hand with the King's desire to put obstacles to the preponderance of the radicals in political matters, and eventually prevailed. The 1901 Constitution introduced a two-house system, thus creating an exception in Serbian constitutional history. King Aleksandar himself granted the Constitution to the people in April 1901, rejecting the idea of convening the Grand National Assembly, which was vested with constituent

74 A. Dragnich, *The Development*, 88.

75 S. Jovanović, *Vlada Aleksandra Obrenovića, druga knjiga* [The government of Aleksandar Obrenović, Book II], Belgrade 1931, 148–65; A. Dragnich, *The Development*, 91–92.

76 S. Jovanović, *Vlada Aleksandra Obrenovića II*, 197–200.

power according to the provisions of the 1869 Constitution that was in force. Making political deals with the Crown, the radicals agreed to this move from the Serbian monarch, despite his usurpation of the constituent power.

Institutions

The core institutions of the 1901 Constitution were the King, the national representation and the ministers. The Council of State should also be mentioned, as well as the judiciary, the latter despite the fact that only one article of the constitution was devoted to it.[77] The provisions concerning the King were put in Section II of the 1901 Constitution, i.e. before the provisions on constitutional rights in Section III. It was different from the 1888 Constitution, where the constitutional rights guarantees found place in Section II and the provisions on the King's powers were in Section IV. The King was vested with executive power according to Article 10 of the 1901 Constitution. That provision went in parallel with Article 38 of the 1888 Constitution, but with a significant alteration in wording. The text of 1888 read that the King 'exercised the executive power through his responsible ministers'. By contrast, Article 10 of the 1901 Constitution provided only that 'the king appoints and dismisses the ministers'. The King was nevertheless limited by ministerial countersignature, according to Article 11 of the Constitution. The question of ministerial responsibility was one of the crucial issues as regards the 1901 Constitution. It concerned the organisation of the national representation body.

The national representation consisted of the National Assembly and the Senate. Article 50 of the Constitution regulated the right to vote and eligibility. For both houses only taxpayers were entitled to vote; however, the requirements were different for each. To be eligible to vote and sit in the Senate, one had to pay three times more taxes than those who qualified for the National Assembly. The National Assembly was composed of 130 elected deputies, whereas the Senate had eighteen elected senators and thirty senators appointed for life by the monarch, as provided for in Article 70 of the Constitution. The Senate could not be dissolved.

Ministers had a slightly different position compared to the 1888 Constitution. Article 132 of the 1888 Constitution provided that the ministers formed the ministerial council, i.e. the cabinet. That was not the case with the provision of Article 76 of the 1901 Constitution, which read that 'the ministers stand under the King's immediate orders'. The same provision empowered the King to appoint one of the ministers to be 'the President'. The provision failed to specify the body that the minister-President was to preside over. There was

77 ibid. 201–04, on the organisation of power in the 1901 Constitution in general.

no mention of a council of ministers. According to Article 79, the ministers were responsible to the King and the national representation. It was, however, doubtful whether that included ministerial responsibility before the Senate, which brought Slobodan Jovanović to conclude that ministerial responsibility under the 1901 Constitution remained insufficiently regulated.[78] There was no ministerial responsibility in the parliamentary sense of the term.

The Council of State preserved more or less the same competence and constitutional role it had under the 1888 Constitution, but with one significant alteration. The King was empowered by virtue of Article 83 of the Constitution to appoint all the members of that body, choosing the councillors of State among the senators for life. The judiciary, as stated above, was hardly mentioned in the Constitution text.

Catastrophe

Although the provisions of the 1901 Constitution were tailored to suit the monarch and his desires, they did not properly fit into King Aleksandar's way of governing the country. He continued to rule on his own, regardless of constitutional constraints. Thus in March 1903 the King performed another coup d'état which would have been reminiscent of the script of a musical, had it not had serious consequences. He suspended the Constitution for an hour at midnight, and during that hour repealed several acts of parliament that he was displeased with. Having repealed them, the King returned the Constitution into force.[79] The burlesque was complete. By that time, however, conspiracy plans of younger officers had already been developing. The Obrenović dynasty was facing its end.

The conspiracy, which originated in the army, targeted both the King and the Queen. The young officers planned the assassination of the royal couple, considering their conduct scandalous and shameful. The officers didn't have any political ideas; their only aim was to eliminate the royal couple. However, at a certain stage of developing their plans, they got in touch with some politicians who were not party leaders, most of them not even radicals.[80] The politicians and other civilians participating in the conspiracy got in touch with Petar Karađorđević (1844–1921), Karađorđe's grandson, who lived in Geneva. He was approached by a representative of the conspirators and informed of the conspiracy, but was not a part of it.

78 ibid. 202–03.
79 A. Dragnich, *The Development*, 93.
80 S. Jovanović, *Vlada Aleksandra Obrenovića II*, 341–42.

In May 1903, the conspirators took action. They entered the King's palace at night and assassinated the royal couple. In turmoil and haste, while searching for the King and the Queen, who were hiding in the palace, the conspirators issued orders to kill the prime minister and the minister of defence. Two of the Queen's brothers, both army officers, were also murdered, so that the whole event ended in horrible bloodshed.[81] The event has been known as the *May Coup*, and its outcome was the extinction of the Obrenović dynasty. Petar Karađorđević was invited to come to the Serbian throne.

2.7 The Line of Evolution of Constitutional Monarchy

When considering the line of evolution of the constitutional monarchy in Serbia, one should take the definition of that notion as a starting point. We have seen above in this chapter that a constitutional monarchy is different from an absolute one primarily because the monarch does not legislate in the same way. The constitutional monarchy in Serbia had three stages of development, and these can be distinguished in respect of the major feature of that form of government, i.e. the organisation of the legislative power. The first stage corresponded with the 1861 constitutional settlement, the second with the 1869 Constitution and the third with the 1888 Constitution.

In the first stage of development of the constitutional monarchy in Serbia the monarch did not legislate himself, but nevertheless appointed the legislators. That form of government was the closest to the absolute monarchy, although not quite the same. Legislating through the intermediary of appointed legislators at the end of the day does not equal legislating alone, despite the fact that appointed legislators are likely to fulfil the monarch's wishes.

In the second stage, under the 1869 Constitution the monarch was empowered to appoint one quarter of the legislators, while in the third stage of evolution, under the 1888 Constitution, the legislators were elected. After the abolition of the 1888 Constitution in 1893 the constitutional system could not stabilise and threatened to return either to the second stage of evolution, or even further back than that. On many occasions the Crown acted of its own initiative and decided at will. The period of ten years between 1893 and 1903 was indeed the aftermath of the unsuccessful attempt to introduce parliamentary government in Serbia.

81 S. Jovanović, *Vlada Aleksandra Obrenovića II*, 350–59; A. Dragnich, *The Development*, 93–94.

CHAPTER 3

Parliamentary Government

3.1 Introduction

The conspirators who had aimed to overturn King Aleksandar Obrenović, and achieved their goal, formed a new cabinet right after the assassination of the King at the end of May 1903. The prime minister became Jovan Avakumović (1841–1928), a former minister and, for a while, prime minister, as well as renowned attorney at law, with his formative legal training in Serbia, Germany, France and Switzerland. He belonged to the Liberal Party, but his cabinet was an all-party coalition.[1] The cabinet issued a declaration on maintaining in force the 1901 Constitution and convened the houses of national representation in session at the beginning of June, just a couple of days after the *May Coup*. The national representation proclaimed Petar Karađorđević to be the new King of Serbia. The houses of national representation ended their session on 5 June, the date of adoption of the new constitution.[2] This was the 1903 Constitution, which indeed represented the 1888 Constitution with slight modifications of the text. The debate in the parliamentary houses was short, because of the unanimous decision of political parties to adopt the 1888 Constitution as a model to be followed.[3] The Constitution text that once served as a foundation of the attempt to introduce parliamentary government in Serbia was thus restored in a somewhat rectified version.

Towards the end of the Obrenović regime and soon after the change of dynasty, on one hand the political parties in Serbia were subject to evolution in the sense that there were splits in some of them, while on the other hand some new parties were formed. The most important novelties were that the Radical Party split into radicals and independent radicals, and that as of July 1903 the social democrats were organised as a political party.[4] The political parties were determined to obey the rules of the parliamentary game. This provided a framework for the provisions of the 1903 Constitution.

1 On the composition of the cabinet, cf. O. Popović-Obradović, *The Parliamentary System in Serbia 1903–1914*, Belgrade 2013 (translated by B. Magaš), 143–44.

2 D. Jevtić, 'Novi vek – Srbija', 186; A. Dragnich, *The Development*, 95.

3 On the debate, cf. J. Prodanović, *Ustavni razvitak*, 414–18.

4 J. Prodanović, *Ustavni razvitak*, 425; O. Popović-Obradović, *Parliamentary System*, 235–37.

 | DOI:10.30965/9783657791026_004

3.2 The 1903 Constitution

Institutions

The pattern of the organisation of power in the 1903 Constitution was the same as in the 1888 Constitution. The legislative power was vested in the King and the national representation (Article 33). The latter returned to the single-chamber system after a short episode of bicameralism in Serbia under the 1901 Constitution. The constituent power was vested in the Grand National Assembly by virtue of Article 130 of the Constitution. For the elections to the National Assembly, the censal regime was maintained. Only taxpayers were eligible and entitled to vote, but the threshold was lowered (Article 95). The National Assembly had to convene on 1 October (Article 101) instead of 1 November, as had been the case according to the 1888 Constitution. The same provision ordered the National Assembly to remain in session until the budget was approved, which was a novelty, replacing the former regulation ordering the National Assembly to sit for at least six weeks. An important alteration of the 1903 Constitution, if compared to the one of 1888, occurred in respect of elections. The regular elections were to take place once in four years (Article 100) instead of three, as was stipulated in the 1888 Constitution.

The executive power was vested in the King (Article 38), who was to exercise it through responsible ministers. According to the provisions of articles 56 and 135 of the Constitution, the King was limited by ministerial countersignature. By the time of the adoption of the 1903 Constitution the crucial rule of parliamentary government was universally accepted by politicians. A cabinet could not stand without support of the majority in the National Assembly. Like in most countries, the parliamentary government emerged in Serbia by way of unwritten rules reminding of constitutional conventions.

By virtue of Article 39 of the Constitution, the judicial power was vested in the courts. Article 146 of the Constitution provided on the independence of the judiciary. Provisions on the constitutional rights of Serbian citizens returned to Section II of the Constitution (articles 6–31). The constitutional guarantees of human rights relied on the independence of the judiciary. The latter was made effective by the mode of appointment of judges, which was the same as the one provided for by the 1888 Constitution. The King appointed judges, selecting the appointees from the lists proposed by their peers.

The Council of State was maintained without significant alterations in respect of its powers. As for the appointments to the Council of State, the 1903 Constitution abandoned the system of 1901 and returned to the mode of appointing councillors provided for in the 1888 Constitution. The latter was more subtle and restricted the Crown in the appointments by way of intervention of the National Assembly in those proceedings (Article 140). The competence of the Council of State in the 1903 Constitution remained in principle the same as it was in 1888. The Council of State was competent to prepare legislation drafts and deliberate on those prepared by other constitutional factors. However, it was clearly stipulated in Article 144 of the 1903 Constitution that it was competent to decide on petitions against ministerial acts issued *ultra vires*. The Council of State thus assumed the role of administrative tribunal.

In sum, there were more than forty alterations made to the Constitution text of 1903 when compared to its role model of 1888. These were minutiously analysed by Jaša Prodanović.[5] Some of the alterations were purely technical, but there were also provisions which were important for the functioning of the mechanism of government institutions. That was the case, for instance, with the period for regular parliamentary elections, or prolonging the National Assembly session until the budget was approved.

The new King, Petar Karađorđević, took oath on the Constitution on 12 June 1903.[6] He became Petar I of Serbia. A day after he had solemnly promised allegiance to the Constitution, the new King declared that he wished 'to be a true constitutional king of Serbia'.[7] Petar Karađorđević was the grandson of Karađorđe, the leader of the First Serbian Uprising of 1804. He had graduated from Saint-Cyr Military Academy and had volunteered on the French side – and was wounded – in the Franco-Prussian War of 1870. He also participated under a false name in the uprising against the Ottoman rule in 1876 in Bosnia and Herzegovina. Besides such features presenting him as a warrior, he was also a distinguished intellectual who had translated John Stuart Mill's essay 'On Liberty' into Serbian. Last but not least, the new King, who was almost fifty-nine years of age at the moment of ascending the throne, came from abroad after long years of exile. He had not been in touch with Serbian internal politics for decades. All these components of the King's personality influenced his conduct and played a role in the functioning of the new constitutional regime, along with the provisions of the 1903 Constitution. Dušan Bataković insisted on the King's personality as the ground for choosing the new monarch.[8]

---

5 J. Prodanović, *Ustavni razvitak*, 418–23; cf. M. Mirković, 'Ustav od 1903. godine [The constitution of 1903]', in: M. Jovičić, *Ustavi*, 193–94; in brief, D. Jevtić, 'Novi vek – Srbija', 187.

6 J. Prodanović, *Ustavni razvitak*, 425.

7 O. Popović-Obradović, *Parliamentary System*, 351, with reference to the memoirs of Prime Minister Avakumović.

8 D. Bataković, 'On Parliamentary Democracy in Serbia 1903–1914: Political Parties, Elections, Political Freedoms', *Balcanica XLVIII* (2017), 126, mentions the new King's 'unwavering

As King Petar I had been absent from Serbia ever since his young days, he had a certain distance from the politicians in the country. He was also modest and pleasant in communications, so that he earned respect of the people. From a constitutional standpoint, his conduct fulfilled the minimum requirement of parliamentary government. The Crown refrained from political issues and the King was not a decision maker in political matters.[9]

The Beginning of Parliamentary Government

The first parliamentary elections after the May Coup were held in September 1903. Their outcome, quite simple at first glance, was indeed peculiar. Out of 160 seats in the National Assembly, the radicals won 144, the liberals seventeen and the progressives and socialists one seat each. The majority would have been clear, had there not been a complex situation among the radicals. The party had two wings that were in significant disagreement on many important issues. The old radical wing had seventy-five seats and the independent radicals had sixty-six.[10] After the elections, the radicals' unity was restored, provided that the main politicians of both wings did not enter into the cabinet. A moderate radical, Sava Grujić, became the prime minister. His cabinet, formed in September 1903, included ministers of both wings of the Radical Party. It was reshuffled at the beginning of 1904, so as to include the key personalities of the two party factions, and eventually split on a draft bill in autumn 1904. Prime minister Grujić stepped down, and the leader of the old radicals, Pašić, formed a new cabinet.[11]

Analysing political facts does not lead to a clear-cut conclusion about the functioning of parliamentary government in Serbia at its beginning under the 1903 Constitution. Formally speaking, the radicals formed one party, so that it looked like the system started functioning as one with the predominant political party. The radicals, taken as one party, had 90% of seats in the National Assembly. However, in reality the cabinet worked as a sort of coalition of two factions of the same party. Its coalition character was confirmed at the end of Grujić's cabinet. Following that line of reasoning, the parliamentary government in Serbia at its beginning gives the impression of a two-party system. The system soon evolved in that direction.

---

committment to liberal and democratic principles'. Cf. M. Mirković, 'Ustav od 1903', 194 in the same sense.

9 For minimum requirements, see the author's stance in: D. Popović, *Comparative Government*, Cheltenham, UK–Northampton MA, USA, 2019, 129.

10 O. Popović-Obradović, *Parliamentary System*, 241; A. Dragnich, *The Development*, 97.

11 O. Popović-Obradović, *Parliamentary System*, 241–55.

Two-Party System

The old radicals and the independent radicals became two distinct parties, which was a prerequisite for remodelling the system of parliamentary government. When Pašić formed his government, succeeding Grujić in November 1904, it included only old radicals. In parliamentary terms, it was a homogeneous cabinet. It obtained a majority in the National Assembly owing to the floor-crossing of some independent radicals, including their leader. The independents chose a new leader – Ljuba Stojanović (1860–1930), a university professor – and made a defection from the Radical Party.[12]

Several months later, in May 1905, the prime minister asked the King to dissolve the National Assembly and convene elections. King Petar refused dissolution. Dragnich wrote that it was 'possibly the only unparliamentary act of his reign'.[13] The prime minister resigned, and the King entrusted the leader of the independents with the formation of the cabinet. Stojanović became prime minister on 29 May 1905. The King promptly granted dissolution at the request of the new prime minister, and the elections were held in July 1905.

Dragnich's above-mentioned statement on the King's unparliamentary move seems correct from the standpoint of parliamentary theory. The Crown should follow the request of the prime minister when advised on dissolution. However, subsequent events portrayed the Crown's refusal of dissolution in a nuanced manner. When Stojanović formed the cabinet, it was clear that the country was on the brink of a parliamentary election. The prime minister of the new cabinet also assumed the portfolio of the interior minister in order to organise free, fair and correct elections. Moreover, prime minister Stojanović promised such an election by a special declaration. When the election was held, its outcome was not disputed and it proved to be probably the fairest election in Serbia in its times of parliamentary government.[14] In the presence of such circumstances, the King's initial refusal of dissolution appears in a new and different light. The Crown did not refuse dissolution; its endeavour was to provide free election that would express the will of the people.

The independents won the elections in 1905 by a small margin. They obtained eighty-one seats in the National Assembly, while the old radicals had fifty-five, the liberals seventeen, the progressives four, the socialists two and the peasant party one.[15] Stojanović's cabinet remained in office until spring 1906. Its majority in the National Assembly was weak from the beginning, but

12 A. Dragnich, *The Development*, 97.
13 ibid. eodem loco.
14 O. Popović-Obradović, *Parliamentary System*, 262–63.
15 ibid. 267.

the cabinet nevertheless survived until March 1906, when Stojanović resigned, confronted with a defeat in a vote in the National Assembly. If we now turn to the mode in which the parliamentary government functioned in Serbia in those days, the conclusion is that it was a two-party system. The cabinet was homogeneous, despite some attempts to return to the coalition cabinets. There were two major parties, whose differences were not of such a degree as to question the maintenance of the system as such. Neither of the parties contested parliamentary rule. However, there were statements of the old radicals tending to deny the fundamental differences of the two major parties, suggesting that the system was not, in their view, a two-party system in the proper sense of the term.[16] This remark seemed exaggerated. It is indeed a requirement of the two-party parliamentary system that the two major players are not totally opposed to each other in terms of the crucial issues of national politics.

However, the two-party system was short lasting. In the middle of political complications, and with a weak cabinet in office, the Crown entrusted the old radicals with the formation of the cabinet. Pašić became prime minister, heading a minority cabinet in March 1906. The National Assembly was dissolved, and the country went to the polls in the early election of June the same year. This was the election that put an end to the functioning of parliamentary government in Serbia as a two-party system.

A System with a Dominating Party

The system switched to another model in June 1906. It was not properly a multiparty system, as some features of the two-party political system were present. The results of the 1906 elections showed a picture quite different from the one of previous year. The radicals won ninety-one seats, defeating the independents, who won forty-seven. The liberals obtained fifteen seats, the progressives five, and two smaller lists won one seat each.[17] The strength of political parties did not change throughout the period of parliamentary government in Serbia. The most important feature of the system was that it turned to homogeneous cabinets. The independents did not return to power, and the radicals were the most influential party on the political scene. With only one exception, all cabinets until World War I were headed by radicals. The exception was the cabinet which had Stojan Novaković as prime minister. It was an all-party cabinet formed as a response to a huge international crisis, provoked by the Austro-Hungarian annexation of Bosnia and Herzegovina. The all-party cabinet was formed because there was pressure on Serbia to accept a *fait accompli.*

16 ibid. 273.
17 ibid. 286.

Between April 1906 and November 1915, when during World War I the King, the cabinet and the National Assembly went into exile, there were a total of seven cabinets. Three of them were headed by Pašić, who was in office as prime minister most of the time.

Two features are important for considering the functioning of parliamentary government in Serbia. The first is the strength of political parties and the second is the character of cabinets. Regarding the first feature, the radicals and the independents mostly repeated their results in the elections held in 1908 and 1912, which were the last before World War I. The radicals won eighty-one seats in 1908 and eighty-four in 1912, whereas the independents had respectively forty-six and forty-eight, out of 160 seats in total in the National Assembly.[18] The radicals had an absolute majority and were able to run the country. If viewed from the standpoint of the strength of political parties, the system showed features of a two-party system rather than a multi-party one.

The second crucial feature is the character of the cabinets. They were mostly homogeneous, except for the above-mentioned all-party cabinet led by Novaković and Velimirović's cabinet, formed in July 1908, which lasted only seven months. Independents participated in the latter, having three ministers out of a total of eight. Homogeneous cabinets characterise the two-party system. In a multi-party system coalitions are frequent, but that was not the case in Serbia. The reason lies in a fact linked to the first characteristic of the political system mentioned. It was the prevailing influence of the Radical Party in the electorate which enabled that party to win the elections in such a way as to obtain the absolute majority of seats in the National Assembly. That is what provided the opportunity to govern the country with homogeneous cabinets. At this point, we come to the crucial characteristic of parliamentary government in Serbia. It was a political system in which there was a dominant party. The dominant party was the Radical Party.

Impediments

Along with the successful implementation of the parliamentary form of government in general, there were impediments to it which to some extent obstructed the functioning of institutions. One of these was socially rooted. Notably, the middle class in Serbia before World War I was weak and not sufficiently numerous. The middle class was mostly urban in a country which had only six cities with populations of over 10,000 people. It was composed

18 For the results of the parliamentary elections of 1908 and 1912, cf. O. Popović-Obradović, *Parliamentary System*, 304 and 336.

of craftsmen (46%), merchants (22%) and civil servants (around 19%).[19] The weakness of the middle class was nevertheless compensated to a considerable extent by the peasants who for the greatest part possessed small plots of land that made them independent.

One of the biggest impediments to the functioning of parliamentary government in Serbia, in the technical sense of the word, was the so-called conspirators' question.[20] The May Coup of 1903 provoked criticism in Europe not only for its brutality but also because of the fact that the army officers plotted against the monarch, to whom they had given a solemn pledge of fidelity. The conspirators' idea was that they would not seek any sort of reward once their task of assassinating the King had been accomplished.[21] Such a stance was not followed after the May Coup. A good number of conspirators wanted to preserve their positions in the army and control it, as well as influence the Crown. This is what antagonised the politicians. The conspirators used intimidation to overstep the rules of the game in a parliamentary monarchy and provoked political tensions. The King was in favour of soothing the tensions by convincing the conspirators to retire; this was a solution applicable to senior army officers, but not to younger. They remained in the army, producing further tensions between the army and politicians, which had repercussions on the functioning of parliamentary government. The Crown was involved in finding a solution: the politicians were dissatisfied with the interference of the army officers in political matters, although the latter were not in a position to threaten the essence of the parliamentary regime.

The conspirators' question was brushed under the carpet during the Balkan Wars of 1912–13, in which the Balkan monarchies first successfullly fought against Turkey (1912) and then got into conflict among themselves (1913). Serbia was both times on the winning side and obtained territorial gains. After the Balkan Wars, the administration of newly liberated territories was at issue. Pašić was the prime minister, and his cabinet insisted on the introduction of civil administration, whereas the army preferred a military rule for a certain period. The cabinet was persistent, and foreign diplomats were implicated in the crisis, which was nevertheless internal. This added a new element to a situation that was already politically complex. The King had to make sensitive decisions on constitutional issues, e.g. dissolution. Eventually the King

19 D. Bataković, 'On Parliamentary Democracy', 124.

20 O. Popović-Obradović, *Parliamentary System*, 458–69; A. Dragnich, *The Development*, 98–99.

21 On the conspirators' original idea, cf. S. Jovanović, *Vlada Aleksandra Obrenovića II*, 341; see also the memoirs of one of the outstanding conspirators, Antonije Antić: A. Antić, *Beleške* (edited by B. Dimitrijević and J. Ilić), Zajecar 2010, 54 ff.

followed the cabinet's advice on dissolution, but soon afterwards he transferred his royal authority to his son, Aleksandar, making him act in the King's stead as a regent.[22]

3.3 Conclusions

An overall conclusion on the functioning of parliamentary government in Serbia under the 1903 Constitution must take into account the short period of its implementation in practice. However, despite the fact that some of the characteristic features of the parliamentary form of government could not be properly shaped, it is possible to notice the line of its development, especially in terms of the model which that form of government obtained in Serbia.

Political institutions in Serbia functioned between 1903 and 1914 as a form of parliamentary government with a dominant political party. In the beginning the trend of developments was not quite clear, due to the existence of two rival factions within the dominating political party; however, even then there was a dominant party. What remained in doubt was whether the two factions would split, or whether they would just remain tendencies within the single party. The latter scenario would have led to the existing system being maintained with a dominant party, and avoided the episode of a two-party system.

After the defection and split within the most influential party, the constitutional system adopted the form of a two-party system for a while. That situation did not last long, and the system soon returned to the form of parliamentary government with a dominating party. One of the previous factions repeatedly won the elections, one after the other. Therefore, an overall assessment should tend towards understanding the brief episode of a two-party system as negligible in the wider context of the evolution of the whole constitutional settlement. Parliamentary government in Serbia between 1903 and 1914 functioned as a system with a dominating party. It was comparable to the way in which that form of government functioned in other countries – for example, Italy, Japan and India – in the second half of the 20th century.

---

22 A. Dragnich, *The Development*, 101–02, 111–12.

PART TWO

The Evolution of Constitutionalism

CHAPTER 4

Human Rights in Serbian Nation Building

4.1 A Prelude

Human rights were constantly present in Serbian constitutions. There were already provisions on human rights in the first constitution of 1835. However, due to many reasons, human rights could by no means decisively influence the evolution of constitutionalism in Serbia. The same applies to the period of Yugoslav monarchy, which was followed by the communist rule in Yugoslavia. That rule took a stand against human rights protection which put the whole concept of human rights in a situation even worse than the one that existed before.

The communist authoritarian regime did not protect human rights because they were considered to be opposed to the officially prescribed ideology and fundamentally bourgeois. It was only towards the end of communist rule, i.e. in the times of transition to democracy, that the academics showed an interest in human rights. The pioneer of the study of human rights in Serbia was professor Vojin Dimitrijević (1932–2012), who started lecturing on the subject in the Law School of Belgrade University in the mid-1990s. Such a belated interest in that area of law had consequences for the opinion of the public at large in the country. Notably, as late as 1998 no less than 36% of Serbian citizens were still hostile to human rights. In the opinion polls of that year, the question was 'What are human rights?' Out of five answers offered, 24.9% of the interrogated persons chose 'Just a piece of paper used by politicians', and 11.1% were in favour of the answer 'An instrument to blackmail small states'.[1] The backward state of mind in Serbia was an outcome of the long-lasting communist regime in the country.

The question of human rights in Serbia can by no means be reduced to a mere reproach to the long-lasting communist system as the origin of evil. Human rights in Serbia and Serbian legal thought have been rooted in history, and can be traced back to the time of Serbian nation building, despite the fact that they did not have a key role in constitutional developments. Besides, the process of the emergence of the idea of human rights and its evolution has

---

1 V. Dimitrijević (ed.), *Human Rights in Yugoslavia – Belgrade Centre for Human Rights Report*, Belgrade 1999, 322. The report referred to what was called rump-Yugoslavia, composed of Serbia and Montenegro.

© BRILL SCHÖNINGH, 2021 | DOI:10.30965/9783657791026_005

been only poorly treated by scholars. The academic contributions in this field are wholly insufficient, and this is due to diverse reasons, such as the lack of training in human rights in Serbian universities until the mid-1990s, and a greater emphasis on other topics within academia.[2]

The idea of human rights first appeared in the works of Serbian intellectuals towards the end of the 18th century. The idea was shaped by the prevailing philosophies of the Enlightenment era, and went on to influence Serbian legal and constitutional thought.

4.2 Developments

Dositej Obradović

On the eve of the national revolution, i.e. the Serbian uprising against the Ottoman rule in the pashalic of Belgrade, Dositej Obradović raised the issue of the role of human rights in the process of nation building. He was aware of the complexity of the problem and clearly outlined it. His starting point was the emergence of new nations in the Balkans and their nation building in the light of future evolution of modern political institutions and the rule of law. Dositej Obradović was a Serb born under the Habsburg monarchy. He was an Orthodox monk living outside the monastery, who travelled a lot across Europe and Turkey in constant search of knowledge and education. 'I am ageing while still learning' were his words towards the end of his life, full of study and intellectual endeavour to spread rational ideas among his Serbian compatriots.[3]

Dositej was of the opinion that the peoples of the Balkans subjugated to the Ottoman rule were to attain liberty in the foreseeable future. New nation-states were to emerge, which compelled Dositej to raise the issue of the foundation of states in general. Notably, he did not put forward the idea of people's self-determination being decisive.[4] His philosophical mind regarded virtue and justice as proper pillars of a polity, which made him approach the concept of human rights in his own way, somewhat different from the approach of a learned lawyer. The idea that Dositej followed had its origins in a metaphor of awakening: new nations will emerge when they awake from their centuries-long dream. This concept took form in his famous poem *Vostani Serbie* (Arise

2 This author can point to some of his works in this respect, e.g. 'The Dawn' and 'Les droits fondamentaux dans les deux premières constitutions serbes (1835 et 1838)' [Fundamental rights in the first two Serbian constitutions (1835 and 1838)], *Etudes balkaniques* 19–20 (2013–14).

3 J. Skerlić, 'Dositej Obradović', 12.

4 For more details, cf. D. Popović, 'The Dawn', 214.

Serbia), in which he praised the Serbian insurrection against the Ottomans in 1804. He portrayed his beloved country of Serbia as a fair lady awakening from a dream in order to show her beauty to the whole of Europe. The beauty indeed consisted in virtue, and the whole poem was based on the idea of a competition of valour and virtue in which Serbia, once liberated, would take part, boldly standing equal with other countries. Being a nation among nations was in Dositej's view a challenge which, if met, would allow Serbia to attain virtue. The virtue would materialise in justice, which was its main substance.[5]

Once the peoples of the Balkans had thus awakened and attained freedom from the Ottoman rule, they would find themselves faced with the foundation of their own states. As regards the founding of new states, Dositej Obradović was concerned that people might make the wrong choice, and pursue a path that would remove them from following the precepts of virtue. Dositej's words sounded like a warning: 'if the people in these countries do not get rid of superstition and do not eradicate the ancient and non-Christian animosity towards the law, they will become their own Turks and tormentors'.[6] The only right choice was, therefore, the foundation of a state based on the rule of law.

The rule of law, for its part, had another precept that was indispensable if a society was to carry out that concept and be based on it. If a polity wished to pursue the rule of law, individual rights had to be protected. Dositej Obradović was not a trained lawyer, so he instead approached the crucial point in this line of developing ideas by way of ethics. He published his *Ethics* in 1803 in Venice.[7] In the chapter of the volume outlining what were called prohibitive duties, the author embraced the idea of human rights. His reasoning was as follows: prohibitive duties are those that require each and every person to refrain from interfering with the three most important values embodied in a human being – personality, estate and dignity.[8] At this point it becomes clear that personality, estate and dignity were perceived as fundamental human rights. Dositej underlined the fact that when these values were in jeopardy a man was entitled to take refuge in the court of law. In other words, the paramount human values were to remain free from any interference and at the same time they were legally protected. Those values were indeed human rights.

Dositej was one of the Serbs from Austria who came to Serbia while the country was temporarily under the rule of the Serbian insurgents at the beginning

5 ibid. 212–13.
6 D. Obradović, *Izabrani spisi* [Selected writings], Novi Sad–Belgrade 1969, 334.
7 The following edition will be used for the purpose of this text: D. Obradović, *Etika*, Belgrade 2007.
8 D. Obradović, *Etika*, 140.

of the 19th century. Having settled in Belgrade, which was liberated from the Ottoman rule, he founded the elite school/grand school in 1808, which was the predecessor of the first Serbian university. In the revolutionary government formed during the First Serbian Uprising, Dositej Obradović assumed the task of education minister and passed away while in office in 1811. He participated in the Serbian national revolution and praised it as an endeavour aimed at the introduction of justice, rule of law and, last but not least, human rights.

Filip Višnjić

The Serbian national revolution had its herald, announcing its goals, in the form of a blind epic singer who recited poems, self-accompanied by his *gusle* and fiddle bow.[9] The singer's name was Filip Višnjić (1767–1834). He was a Serb from Bosnia, who came to Serbia in 1809 during the First Serbian Uprising.[10] Many of the poems he reproduced have become widely known across the population. It was in 1815 that Vuk Karadžić, who was to become the Serbian language reformer in the mid-19th century, listened to the blind singer, who performed for him. They were both in exile in the Habsburg territory after the defeat of the Serbian insurgent troops by the Ottomans in 1813. Vuk Karadžić recorded the poems. One of the best known among these was *Beginning of the Rebellion against the Dahis*. The dahis were military commanders in the Ottoman *corps d'élite*, called janissaries.[11] Towards the end of the eighteenth century a group of them residing in the Pashalik of Belgrade had disobeyed the Sultan's imperial power. The Serbian insurgents had declared at the beginning of their insurrection that they were opposed to the terror of the dahis, and not to the Sultan's rule. However, they altered their previous stance later on, and their goal changed to the liberation of the country. This shift in their aims came as a consequence of their success in the warfare.[12]

At the beginning of the poem, Višnjić endeavoured to explain the cause of the Serbian insurrection. His leading idea was that of justice, which was to some extent combined with a certain social attitude. Among the strata of

9 The *gusle* is a popular Serbian single-stringed instrument. A person who plays the *gusle* is *guslar*.

10 For the singer's biography, cf. M. Panić-Surep, *Filip Višnjić – život i delo* [Filip Visnjic – Life and work], Belgrade 1967, 23–45.

11 In the English language of the 19th century, *dahis* were sometimes called *deys*.

12 The classical academic authority on the subject is L. Ranke, *Die Serbische Revolution*, Hamburg 1829. Cf. in English: L. Ranke, *The History of Servia and the Servian Revolution*, Henry G. Bohn 1853. On constitutional developments during the First Serbian Uprising, cf. S. Šarkić, 'The Beginning', 233–79. On social and political ideas and the national programme, cf. V. Stojančević, 'Srpski narod pred prvi ustanak', 88–93.

society in the pashalic, those who were in favour of the uprising were indeed only the *sirotinja raja* (poor commoners). According to the poem, the causes of their sticking to arms were, however, twofold. On the one hand, the taxes were raised by the dahis' oppressive regime, and on the other, there was an idea of ethnic revenge. The respective expressions were 'koja globe davati ne može, ni trpeti turskoga zuluma' ('for they were unable to pay the taxes and endure the Turkish terror') and 'svaki svoje da okaje stare' ('so that each and every person should atone for his ancestors').[13] This twofold interpretation of the just cause of the insurrection seen at the beginning of the poem somehow diminishes as the poem progresses. The poem perceived the justice exclusively in the way that we would today call 'good governance'.

The reducing of the concept came in lines 108 to 131 of the poem, which narrated the Battle of Kosovo of 1389 as the beginning of the Ottoman rule over the Serbian people. The Serbs were defeated in the battle and became subjugated to the Ottoman Empire. However, one of the Serbian knights managed to slay the Sultan during the battle. The imagination leads us in the narrative to the last moments of the Sultan's life, in which he allegedly advised his dignitaries on how to rule in the country which they had conquered in the battle. At that point the dying Sultan's advice appears to be based on ruling fairly, i.e. in accordance with the precepts of justice. This was summarised in lines one-hundred-sixteen to one-hundred-nineteen of the poem, which read: 'Impose neither fines nor taxes/ Torment not the commoners/ Interfere neither with their churches/ Nor with their customs and honesty.'

The whole context must be taken into account so as to properly understand the idea of justice as fair rule. A reading of the text that might find traces of human rights in it should not be excluded. For instance, the last line might lead us to find protection of private life, whereas the first one reminds us of some kind of protection of property. The ideas were those spread among the masses, and expressed the sentiment of the people.

However, a thorough and more critical reading of the four lines makes us conclude that the human rights as understood in the time when the blind singer reproduced the poem were not the object of his reciting. It was a period of turbulence in Europe, provoked by the great French Revolution of 1789 and its aftermath. Human rights in Europe were then perceived as individual rights. The French had proclaimed a Declaration of the Rights of Man and of the Citizen. The Serbian poem was to some extent close to such a stance towards human rights, but owing to the situation of the Serbs in those times

13 For the text of the poem in Serbian, cf. 'Početak bune protiv dahija' [The beginning of the revolt against the dahi], in: V. S. Karadžić, *Srpske narodne pjesme IV*, Belgrade 1985, 100–14.

it nevertheless favoured collective rights. That is why the dying Sultan in the poem refers to the people defeated in the battle in group terms – 'their' churches, 'their' customs and honesty. It has been remarked in academia that the concept of human rights made a slow transition from societal understanding to the individualistic approach.[14] The fact can be established in Serbian historical developments, as witnessed by the epic singer presenting the goals of the Serbian national revolution. It seems that the transition from societal to individual rights was underway, but it had not yet been achieved.

If we are to compare at this point the attitudes of a learned monk such as Dositej Obradović with those of the epic singer that Filip Višnjić was, there are elements of difference that come to light. Dositej Obradović, as a learned man, reflected ideas prevailing in Europe in his time, whereas Filip Višnjić was a singer, expressing sentiments of the people's soul. That is why the latter remained faithful to the concept of collective rights that were probably easy to explain to the people, whereas the former reached the idea of individual rights in his *Ethics*. It would probably be going too far to conclude on the grounds of this difference between the two persons mentioned that there was a gulf between the Serbian masses and the learned elite, but it was nevertheless the germ of such a distinction. In the time of the Serbian national revolution the question of whether collective rights should serve as pillars of a nation-state was confronted with the concept of individual human rights inherent to each and every human being.

Božidar Grujović

The Serbian insurgents of 1804 were successful in fighting the Ottoman troops. By mid-December 1806 they had liberated the Belgrade fortress, put the whole of the *pašaluk* under their rule and started governing the country from Belgrade. Even before they got hold of the Belgrade fortress, the insurgents had made efforts to construct the Serbian nation-state. One of the first steps on that path was the introduction of a central government, separate from military command, which spontaneously emerged among the insurgents. In the summer of 1805, the *Praviteljstvujušči sovjet* (Government Council) was founded. Karađorđe had previously been proclaimed by the people to be their leader and was given the title of *vožd*.

Instituting a governing body for the first time in the liberated country was an event that indeed represented the introduction of the national revolutionary government, a clear sign of the process of modern nation building and

14 Cf. H. Dippel, 'Human Rights – From Societal Rights to Individual Rights', *Universidade de Coimbra, Boletim da Faculdade de Direito*, Vol. LXXXIV 2008, 16.

creating political institutions in Serbia. The importance and the serene character of the event called for some elements of ceremony, which probably was the reason why one of the learned men who participated in the undertaking had prepared a speech to pronounce the occasion. His name was Božidar Grujović (1778–1807), and he was then appointed secretary of the Government Council. Grujović was a learned lawyer, a Serb from the Habsburg monarchy who graduated receiving his PhD from the university in Pest. He was then appointed professor of history of law in the Russian university in Harkov in 1803. While in Russia, he met with a delegation of Serbian insurgents on their mission to beg the Russian tsar for help. Grujović joined the delegation, serving as counsel and interpreter, and returned with its members to Serbia in March 1805. The head of the Serbian delegation was an Orthodox priest, Mateja Nenadović, the chair of the Government Council as of summer 1805: in other words, the first prime minister in modern Serbia. Grujović was then appointed to the post of secretary of the Government Council.[15] The text of the speech has not been preserved in its original version. The only source we have today is the book of memoirs of Mateja Nenadović, who preserved the speech entitled 'A Word on Freedom' in his book. The memoirs were first published in 1867, but the importance of the speech was so great that it has been republished separately on various occasions. 'A Word on Freedom' is considered to represent a landmark in Serbian constitutional history.[16]

The concept of state Grujović favoured in the speech relied first and foremost on the rule of law. Grujović praised the law to be, as he put it, 'overlord and judge' in a polity. He also expressed the view that reason and justice were the foundations of both law and welfare. Grujović is considered to be the first in Serbian history to mention the word constitution in its modern sense.[17] He was prepared to pronounce the following words: where there is a good constitution, i.e. where the law is solidly established and where the power is well settled under the law, there is freedom. Freedom was his ideal which in his view could be achieved exclusively under a constitutional government. Grujović's attitude on sovereignty, however, remains open to discussion. The author of

15 For the biography of Božidar Grujović, cf. D. Basta, 'Životni put Božidara Grujovića (Teodora Filipovića)' [Life of Božidar Grujović (Teodor Filipović)], in: J. Trkulja and D. Popović, *Liberalna misao*, 11–13; S. Savić, *Počeci teorije i filozofije prava u Srba* [The beginnings of the theory and philosophy of law in the Serbs], Banja Luka, 1998, 141–43; M. Đ. Milićević, *Pomenik znamenitih ljudi u srpskom narodu* [Monument to famous people in the Serbian population], Belgrade 1959, 358.

16 D. Basta, 'Životni put Božidara Grujovića' 16. The text of the speech is in *Hereticus*, 2005/3–4; see also the edition of the memoirs: M. Nenadović, *Memoari*, Novi Sad–Belgrade 1969.

17 S. Savić, *Počeci teorije*, 148, 160.

this volume is of the opinion that he advocated what we would call today constitutional supremacy, rather than popular sovereignty.[18]

However, regardless of his attitude towards the question of ultimate power, Grujović was convinced that the most important feature of a state was the rule of law.[19] At the same time, the issues of sovereignty and the rule of law were in his view inseparable from the concept of human rights. That is why he developed the thesis as follows: the sovereign's first duty is to ensure that everyone in the community is secure in terms of himself and his life, as well as his wife, his home, his property and dignity. At this point of the speech, Grujović finds it essential to add that human rights are susceptible to being claimed before a court of law: in other words, they are enforceable. The sovereign, to whom he referred as commander at this point, is indeed under obligation to secure the enjoyment of human rights. Moreover, the sovereign will be entitled to maintain his position insofar and as long as he ensures the protection of human rights. Grujović also considered it important to reiterate the stance, and in this short passage he twice reproduced the enumeration of human rights, which in his view were the most important of all. These rights are: 1) life, 2) estate and 3) dignity.

This triad suggests a possible Anglo-Saxon, or rather American, influence on Grujović, but the state of our sources does not offer the possibility of researching this thoroughly. Despite the mystery of the origin of his opinion, it remains beyond doubt that Grujović perceived human rights as being efficiently protected, for they could be claimed, which means enforced through the administration of justice. They are acquired at birth, for Grujović says that even a child who hasn't been born yet will be entitled to claim their rights. However, the crucial argument on the role and function of human rights in the society is to be found in the stance that has been mentioned above. The sovereign will remain as such, provided he secures the enjoyment of human rights for the members of the community. This leads to the conclusion that human rights serve the role of providing legitimacy to the sovereign power.[20] Human rights are thus figured as the pillar of a modern state. They seem to have reached a peak in importance in the opinion of the secretary of the Government Council as early as in the time of the formation of the first government in the Serbian national revolution.

The peak was indeed reached in the brilliant mind of an intellectual. The ideas exposed by Grujović nevertheless had to face the reality, which was

18 See Chapter 2. Cf. also D. Popović, 'The Dawn', 222–26.

19 ibid. 226.

20 cf. D. Basta, 'Životni put Božidara Grujovića', 24.

complex and different from the realm of philosophical concepts developed by a learned lawyer. Although the first Serbian prime minister saved the speech for posterity, the secretary of the Government Council was deprived of the possibility of delivering it in front of the audience. The leaders of the national revolution were reluctant to hear the speech. It is somehow significant that 'A Word on Freedom' has been preserved in writing, but was never pronounced, which seemed to be a bad omen for human rights. The idea that the Serbian nation-state should be based on the protection of human rights was put aside and did not materialise at the beginning of Serbian modern history. Grujović passed away in 1807 and was unable to advocate the concept any more. Nevertheless, it persisted, and human rights re-emerged in subsequent political developments.

Vuk Karadžić

After the Second Serbian Uprising, the Turks made a compromise with the insurgents, whose leader was Miloš Obrenović. The deal was to institute home-rule for the Serbs as a specific form of power sharing. Miloš was competent to rule over the Serbs and the Turkish pasha, residing in the Belgrade fortress oversaw all the Turks in the country.[21] The power sharing was based on an agreement made between Miloš and the commander in chief of the Turkish troops, and was never put in writing. It nevertheless proved to be operative. The Serbs then started striving for the introduction of a proper autonomous status of their land. Pursuing such a noble cause provided an opportunity for Miloš Obrenović to institute an autocratic regime in the country.

The regime that Prince Miloš instituted in the country may be labelled as an authoritarian patriarchal government which lacked checks and balances.[22] The fact that Serbia had to launch into a diplomatic struggle to achieve this autonomous status made room for authoritarianism, favouring a strong ruler that was capable of providing for the national interests. Miloš was illiterate, and an ordinary man, who maintained good contacts with the masses. Under his rule, Serbia underwent a system of nation building in which divergent processes were intermingled. Serbian families occupied the plots of land that the Turks had left during the time of the uprisings. They needed confirmation of their recently acquired titles. The trade with Austria was renewed and showed signs of growth. With the restoration of peace, the Serbs from Austria

21 V.S. Karadžić, *Istorijski spisi*, 127.

22 Cf. Part One Chapter 1 of this book. For a brief sketch of the regime, see also A. Dragnich, *The Development*, 16–18. For a more detailed account on Miloš's arbitrary rule, see V. S. Karadžić, *Istorijski spisi*, 184–98.

started coming to Serbia to settle for good. Many of them were educated or had some kind of business. All of this laid down foundations for the emergence of a middle class. Little by little, an opposition to the Prince's authoritarian rule emerged, contesting the old patriarchal mode of running the affairs of the nation. As discontent was rising in the country, the question of adopting a constitution came to the agenda, for it appeared to be necessary to impose limits on the Prince's power. The idea of constitution was linked to the concept of human rights.

It was in such circumstances that Vuk Karadžić decided to address the Serbian Prince in a letter dated April 1832. Karadžić was in exile in the Habsburg monarchy at the time. The letter has become a vestige of the situation in Serbia under the rule of Prince Miloš during his first reign, which ended in 1839.[23] The reason for addressing the Prince was the poor state of the society and governance in Serbia, where, according to Vuk, no one was satisfied with the Prince's rule. The author of the letter mocked the Prince by saying that the only persons satisfied with the situation in the country were the Prince's two sons, adding that even they would have been dissatisfied, had they been older and more mature. At the origin of dissatisfaction was the fact that there was a lack of security in the country, provoked by the way in which the Prince exercised his powers. Arbitrariness was elevated to such an extent that it became a rule in the exercise of power. That made Vuk reproach to the Prince: 'no one is secure for his life, for his dignity, and nor is anyone the master of his estate acquired by his blessed and just endeavour'.

At this point, the expressions that Vuk Karadžić used in his letter make a clear allusion to human rights. The absence of their protection created an atmosphere of uncertainty in Serbia. The idea of human rights becomes even more transparent as a guideline when Vuk shifts from the statement of facts to the proposals for improvements and overcoming the misfortune of the country. In exile, beyond the Prince's reach and safe from his anger, the author of the letter suggested the adoption of a constitution as the solution to the problems in Serbia: 'The people should be given the right, or as it has currently been the expression in Europe – a constitution.' This was the main stance, from which Vuk later proceeded to explain the substance of the notion of the constitution. In this regard Vuk showed that he was well informed in constitutional matters, for he tackled the two traditional areas of constitutional law, somehow explaining them to the illiterate Prince. These were the organisation of power and human rights.

---

23 The text of the letter in: V. S. Karadžić, *Istorijski spisi*, 215–29.

As for the organisation of power, Vuk criticised the Prince for his practice of arbitrary rule and the introduction of a personal regime. He stated that there was no proper government in the land. 'You are the government yourself,' Vuk wrote, 'and therefore when you are in Kragujevac, the government is in Kragujevac. If you move to Požarevac, then the government moves to Požarevac ...' Vuk suggested instead the introduction of the institution of government and also of a form of government: 'a form of government should be determined and a government set up'.

As regards human rights, Vuk was as resolute as he was accurate. Human rights were to be protected, and Vuk pinpointed in the letter which among such rights were the most fundamental: 'To everyone must be secured life, estate and dignity.' This was strikingly repeating what Božidar Grujović had been prepared to declare in his unpronounced speech, 'A Word on Freedom'. The enumeration of human rights is the same for both authors. There is no trace in the sources indicating that Grujović was a possible influence on Vuk's opinion on the subject – almost twenty-seven years had elapsed between the moment of founding the first revolutionary government and the time in which Vuk wrote his letter to the Prince. Another possibility is the existence of a common source of inspiration for both. That assumption also appears to be problematic. Grujović was a learned lawyer, which Vuk was not. We have seen above that the sources of inspiration influencing Grujović remain unknown to date. The same applies to the question of Vuk's possible sources. However, irrespective of the way in which the idea of the triad of human rights penetrated Serbian legal thought, it is very likely that its origin points to the English and American legal treasury. John Locke and the Declaration of Independence may have influenced the Serbs in the time of nation building in a way that we are unable to grasp today, due to the lack of reliable sources.[24]

If we are ready to accept the idea that a threefold enumeration of the most fundamental human rights may have been received from England or America, the issue of its substance will inevitably arise. Should the Serbian enumeration of life/estate/dignity be considered equal, or at least sufficiently comparable, to Locke's formula of life/liberty/estate or the American founding fathers' principles of life/liberty/pursuit of happiness? Could the notion of life in the Serbian list embrace liberty as well? Or should dignity stand for liberty? The latter seems to be more likely. However, the omission of the notion of liberty in the Serbian formula may be significant if we consider subsequent developments. Comparing the stances on human rights and the constitution, as well as on the role of those two concepts in the course of Serbian nation building, we

24 For more details, cf. D. Popović, 'The Dawn', 227–28.

may conclude that the ideas of the two authors went hand in hand. Grujović was the first among the Serbs to mention the notion of constitution. A quarter of a century later, Vuk raised his voice to demand its adoption. In respect of human rights, the two authors were rather close to one another. Grujović understood the human rights as pillars of a state, whereas Vuk held them as indispensable in a constitutional settlement and indeed a cornerstone.

Dimitrije Davidović

Serbian nation building during the time in which Prince Miloš ruled had diverse aspects and materialised in different activities. On the one hand, the country was striving for autonomy that would be recognised by the Ottoman Porte, while on the other some elements of modern life and institutions were introduced. Dimitrije Davidović took part in both activities. He distinguished himself as a skillful diplomat and the founder of the Serbian press.[25] He conducted negotiations with the Ottoman Porte between 1829 and 1833, ultimately obtaining the status of vassal state for Serbia in 1830, which was supplemented in 1833 by another imperial act of the same kind. As of 1834, Davidović was the editor of the first Serbian newspaper published in Serbia, *Novine Srbske*. In the first half of the 1830s he was also committed to draft the text of the First Serbian Constitution, which was adopted in February 1835. The 1835 Constitution was adopted by acclamation in the session of the National Assembly, which began on *Sretenje* (the Candlemas). For that reason it became known as *Sretenjski Ustav* (the Candlemas Constitution).

Davidović was a patriot and a convinced liberal at the same time. He never accomplished his study of medicine at the University of Vienna because he had got involved in the activities supporting the Serbian national cause. His perception of home-rule and nation building in Serbia was to understand the latter process as one of national emancipation and liberation at the same time. The freedom of the Serbian nation was in his view reliant on the freedom of each and every individual inhabiting Serbia. When requested to draft a constitution, he was determined that it should provide for both. In other words, the constitution was to cover both areas of constitutional law, namely the organisation of power and human rights.

---

25 On Dimitrije Davidović, cf. R. Ljušić, *Orijentalni novinar, evropski političar – Dimitrije Davidović (1789–1838)* [Oriental journalist, European politician – Dimitrije Davidović (1789–1838)], Belgrade 2006, 91–134. See also D. Popović, 'Od narodne k pojedinačnoj slobodi' [From national to individual freedom], in: J. Trkulja and D.Popović, *Liberalna misao*, 36–42.

We have seen above that Vuk Karadžić, although not a learned lawyer, explained in his letter of 1832 to the Serbian Prince that it was necessary to provide for the two respective areas of constitutional law in a constitution and suggested its adoption. However there was a line of development in that regard which preceded the letter of 1832, and it is very likely that Vuk was aware of it. In brief, those who were in charge of preparing draft constitutions in Serbia in the times of home-rule more or less disregarded human rights. Their preoccupation was in dealing with the issue of the organisation of power alone. The first draft constitutions, made by unknown authors in 1831, were designed in such a way. That was also the case for a draft that was shown to a French diplomat who was in a mission to Serbia in 1834.[26] The attitude of the Serbian Prince must have been reflected in such an approach to the concept of constitution. From the standpoint of nation building, the constitution was understood in a twofold way. The one favoured by the Prince saw the constitution as, above all, a token of state prestige and a way of placing Serbia on a level with other European nations. The goal of nation building would be attained in this view by adopting a constitution that provided for the organisation of power and somehow solemnly approved the Prince's decisions. Human rights were strikingly absent in this, and indeed neglected.

However, Vuk's approach returned to the idea put forward by Grujović, although without mentioning him. That concept was different from the one developed among the circles surrounding the Prince. Those were indeed the human rights that should represent the foundation of the whole enterprise of constructing the Serbian nation. When tasked with drafting a constitution, Davidović attempted to embrace the stance of Grujović and Vuk Karadžić, or at least to reconcile it with the opinion prevailing among the Prince's friends and supporters. This was by no means an easy path to follow.

We are unaware today of the mode in which Davidović performed his task. Our only guide is the outcome of his endeavour, i.e. the text of the 1835 Constitution. Two main remarks seem to be relevant in that respect, so far as human rights are concerned. Davidović included a whole chapter on human rights in the Constitution text and provided for a catalogue of human rights. At the same time, the provisions on human rights were somehow pushed towards the end of the Constitution text. Davidović assumed the role of the Prince's secretary while drafting the constitution. He must have read to the Prince what he had put into the draft, because the latter was unable to read

26 For details, cf. D. Popović, 'Arduous Path to Constitutionalism – Serbian constitutional developments in the first half of the nineteenth century', *Pravni zapisi* (The Union University of Belgrade Law Review) 1/2019, 13–19.

it on his own. Imagining the two in such a situation, one can understand why the provisions on human rights had to be placed in Chapter 11 out of the fourteen chapters the Constitution text was composed of. The authoritarian Prince could not have been enthusiastic about the inclusion of human rights in the text. It is therefore difficult to understand how the skillful secretary managed to convince the Prince not only to allow provisions on human rights to be included in the Constitution text, but also to agree on an ample catalogue of such rights. Many provisions on important human rights found their place in Chapter 11 of the 1835 Constitution. Those were, for instance, equality before the law (Article 111), the legality of criminal pursuit (112), a *habeas corpus* guarantee (113), the legality of criminal sanctions (114), prohibition *ne bis in idem* (115), prohibition of slavery (118), protection of property (119) and the right of petition (126). Notably, the human rights provided for in the 1835 Constitution were all civil rights; political rights did not find a place within the catalogue. We do not know whether Davidović made an attempt to introduce those as well, but it remains doubtful, for he had to remain realistic. Prince Miloš was not ready to go too far, and Davidović's liberalism had to cede. Moreover, if we consider the human rights that were inserted in the Constitution text, we are bound to conclude that many provisions on those were in essence a political programme rather than proper provisions. An example of this is the legality of criminal sanctions in a country which did not have a criminal code or even a well-developed legislation in the area of criminal law.

The 1835 Constitution, which had been adopted in February, was suspended in April of the same year. The Prince had to proceed to the suspension under the pressure of foreign powers. However, since the provisions on the organisation of power in the 1835 Constitution were favourable to him, the Prince tried to maintain the constitution in force. His diplomatic action, consisting of sending a special envoy to Constantinople which was aimed at preserving and maintaining the constitution in force, however, failed.[27] The sources nevertheless show beyond doubt that the provisions on human rights were not the cause of suspending the 1835 Constitution. The reasons for that lay in the political considerations of the great foreign powers and their estimations of the influence they might be able to have over a small and vassal country such as Serbia. If those reasons were to be found in the Constitution text itself, they

27 The academic article which is still the most relevant authority in this respect is: M. Gavrilović, 'Suspendovanje Sretenjskog ustava' [Suspension of the Sretenje constitution], *Iz nove srpske istorije*, Belgrade 1926, 190–209. Cf. also D. Popović, *Prapočetak*, 93–98; M. Pavlović, *Pravna evropeizacija Srbije* [The legal Europeanisation of Serbia], Kragujevac 2008, 51.

would concern the provisions on the organisation of power. An illustration of this is the conversation that a Serbian diplomat, the Prince's special envoy to Constantinople, had in that city with the Russian ambassador to the Ottoman Porte. The Russian diplomat reproached his Serbian interlocutor for Serbia's alleged adoption of the concept of ministerial responsibility in the constitution. That was by no means true, but such a statement nevertheless served the Russian ambassador as an argument in the discussion with the Serbian diplomat.[28]

In light of the poor destiny of the short-lived First Serbian Constitution, a question must be raised regarding the attitudes of its author towards human rights, as well as regarding his perception of their function in Serbian nation building. It is commonplace to say that Dimitrije Davidović was a liberal. However, liberal as he was, he served an authoritarian Prince – a sacrifice he made in the interests of Serbia. He wished to contribute to Serbian nation building, which he did as a diplomat who brokered the introduction of autonomy for the vassal state, to be granted by an act of the Ottoman imperial power. As a diplomat, he did not have to hesitate in defending the national cause, for his work was performed for the sake of protecting the emerging nation from others. On the other hand, when he was tasked with drafting a constitution, this appeared to be more complex. The principal question was how to set up the relations of individuals within Serbia, as well as their relationships to the political power.

Davidović was a partisan of human rights and considered them to be the foundations of freedom. At this point a question should be raised as to whether Davidović was inclined towards the concept of constitutional supremacy, which seemed to be the case with Božidar Grujović thirty years before? A clear-cut answer is impossible to give, but it seems more likely that Davidović was more in favour of popular sovereignty. However, the concept he adopted in the 1835 Constitution remains somewhat unclear in that regard. The National Assembly adopted the constitution, albeit by acclamation and in an atmosphere that could not match the idea of a proper exercise of constituent power by the people. Another important remark is that Grujović was a learned lawyer, which was not the case for Davidović. That is why it remains doubtful whether their attitudes were identical at this point. Grujović, the lawyer, seems to have favoured a principle superior to the will of the people, whereas Davidović, a liberal and a patriot of practical skills, seems to have given precedence to the will of the people. That is why it is difficult to say that the latter thoroughly considered human rights to be the foundation of the nation.

28 M. Gavrilović, ibid.

However, Davidović realised that human rights were provided for in foreign constitutions at the beginning of the texts and represented the foundations of respective nations. Davidović was familiar with foreign constitutions and commented on these in Novine Srbske.[29] At the same time, he had to be practical, for he was aware of the fact that the time was not ripe for human rights in Serbia. The country was under-developed, lacked a proper middle class and educated people were few among the population. He nevertheless did not want to give up introducing provisions on human rights in the constitution. The word may not be appropriate, but he somehow smuggled human rights into the Constitution text; although not at the beginning, as in many other constitutions of that time, human rights were provided for in Chapter 11 of the Serbian Constitution of 1835, towards the end of its text. It must have taken some effort to convince the Prince of Serbia to leave the text as proposed by the drafter.

The provisions on human rights are not the only example of the method which Davidović applied. The same method is evident, for instance, in drafting Article 5 of the 1835 Constitution, in which its text solemnly declared that 'Serbian powers are three: legislative, executive and judiciary'. The expression is quite clear, and the article announced the concept of the separation of powers, which Davidović could not carry out when formulating provisions on the three powers mentioned. Davidović provided for a confluence of powers to satisfy the Prince, who was by no means willing to accept any settlement in which his role in the government would not be preponderant.[30]

Davidović may appear to be naïve from a historical perspective, but indeed he was not. He seems to have been inclined towards transforming the authoritarian Prince into a constitutional monarch, or rather into a ruler of a state governed by the constitution. His problem with the Prince was in a way semantic, for there was some misunderstanding between the Prince and the drafter on the meaning and the notion of constitution. Miloš was ready to pass a constitution and rule under its provisions, so far as the latter were favourable to him. In that sense, he was prepared to rule in the presence of a constitution. Davidović advocated another concept, namely using the constitution as a lever, to check the monarch's power. Driven by a situation he was fully aware of, Davidović made a compromise and chose to cede his liberalism. He drafted a Constitution text providing for the confusion of powers and the Prince's preponderance. However, he did introduce some modern ideas in that same text

29 cf. D. Popović, 'Arduous Path', 5–15.

30 For a more detailed analysis of the organisation of power in the 1835 Constitution, cf. D. Popović, *Prapočetak*, 83–92; D. Popović, 'Les droits fondamentaux', 290–91.

which probably could not have been effectuated, but it was important for the drafter of the text that they should find their place there. Among these were human rights, to which Davidović intimately adhered as one of the elements of foundation of a modern nation, which he wished Serbia to become. His efforts were fruitful. Human rights remained in Serbian Constitution texts after 1835, even though it was still too early for their proper implementation in everyday life.

Human Rights in the 1838 Constitution

After the suspension of the First Serbian Constitution in April 1835, the country entered a period of constitutional crisis. The issue of adopting a constitution became the key focus in the process of nation building. It became clear that the constitutional question in the vassal state was not to be resolved by the domestic political factors, but rather with the assistance of foreign powers. The issue was eventually entrenched by the sovereign, i.e. the Sultan, who granted a constitution to his faithful province of Serbia in December 1838. Its text emerged as an outcome of diplomatic negotiations in Constantinople.[31] The 1838 Constitution provided for an oligarchy, concentrating the most important portion of power in a body called the *Sovjet* (Council), which was composed of seventeen immovable councillors who were independent from the Prince of Serbia and in principle accountable only to the Ottoman Porte. Prince Miloš decided to abdicate some months after the constitution had entered into force, for he was unable to continue ruling in the patriarchal way he had been used to. The oligarch counsellors were aware of the importance of preserving the constitutional settlement, which was favourable to them. They therefore cherished the 1838 Constitution to such an extent that they were given the name of *ustavobranitelji* (constitution defenders).[32]

The 1838 Constitution was peculiar in its form. Its text appeared as a Sultan's letter sent to his vassal, the Serbian Prince. It consisted of more than sixty provisions and had very little structure; it also did not follow the pattern of European constitutions at that time. The provisions concerning human rights were included in the Constitution text, but they were scattered all over it. Nevertheless, their number was not negligible. There was indeed a catalogue of human rights. The provisions on human rights in the 1838 Constitution

31 On the emergence of the 1838 Constitution, cf. R. Ljušić, *Kneževina Srbija*, 165–83; Lj. Kandić, 'Turski ustav', in: M. Jovičić, *Ustavi*, 63–64.

32 The classical academic authority for the whole period of the rule of the oligarchs is S. Jovanović, *Ustavobranitelji* (1990). This is a modern edition of the volume published for the first time towards the beginning of the 20th century.

had an important feature in common with the 1835 Constitution. There were no provisions on political rights in either of the texts. As for the catalogue of human rights in the 1838 Constitution, it was similar to the one of 1835. The legality of sanctions was provided for, as was the ban on confiscation of property as a sanction (Article 28). There were also provisions on the *habeas corpus* and the prohibition of arbitrary pursuit (65 and 66). The independence of the judiciary was guaranteed (44), as well as freedom of trade (45) and the freedom of the Orthodox religion (57). The latter was important, since it was the Turkish Sultan who granted the 1838 Constitution for Serbia.

The text of the 1838 Constitution tackled the concept of human rights in connection with the rule of law in two articles. In those articles the unknown drafter of the text seemed to have been inclined to point out by way of enumeration the most important human rights. Thus in Article 27 of the constitution there was a reference to the 'estate, person, honour and dignity' of each and every inhabitant of Serbia. In a similar manner, Article 66 provides that the 'status, honour, rank and service' of everyone must be conserved. By protecting rank and service, the Sultan wished to put an end to the arbitrary rule of the Serbian Prince who on many occasions regarded the civil servants as being his own personal service. Notably, in the same articles there were references to the concept of the rule of law, although somewhat vague. Thus in article 27 the Sultan declared that 'the Imperial will is opposed to depriving any person of his right without a court ... or exposing them to pursuit or punishment without judgment rendered according to the law and principles of justice'. This goes along with Article 66, which concludes the text by stating that the 'constitutional paragraphs and conditions mentioned above are to be executed in full and forever'.

On the one hand, the idea was clear that the rule of law should be instituted in Serbia, while on the other, the understanding of the concept of the rule of law which the Serbian oligarchs had in mind was not exactly modern. It has been rightly remarked in academia that the oligarchs were more in favour of passing legislation than of instituting a regime of the rule of law in the substantial sense of the term.[33] To this it should be added, as has been previously mentioned, that due to the state of development of the country and society, the time was not ripe for a proper protection of human rights in Serbia in the 1830s. Nevertheless, the fact that the provisions on human rights found their place in the 1838 Constitution, which remained in force for more than twenty years, led to an increased awareness of human rights in the everyday life of the citizens of Serbia. The provisions were there, the public at large was aware of

33 Cf. M. Pavlović, *Srpska pravna istorija*, 284.

them and the patient and dedicated researchers of the past have found traces of their influence, if not their implementation in practice.[34] However, that was only part of a broader image in which human rights did not appear to be dominating the scene of the nation building in the Principality of Serbia. Other topics were more advanced and prioritised.

Stefan Radičević

Stefan Radičević (1800?–71), who was, like Dositej Obradović, Grujović and Davidović, a Serb from the Habsburg monarchy, had also come to the Principality of Serbia and played a role in nation building especially in connection to human rights. Little is known about his life. Vuk Karadžić related that Radičević, having served a prison sentence for theft in Austria in his younger days, could not prosper in the Austrian public service. However, having served at the lowest level in the administration he read a lot and spoke German very well. He came to Serbia in 1830 and became one of the Prince's secretaries, indeed the highest ranking secretary after Davidović. Vuk Karadžić considered him an honest man and a capable public servant.[35] He was a minister of justice and education of the principality of Serbia between June 1840 and September 1842, and a close collaborator of Mihailo Obrenović. When Prince Mihailo abdicated in 1842 and went into exile in Austria, Stefan Radičević followed him.[36] Radičević later returned to Serbia in the 1850s and passed away in Belgrade in 1871.

The activity of Stefan Radičević in respect of human rights in Serbian nation building was marked by an early episode. He was among the persons whom Prince Miloš entrusted with the task of preparing a new Constitution text in times of constitutional crisis after the suspension of the 1835 Constitution. The ruling Prince had no more confidence in Davidović, whom he reproached for the failure of the First Serbian Constitution. Having fallen into disgrace in the eyes of the Prince, Davidović had left Belgrade to live in Smederevo, where he died young in 1838. The persons surrounding the Prince tried to develop new texts aimed to serve as a replacement for the one of 1835, which had evidently been at odds with the attitudes of foreign powers. Radičević was the author of one such text. The curious thing about his work was that the draft he had prepared appeared to be more liberal than the text of the 1835 Constitution.

34 For one of the examples, cf. D. Popović, 'Les droits fondamentaux', 300–01 and the references made there.

35 V. S. Karadžić, *Istorijski spisi*, 206.

36 Cf. Lj. Krkljuš, 'Proekt Ustava za Vojvodovinu Srbsku Stefana Radičevića' [Draft constitution for Serbian Vojvodovina by Stefan Radičević], in: SANU, *Ustavni razvitak Srbije u XIX i početkom XX veka*, Belgrade 1990, 77–84.

It remains unclear how Radičević could expect his draft to replace the 1835 Constitution, but for our topic here it is of twofold interest. Radičević boldly moved forward the chapter providing on human rights in the text of his draft, where it figured as Chapter 2. Apart from that, Radičević provided in clear-cut terms for the concept of the separation of powers.[37] Needless to say that the draft was abandoned in the course of discussions, but it nevertheless brings evidence on the attitude of its author towards human rights and liberal ideas in times of constitutional crisis in the Serbian principality.

The political aspect of Serbian nation building was primarily linked to the vassal Principality of Serbia, which remained under the sovereign power of the Turkish Sultan who granted it semi-independent status. The cultural component of that process was for a considerable part also connected to Austria, the neighbouring empire that had sheltered many Serbs ever since the Middle Ages. The Serbian population in the Habsburg monarchy grew as a result of waves of Serbian newcomers arriving after the Austrians were defeated several times in their wars against the Ottoman Empire in the sventeenth and the eighteenth centuries. The Serbs who had supported the Christian empire in these war campaigns against the Turks had to flee to the territory of the Habsburg monarchy, where they mostly settled as members of the special military frontier corps. In the course of time, however, the Serbs formed a middle class of traders, merchants and artisans from which originated the intellectuals already mentioned in this text. The Austrian Serbs participated strongly in Serbian nation building, despite the fact that they did not have a political unit of their own in Austria, as was the case for their brethren, who were Turkish subjects.

It was towards the mid-nineteenth century that the Serbs in Austria achieved the stage of having a political unit, although for a very short period. Their participation in Serbian nation building remained mostly within the cultural sphere, but the short-lived Serbian political unit also contributed to the process. Stefan Radičević played a role in those events that is of interest for our story. The creation of the Serbian political unit took place during the Hungarian revolution of 1848. The Hungarians living in the Habsburg Empire attempted to secede with arms in hand, and lay down the foundations of a Hungarian nation-state. The Imperial Court of Vienna then invited the Serbs and the Croats who were the subjects of the Habsburg Empire to fight the Hungarian insurgents and help the imperial cause. Both the Croats and the Serbs accepted the call and fought against the Hungarians. Serbian volunteers from the Principality of Serbia crossed the Danube and the Sava rivers to help

37 On the draft prepared by Radičević, cf. D. Popović, *Prapočetak*, 106–14.

their brethren on the battlefield. While engaged in the warfare, the Serbs from the Habsburg Empire proclaimed in May 1848 the foundation of their own political unit within the Habsburg Empire. It was called Serbian Vojvodovina. The name comes from the Serbian word *vojvoda*, meaning 'duke' in English. The Serbs elected a duke to be their leader in the war against the Hungarians; this is why the word was at the origin of the name given to their political territorial unit. However, the Vojvodovina did not last long. The Austrian Emperor granted its status in December 1848, but abolished it the next year, once the Hungarians were defeated and their rebellion was put to an end.

In those turbulent times Stefan Radičević, a Serb from the Habsburg Empire and an ex-minister of justice of the Serbian principality, undertook efforts to draft a constitution for the emerging political unit comprising Serbs inhabiting the Habsburg lands. He accomplished his work and published the draft in Zemun/Semlin in 1849.[38] The organisation of power within Serbian Vojvodovina was envisaged to rely on two main organs – the vojvoda and the national representation, both directly elected by the people. The vojvoda would represent the Habsburg crown within Vojvodovina, but his competence was also similar to those of a head of state in a certain manner.[39] The draft also contributed to the development of the concept of human rights. Radičević put the provisions on human rights in Chapter 4 of his draft constitution, which contained a catalogue of human rights consisting of sixteen provisions. However, some provisions concerning that area of law found their place outside Chapter 4. That was, for instance, the case of the provision on equality of all Christian religions found in Article 178 of the draft constitution.

The catalogue of human rights encompassed personal liberty (Article 33), security (34), as well as the right to property (39–40) and equality before the law (41). Capital punishment was prohibited for political offences, i.e. high treason (44). There were no provisions on political rights, except one: Article 45 of the draft constitution guaranteed the freedom of the press.[40] That was a novelty from the standpoint of Serbian constitutional developments. There were no such provisions in the constitutions of the Serbian principality. This provision was probably introduced under the influence of the text of the March Laws (also called the April Laws), enacted by the Hungarian Diet in 1848, which were the Hungarian revolutionary constitution. They provided for the freedom of

38 S. Radičević, *Proekt ustava za Vojvodovinu Srbsku sa državoslovnim primetbama* [Draft constitution for Serbian Vojvodina with state scientific remarks], Zemun 1849.

39 ibid. 41–65.

40 ibid. 77–80.

the press.[41] Radičević distinguished himself not only as a skillful constitution drafter but also as a follower of modern, liberal ideas. Although he contributed to the nation building both in the Principality of Serbia and among the Serbs in Austria, during the brief history of Vojvodovina his work was not considered much of a success. He was nevertheless the first to include political rights, along with civil rights, in a draft constitution.

Radičević made a step forward as regards human rights in Serbian legal developments. In the draft Constitution for *Vojvodovina Srbska* (Serbian Dukedom/Duchy) he inserted a provision on the protection of human rights. Article 139 of the Constitution read 'Svakome je put pravice kod suda otvoren protivu Praviteljstva' ('Everyone is entitled to challenge a government's act before a court of law'). This was a complete novelty which provided for judicial review of administrative acts in the form of a right to legal remedy. Radičević was indeed a pioneer on the path of protection of human rights. His work marked the evolution of Serbian legal thought, although it still remains only poorly researched in Serbian historiography. Some of his contributions to the Serbian legal developments announced the approach of modern times towards the end of the first half of the nineteenth century. In its second half the nation building would be completed, but the attitudes on human rights would, in the 1840s and 1850s, be connected to other legal concepts, especially in the work of Serbian professors of law.

4.3 Conclusions

The concept of human rights emerged among the Serbs at the very beginning of the process of nation building. Dositej Obradović put it forward, connecting it to the rule of law. Dositej referred to individual rights that should be protected by the judiciary. He wrote on the subject on the eve of the Serbian national revolution, which began in 1804. In those times, however, another idea seemed to have spread among the population. The masses were in favour of collective rights, whereas the educated and enlightened intellectuals, like Dositej Obradović, favoured individual rights. The standpoint of the masses was reflected in the poetry and formulated by the epic poet, Filip Višnjić.

What appeared to be a gulf between the masses and the learned men seemed to be overcome when Grujović, on the occasion of forming the revolutionary government, intended to proclaim human rights to be the foundation of a modern nation. He was deprived of the possibility to deliver his speech,

41 Cf. www.britannica.com, 'Revolution and counterrevolution 1848–59' and 'March Laws'.

but the latter was preserved in writing as a token of the position his author had taken on the subject. However, the fact that Grujović was not given the chance to speak suggests that ideas other than the protection of individual rights prevailed among the leaders of the national revolution. The popular sentiment seemed to have been given precedence.

At a later stage of development, after an authoritarian regime had been put in place in the period of home-rule in the Principality of Serbia, Vuk Karadžić returned to the stance of individual rights as foundations of a constitutional state, although without mentioning Grujović. Their attitudes were identical in many aspects, and especially in how they approached the issue of human rights and their role in Serbian nation building.

The intellectuals who were close to the Serbian Prince, such as Davidović and Radičević, endeavoured to introduce human rights in the draft constitutions by way of enumeration. Their method was to compromise and look to avoid the fundamental question of the role of human rights in a practical way. This was evidenced by the fact that they almost entirely considered civil rights and were anxious not to mention political rights. Despite their insufficient approach, the outcome of their efforts consisted in the fact that the provisions on human rights found a place in Serbian constitutions. Notably, both for Davidović and Radičević it should be highlighted that their liberalism was greater in their convictions than in appearances. Davidović tried to reconcile the Prince's wishes with modern ideas, while Radičević was the first to introduce a provision on a political right in a draft constitution, as well as to provide for judicial review of administrative acts in a draft constitution. Their main contribution to the evolution of the concept of human rights consisted in the fact that human rights remained in the Serbian constitutions adopted later, in 1869, 1888, 1901 and 1903.[42]

Human rights have never become a pillar of the Serbian nation-state. They were present as a concept competing with other ideas during the nation building, but were nevertheless unable to prevail. The reason for their weakness originated in the lack of social and political forces which could promote them and impose the respective narrative on the political agenda; the isolated voices of the intellectuals were much too weak for such a task. In the time that the nation building was completed, human rights were hardly making their steps in practice in an atmosphere in which the constitutional provisions on human rights did not apply before the courts of law. It was only exceptionally that the

42 Cf. articles 22–40 of the 1869 Constitution, articles 6–31 of the 1888 Constitution, articles 25–42 of the 1901 Constitution and articles 6–31 of the 1903 Constitution.

parties invoked constitutional provisions in litigation. Human rights were proclaimed in constitutional texts, but remained mostly ineffective.

To this it should be added that Serbia in this respect followed the mainstream of European constitutional developments in the second half of the 19th century. There was no immediate application of the constitution provisions by the courts, which was detrimental to the protection of human rights. Such a state of evolution was reflected in the stance of Slobodan Jovanović in his book *On the State* (*Foundations of a Legal Theory of State*). He wrote at the beginning of the 20th century, comparing America and Europe as regards the immediate implementation of constitutional provisions, 'In the United States of America ... the courts are empowered to refuse implementation of a statute they find unconstitutional. In Europe however ... the courts are bound exclusively by legislation and not by the constitution.'[43] The constitutional provisions on human rights contained mostly proclamations and could not serve as a functional Bill of Rights. As an outcome of such developments, an effective protection of human rights was to come to Serbia as a novelty imported from the West more than a century after the completion of the Serbian nation building. Although it should be subject to research, it seems likely that the Serbian historical evolution in this particular aspect had traits in common with those of the neighbouring nations. Serbia was not an exception, but rather confirmed the rule.

43 S. Jovanović, *O državi – osnovi jedne pravne teorije* [About the state – The basis of a legal theory], Belgrade 1922 (the first edition of the volume appeared in 1912), 232. The edition used in this book is the one published in 1922.

CHAPTER 5

Sovereignty and Rule of Law in the Time of Nation Building

5.1 The Approach to the Problem

Sovereignty is the supreme authority over a polity. Discussing the notion of sovereignty in Serbian constitutional history raises two major questions. First, who was in possession of the supreme authority, i.e. with whom was the ultimate power in the society vested? Secondly, how was the sovereignty legitimised?

As to the first question, the answers may point to a physical person, or to a group, no matter how small or large it may be, or to a document which provides guidance and streamlines the power holders' actions. The physical person is the monarch. Serbia was a monarchy which emerged as an outcome of a national revolution. The revolution took place in a country of peasants in which the social strata were not sufficiently developed, at least not at the beginning of the nation-building period. The insurgents in the national revolution chose their leaders in 1804 and 1815. The leaders founded dynasties in the course of time. That is why the idea of a monarch's sovereignty was somehow adopted as natural, even without being exclusively connected with a certain dynasty. Two dynasties altered the governance of the country during the nineteenth century, and the people stood behind the alterations as their cause.

Another possibility is to understand the people as a whole to be the holders of the ultimate power. The idea of popular sovereignty existed among the masses in the time of the national revolution in a rudimentary way. However, in the legal thought it was linked with the notion of a republic, which Serbia never was, throughout the time of the nation building or later on – indeed not until the mid-twentieth century. The concept of sovereignty of the people was nevertheless eventually harmonised with the idea of the monarch's sovereignty. In all the Serbian constitutions of the second half of the nineteenth century, Article 1 was the same. It read 'The Kingdom of Serbia is a hereditary constitutional monarchy with a national representation.' The constitutions provided that the monarch was under obligation to rule according to the constitutional provisions.[1]

1 Cf. articles 91 (Constitution of 1869); 125 (Constitution of 1888); 169 (Constitution of 1901); 199 (Constitution of 1903). In 1869, Serbia was a principality.

 | DOI:10.30965/9783657791026_006

Last, but not least, there is a third answer to the question regarding the sovereign, i.e. the supreme authority, posed above. The sovereign could be the law, which means that the sovereignty could be vested in the constitution. This way of answering the first question also showed up in Serbian legal and constitutional developments. It led to the idea of constitutional supremacy.

The question of legitimacy of the sovereign power posed above is also complex. It could be answered in different ways. The old medieval idea was that the Divine Power was indeed the true source of sovereignty. It was the Divine Power that provided legitimacy to the entitlements of the sovereign or, in other words, provided a proper justification for the acts of the sovereign as a decision maker.[2] The idea was developed in the times of rationalism. It was transformed in the attitude that sovereignty had to be based on reason. Originally reason had been identified with the Divine Power, before it evolved into a separate and not necessarily religious concept. At the same time, reason was understood as a source of justice: only something that was just could be perceived as reasonable and vice versa. Therefore, the main question on the legitimacy of the sovereign power was connected with two notions, covering the substance of reasonableness and justice: these were the protection of human rights and the rule of law. As we have seen in the previous chapter, the notion of human rights was unable to prevail and decisively influence the evolution of Serbian constitutional law. On the other hand, the concept of the rule of law was much more widely discussed and was one of the levers of the developments. This was rather complex and showed specific traits of the Serbian society. That is why, if we were to distill an overarching principle as a source of the legitimacy of the ultimate power, that principle would not be found in the protection of human rights, but rather in the rule of law.

5.2 Sovereignty of the People

The idea of popular sovereignty existed among the Serbian masses at the beginning of the national revolution in some form, but was not yet properly developed in the modern sense of the term. When hostilities broke out in the First Serbian Uprising against the Ottomans of 1804, the people became aware of the possibility of putting an end to Ottoman rule in the country in the simplest way possible: by replacing the government of the foreigners with a Serbian government. Such a stance was reflected in the popular poetry. The singer of

2 The idea was present in the works of the earliest Serbian legal philosophers preceding the national revolution; cf. D. Popović, 'The Dawn', 183–87.

the Serbian revolution, Filip Višnjić, expressed it in the first lines of the well-known poem *Beginning of the Rebellion against the Dahis*, which recites and describes the events of 1804 in a poetic way.[3] The very beginning of the long poem reads as follows:

Bože mili! Čuda velikoga!	O, dear Lord, what a miracle
Kad se ćaše po zemlji Srbiji,	Took place in the land of Serbia,
Po Srbiji zemlji da prevrne	In Serbia when it was to overthrow
I da druga postane sudija.	So as to install another justice.

The main idea was clear. The existing government will come to its end, so as to make room for installing a new order, or another justice, as is seen in the poem. Notably, the text of the poem used the expression *justice* to describe the new order that was envisaged to be instituted in the country.[4] The poetry is emotional and not rational, but it nevertheless provides evidence in a historical perspective.[5] The Serbian people could not conceive of a government overseen by their compatriots as being anything other than laid on justice and therefore rooted in fairness. The shift in power from foreigners to compatriots was for that reason supposed to bring justice in the sense of good governance.

However, the shift of power from foreigners to nationals was exactly the circumstance which led the intellectuals to raise significant fears. As we have seen above, the first Serbian minister of education in the revolutionary government, Dositej Obradović, expressed his fear about the future developments of the Balkan nations once they became liberated from the foreign rule: 'if the people in these countries do not get rid of superstition and do not eradicate the ancient and non-Christian animosity towards the law, they will become their own Turks and tormentors'.[6] Passing of the power to local compatriots was by no means a guarantee of introducing good governance and fairness. However, the romantic attitude of the popular poetry, reflecting the opinion of the masses, neither went into detail, nor was it burdened with the subtle considerations of learned men. The latter were, however, right in raising important issues concerning the future government. Indeed, the valid questions were: Who is going to hold power? And how was the power to be organised after the liberation from foreign rule? In other words, the form of government, once it

3 The text in: V. S. Karadžić, *Srpske narodne pjesme IV*, 100.

4 In the original text in Serbian, the word used is *judge*. However, a judge is the symbol of justice. The new order was supposed to be fair.

5 Višnjić's biographer raised and thoroughly discussed the issue of poetic and historical truth in his work; cf. M. Panić-Surep, *Filip Višnjić*, 87–102; the veracity of his reports was praised by historians, ibid. 88.

6 D. Obradović, *Izabrani spisi*, 334.

became national, was not among the considerations of the masses. The masses were in favour of the shift of power from the Ottomans to the Serbs, and had little awareness of the issues concerning the form of government.

The same applies, for the most part, to the concept of sovereignty. Striving for the shift of power from the imperial court in Istanbul to the nationals or compatriots did not necessarily mean advocating the popular sovereignty. This was even more the case in light of the fact that, although their ideas on statehood were vague, the Serbs were at first ready to accept the power of a Christian emperor, either Russian or Austrian, to replace the Ottoman rule. It was only in the course of events concerning the warfare against the Ottoman troops that the idea of founding a nation-state indisputably prevailed.[7] It is therefore necessary to be cautious when assessing the concept of popular sovereignty in the Serbian national revolution. It found an adequate expression in the epic poetry of the period of the First Serbian Uprising, but at the same time it was neither properly shaped in modern terms nor complete enough to inform ideas and concepts concerning the form of government. The popular sovereignty was derived from the revolt of the masses and remained without proper doctrine. Its core consisted in the sentiments leading to the action of the masses that were willing to fight in the rebellion against the Ottoman rule. It was nevertheless present in the Serbian constitutional history at the beginning of the national revolution.

5.3 Between Sovereignty of the People and the Monarch

During the time of home-rule, which began in 1815, the question of sovereignty was not on the agenda. Serbia was a province of the Ottoman Empire without legal guarantees of its status, a fact which made the Serbian political factors strive for autonomy that would rely on an act of the imperial court in Istanbul. Once that task was achieved in the first half of the 1830s, the concept of sovereignty re-emerged in a specific way. It was connected with the adoption of the First Serbian Constitution in 1835. The adoption of the 1835 Constitution was marked by a legal controversy. It was doubtful whether an autonomous unit, i.e. a vassal state, as Serbia was at that time, was entitled to pass a constitution. The vassal status of the country relied on the Sultan's act of 1830, and only according to the Serbian interpretation of the act was the vassal country entitled to adopt a constitution.

7 For more on the subject, see D. Popović, 'The Dawn', 193–98.

The Prince's secretary, Dimitrije Davidović, drafted the constitution, and it is most likely that he had a decisive role in the ceremony of adopting the First Serbian Constitution in Kragujevac in February 1835.[8] The secretary convinced the Prince to comply with the idea of a constitution adopted by the national representation organ, as well as to take an oath on the constitution. One could consider today that Davidović stood between the ideas of the monarch's sovereignty and that of the people. The whole atmosphere in Kragujevac was serene. The National Assembly was convened. It was a traditional state organ consisting of a huge number of members elected for the occasion. Its session was opened by the Prince's speech, which consumed the first working day. On the second day, Stefan Radičević, one of the Prince's secretaries, read aloud the whole of the Constitution text, which was adopted without any discussion, i.e. by acclamation. Immediately after that, the Orthodox metropolitan bishop of Serbia, who was present at the session of the National Assembly, loudly read the Prince's oath. The Prince repeated the oath word by word, and then the members of the National Assembly also took a unison oath in the name of the Holy Trinity.

The events, as shortly described here, are reminiscent of the idea of popular sovereignty, at least to some extent. The monarch undertook certain commitments in a solemn and ceremonial way, and these were accompanied by the oath of the representatives of the people, a reminder of the fact that this was a constitutional pact concluded between the monarch and the people. However, to complete the image of the adoption of the constitution, one should take note of the report on the event which appeared in *Novine Srbske*, the only newspaper in the country, which assumed the role of an official herald as well.[9] The report referred to the metropolitan bishop's words addressed to Prince Miloš: 'Thou hast completed the salvation of the country, by solemnly granting the Constitution', and, further on, 'The Constitution that we have now received from the hands of our legitimate ruler'. At the time of adopting the 1835 Constitution, Serbia was a vassal country and its sovereign was the Sultan. However, the Serbs neglected that fact to a certain extent. They were inspired by the pattern of German principalities, because those in principle submitted to the imperial power of the German-Roman emperor. The passing of the constitution in Serbia was indeed an effort made on the road to sovereignty. That

8 Cf. B. Cunibert, *Srpski ustanak i prva vladavina Miloša Obrenovića 1804–1850* [The Serbian Uprising and the first rule of Miloš Obrenović 1804–1850], Belgrade 1901, 394–95. This is still the most reliable source, stemming from a witness to the event. On the ceremony and the adoption of the 1835 Constitution, including the Prince's speech, cf. D. Popović, *Prapočetak*, 81–83; R. Ljušić, *Kneževina Srbija*, 137.

9 *Novine Srbske* 7/1835, 52–53.

is why the question appeared in the light in which it would have appeared in a truly sovereign country.

It is not of prime importance for this volume to establish whether the 1835 Constitution was granted by the monarch or adopted by the national representation.[10] What is of interest, is the fact that the driving force of the adoption of the 1835 Constitution, Dimitrije Davidović, proved to be inclined towards the concept of popular sovereignty, although his opinion stood between that concept and the idea of the sovereignty of the monarch. Davidović's attitude on the subject can, however, be properly reconstructed only in the light of the contributions he had made as the editor of *Novine Srbske* in which he published a series of articles under the title of 'Kratko opisanije strani zemalja' ('Short Description of Foreign Countries'). Although written in a popular manner, the articles were mostly academic in substance, with the aim of enlightening the public at large in Serbia on the forms of government in foreign countries.[11]

In his articles, Davidović distinguished the notion of absolute monarchy from a limited one. In the former, the monarch was vested with all three branches of power: the legislative, executive and judiciary. In the latter, the monarch shared the power with the national representation. Davidović even went so far as to tackle the issue of sovereignty, stating that in the limited monarchy the ultimate power was shared between the monarch and the representatives of the people.[12] This clearly shows his opinion sat halfway between the concept of the monarch's sovereignty and that of the people, despite the fact that at the same point he praised the monarchy as the best form of government. He was indeed a partisan of the system of representative government, for which he invoked several examples, pointing above all to England and France. The inclination towards representative government was underlined in a certain manner when Davidović discussed the notion of the republic. Davidović's main stance was that in a republic the people were vested with the sovereign power.[13] Notably, Davidović was an adamant supporter of the representative form of government. He insisted on the fact that the system of representative government could exist in a monarchy as well as in a republic. That seemed to be of utmost importance for the drafter of the First Serbian Constitution, and that is why at this particular point in his series of articles he came close to the views of Benjamin Constant. Constant insisted on the idea that the

---

10 For the author's view on the issue, cf. D. Popović, *Prapočetak*, 83.

11 The articles appeared in 1834 in *Novine Srbske* 4, 5, 6, 10, 11, 13, 14, 15 and 17. For comments on the articles, cf. D. Popović, ibid. 40–48.

12 *Novine Srbske* 10/1834, 40.

13 *Novine Srbske* 11/1834, 44.

difference between a constitutional monarchy and a republic was smaller than the one between a constitutional and an absolute monarchy. For the French philosopher, the difference between a constitutional monarchy and a republic existed merely in form, whereas the difference between the two types of monarchies was indeed fundamental.[14] Although it cannot be established whether the French author had an immediate impact on the Serbian, the latter's view provides evidence that Davidović connected the question of sovereignty with the forms of government. He took account of the mode in which the powers were exercised, which was within the realm of the rule of law, a notion that Davidović did not use, but nevertheless seemed to understand.

Davidović was a convinced liberal, influenced by the Western political and constitutional concepts. His liberalism may appear today to be somewhat romantic, because he was, above all, a Serbian patriot. He nevertheless properly understood the problem of the organisation of power, and was essentially in favour of putting checks and balances on the Prince's powers. At the same time, his position as the Prince's secretary made a strong impact on his activities and writing. Drafting the text of the 1835 Constitution, he attempted to reconcile the irreconciliable – the Prince's style of governance – for Prince Miloš exercised his powers in the old, patriarchal way using the modern institutions of government. Davidović's opinion on sovereignty stood between his liberal attitude and his support for the Serbian Prince, which was based on the Prince's role in the liberation of the country, national emancipation and nation building.

5.4 Monarch's Sovereignty

Throughout the nation-building period in Serbian history, there were thinkers who favoured the concept of the monarch's sovereignty. They form a line which begins with Dositej Obradović, the first education minister of modern Serbia, who lived in the eighteenth and early nineteenth centuries. The line stretches throughout the nineteenth century, even to the time in which the nation building was over. The views of the authors belonging to this group were diverse in substance and nuanced, but they had one important point in common. Apart from the fact that they were supporters of the monarch's sovereignty, the followers of that idea also connected the notion of sovereignty with the concept of the rule of law in a specific way. Despite the fact that for the most part they did not mention the rule of law, a thorough analysis of their attitudes shows

14 Cf. B. Constant, *Cours de la politique constitutionnelle*, Paris 1861, II 70.

that the rule of law was, according to them, an essential feature of the substance of the notion of sovereignty.

Dositej Obradović expressed his views on sovereignty following the precepts of the leading doctrine in the times of absolute monarchy. His fundamental ideas were those of tolerance and enlightenment, which he found in Christianity. A Christian absolute monarchy was his ideal, and he was of the opinion that this had been realised in Europe in the eighteenth century. Dositej Obradović highly praised the rule of Joseph II of Austria and Peter I of Russia.

One of the best known of Dositej's publications was his *Fables*, which appeared in Leipzig in 1788.[15] In the morals of one of his fables, he tackled the issue of the form of government, portraying the whole atmosphere of an absolute monarchy. His presentation suffers from an idealistic approach, but nevertheless clearly displays his opinion on the subject. The title of the fable was 'A Lion, a Wolf and a Fox' and the core part of its *naravoučenije* (morals) read: 'in a nation governed by an enlightened ruler attached to justice, where just laws are in force, and where the subjects themselves are enlightened and industrious ... they know what they owe to their emperor, as to a father, and the emperor knows what he owes to them as to sons and family'.[16]

The monarch was thus portrayed as a father of the family, and the whole idyllic presentation of the state was styled in such a way as to compare the two institutions – the state and the family. The author insisted on the mutual obligations of the monarch/father and the subjects/sons. The whole relationship between the two was accentuated by the idealistic stance that not only the emperor but also the subjects were enlightened and industrious. The starting point for Dositej was the reciprocity of the duties of a monarch and his subjects, which echoed the situation in a family, and the roles of a father and his sons. Notably, on the side of the monarch there are in Dositej's view two important features which invite comments. The monarch is attached to justice, and in his realm just laws are in force. Those two features were indispensable for Dositej in the form of government that he considered to be superior to all others.

Since the sovereign monarch is attached to justice, the first issue to discuss is the one concerning Dositej's understanding of the notion of justice. That notion was placed at the highest possible level in Dositej's line of developing ideas. He departed from the idea of distributive justice, consisting in the concept that everyone receives their just deserts. 'Pravedan je koji svakom svoje

15 For Dositej's bibliography, cf. M. Pavić, *Rađanje nove srpske književnosti* [The birth of new Serbian literature], Belgrade 1983, 600–01.

16 D. Obradović, *Izabrani spisi*, 286.

ostavlja i daje' ('Just is the one who grants and gives to everyone his own') was his stance in *Sovjeti zdravago razuma* (*Counsels of the Sound Mind*).[17] This goes along with his opinions expressed in the *Fables*.[18] The concept of distributive justice appeared to be fundamental, because it was purely logical and could not be contested as the substance of the notion of justice.

However, both in the *Counsels* and the *Fables* Dositej Obradović insisted on the idea that God Almighty and justice were inseparable. In other words, he either identified God with justice or at least considered justice to be a constitutive feature of the Almighty. In the *Counsels* Dositej stated: 'A reasonable and benevolent man believes that God exists and that He is perfectly good and perfectly just.'[19] If the emperor, i.e. the sovereign, is attached to justice and inspired by it, then he will find inspiration in justice when fulfilling his task as legislator. This further means that the sovereign will inevitably pass just and equitable laws, which brings our writer to connect the notions of sovereignty and the rule of law. In the passage from the fable 'A Lion, a Wolf and a Fox' quoted above, the author portrayed the enlightened ruler as attached to justice, but at the same time he stated that just laws were in force in the realm of such a sovereign. An enlightened sovereign monarch was thus perceived as someone who ruled according to the precepts of the rule of law.

It was, however, not enough in Dositej's view that the enlightened monarch ruled by way of enforcing laws he had passed himself. The fact would by itself lead to an impartial governance, since the legal rules would apply to each and every one of his subjects.[20] Dositej Obradović went a step further, insisting on the substance of the emperor's enactments. Notably, the laws in force had to be just: as the author puts it, in the best of governments 'the just laws are in force'. We have seen earlier in this volume Dositej's entire opinion on the subject. He considered the substance of the just laws to be the protection of human rights. It is essential at this point to underline the fact that this offers evidence that Dositej Obradović understood the rule of law in a substantive way. The enforcement of laws was not enough to achieve the task of good governance in the best form of government, which for Dositej was the absolute monarchy.

17 D. Obradović, *Izabrana dela*, 230.

18 For comments on the relevant points in the *Fables*, cf. D. Popović, *Misao o pravu u delima srpskih pisaca* [The idea of law in the works of Serbian writers], Belgrade 2011, 22.

19 D. Obradović, *Izabrana dela*, 235; for the comments on the same idea expressed in the *Fables*, cf. D. Popović, 'The Dawn', 206.

20 Rade Radović insisted on the stance that Dositej Obradović was a supporter of the rule of law. Cf. R. Radović, 'Prirodnopravna teorija monarhiskog apsolutizma u političkoj filosofiji vojvođanskih Srba' [The natural law theory of monarchical absolutism in the political philosophy of Vojvodina Serbs], *Arhiv za pravne i društvene nauke* 5/1939, 414.

The sovereign was to enforce the law, but at the same time the law in the sense of legal order had to be just and equitable. That was indeed what qualified the absolute monarchy of an enlightened monarch to be the outstanding form of government. However, as we have seen in the previous chapter, Dositej Obradović reached the idea of protection of human rights in his *Ethics*, which was published in 1803. There seems to have been an evolution of his opinion towards the understanding of the rule of law in a substantive way, i.e. in connection with the concept of human rights.

The whole of Dositej's opinion on sovereignty as related to the concept of the rule of law aligns with the contemporary philosophy of natural law.[21] This is evidenced, for instance, by his reference to Christian Wolff in the morals of one of his fables. It remains difficult, nevertheless, to assess the scope and the degree of influence of the German philosopher on Dositej Obradović. The Serbian author was by all means a dedicated follower of the philosophy of the Enlightenment and natural law. Therefore, the absolute monarch who reigns rationally and justly was the sovereign in his opinion. The sovereign's rational and just reign was the rule of law, as Dositej Obradović understood it. His opinion was in line with the spirit of the eighteenth century. It was commonplace in that time that the state should be governed according to laws, so as to rule out the arbitrary.[22]

Soon after the insurgents of the First Serbian Uprising got hold of the Belgrade fortress and liberated the city from the Turks in December 1806, the first institution of higher education was launched in Serbia. It was called the *Velika škola* (Grand School). Dositej Obradović gave the opening speech on the occasion of its opening in autumn 1808.[23] That was the year in which the teaching of law was launched in modern Serbia. A learned Serb who came from abroad was among the first professors of the Grand School. This was Lazar Vojnović (1783–1812) whose course was the one in *državno pravo*, which was a translation from the German *Staatsrecht*. The German term may be considered

---

21 For more comments on the issue, cf. D. Popović, 'The Dawn', 211.

22 The expressions are borrowed from Kelly, who refers to M. S. Anderson. Cf. J. M. Kelly, *A Short History of Western Legal Theory*, Oxford 1999, 282.

23 A. Gavrilović, *Beogradska Velika škola 1808–1813* [The Belgrade Grand School 1808–1813], Belgrade 2013 (a reprint of the volume which appeared in 1902), 16–18. On the beginning of legal studies in Serbia, cf. Z. Mirković, 'Die Anfänge des Rechtsstudiums im Serbien der Neuzeit und die Juristenausbildung in der Habsburger Monarchie (Ein Beispiel des Rechtstransfers)', *Annals FLB, Belgrade Law Review LVIII*, 2010/3, 151–62. See also: Ž. Bujuklić, 'Nation-building and the emergence of Serbian Legal Studies', in: Th. Simon (ed.), *Konflikt und Koexistenz*, 553–54 and the scholarship referred to.

to cover the expression of Law on State Organisation in English. Vojnović also taught International Law and Criminal Procedure.

Lazar Vojnović was born in Sremska Mitrovica, the son of a Serbian military officer committed to the Austrian frontier troops. He had attended the grammar school in Sremski Karlovci where he was a pupil of Ivan Jugović, who was among the founders of the Grand School in Belgrade in 1808. Having completed his grammar school studies, Vojnović afterwards studied in Pest, where he graduated in law and philosophy from the university. He had come to Serbia in 1807, became involved in politics and diplomatic affairs, taught in the Grand School and passed away young in 1812.[24]

The material covered in Vojnović's course in the Grand School could best be described as a rather short introduction to what the Germans call *Allgemeine Staatslehre* (General Theory of State). The Grand School historian, Andra Gavrilović, who consulted the manuscript of the course, reports that the manuscript consisted of thirty-five and a half sheets of paper, written in elegant handwriting.[25] The manuscript had been preserved in the National Library of Serbia and was destroyed with the whole library book fund during the German bombing of Belgrade on 6 April 1941. The last author who consulted the manuscript and afterwards published an article based on it was Rade Radović.[26] However, Andra Gavrilović reproduced most of the substance of the manuscript in his book of 1902, which enables us today to have a proper insight into Vojnović's attitudes on many important issues that are relevant for this volume.[27]

When treating the issue of the forms of government, Vojnović followed the Aristotelian pattern. The forms of government were three – republic, oligarchy and monarchy. Vojnović had been teaching his course before the standard legal terms developed in Serbian language. The foundations of Serbian legal terminology were laid down decades afterwards, under the Austrian impact and the influence of German language. The first German-Serbian legal dictionary was published in Vienna in 1853. It was based on a project that had been launched in 1849.[28]

Since the standard legal terms were lacking, Vojnović used expressions which are no longer used in Serbian vocabulary for teaching purposes: *narodo-deržavije* for republic, *pravlenije boljarov* for oligarchy and *jedinonačalije*

24 For biographical data cf. S. Savić, *Počeci teorije*, 119–20. On Vojnović as professor of Criminal Procedure, cf. Z. Mirković, 'Die Anfänge des Rechtsstudiums', 159.

25 A. Gavrilović, *Beogradska Velika škola*, 49.

26 Cf. R. Radović, 'Prirodnopravna teorija'.

27 A. Gavrilović, *Beogradska Velika škola*, 49–69.

28 Cf. Ž. Bujuklić, 'Nation-building', 522–31.

for monarchy. It was only for the latter notion that he informed the students of the Greek word *monarhija* as an alternative.[29] To distinguish the three forms of government, Vojnović resorted to the concept of sovereignty as a lever. He explained to students that in a republic the sovereign power was vested in the people, or as the author put it, 'prava veličestvena su u saboru' (in the Congress). In an oligarchy says Vojnović, 'boljari u jedno uzeti čine veličestvo' (the noblemen taken together are the sovereign), whereas in a monarchy 'sva prava načalstvujuštega ima samodržac' (the monarch is vested with the sovereign power). Vojnović was wholeheartedly in favour of the monarchy as the best form of government. His reason for this was the rational advantage that he found in that form. It primarily consisted in the fact that the monarch would usually be inclined to rule upon the advice of the outstanding and wise. However, despite the latter remark, Vojnović was against mixed forms of government, relying on the separation of powers that was founded on the division of the sovereign power between the monarch, the people and the noblemen. The noble and the wise should act as counsel to the ruler, but they should not share the sovereign power with him.

Since Vojnović was of the opinion that the concept of sovereign power was the decisive feature when classifying the forms of government, it is of paramount importance to study his attitude on the notion of sovereignty itself. For the purpose of displaying that concept he again used terms that no longer exist in modern Serbian language. The first of those was *načalstvo*, and the second was *veličestvo*. Our author appeared to have been a supporter of the idea of state sovereignty, a doctrine, which tends to understand the sovereign authority as superior to all other powers existing within a state. Therefore, Vojnović says, 'načalstvo deržavno mora biti najveće nad svim graždanskim vlastma' (the state power must be paramount to all civil powers). Because of being superposed and superior to all other powers within the state, it takes the name of *veličestvo* (sovereignty), explained the author.[30] This stance made him close to the theory of state sovereignty. It is based on the opinion that the sovereignty is a fundamental element of the modern state, despite the fact that it did not play a primary role in its emergence.[31]

At that particular point in his lectures, Vojnović proceeded to enumerate the specific features of the sovereign power. Those were six in his view. The first three of the enumerated features are of the greatest interest for this volume.

---

29 A. Gavrilović, *Beogradska Velika škola*, 65–66.

30 A. Gavrilović, *Beogradska Velika škola*, 52.

31 On the theory and its origins, cf. J-L Thireau, *Introduction historique au droit*, Paris 2009, 155–58.

Notably, Vojnović understood the sovereign power as being paramount, unique and inseparable from the state. This corresponds with the ideas that we still have today on the same issue.

Having thus defined the notion of sovereign power, Vojnović went to the next topic in his course, which was devoted to the entitlements of the sovereign. It was probably because of his inclination towards monarchy as the best form of government that Vojnović used an old word, nonexistent in modern Serbian, to denote the holder of the sovereign authority. The word was *načalstvujušti*, and roughly speaking it personifies a man who is the head of state. Our author then wrote in detail about *prava načalstvujuštega* (the powers of the head of state). In his opinion, the sovereign powers of the head of state were three. The sovereign was entitled to legislate, he had the power of control and he also had the ability to execute laws.[32]

Vojnović's views on the monarch's entitlement to legislate showed the influence the school of natural law had had on him. He explained that the laws (*zakoni*) were either natural (*jestestveni*) or positive (*položitelni*). The latter, says the author, should be drafted in view of the former.[33] The sovereign's power to execute laws supplements his legislative power. Vojnović raised a simple question: why should the head of state legislate if not to execute his own legislative acts? The purpose of legislation lay in its enforcement. At the same time, our author understood the judicial power as one among the entitlements of the executive.[34] That was also in line with the prevailing opinions among lawyers in the eighteenth century, at least in German lands. Vojnović had received his PhD in Law from the Pest University, which was under the influence of the Austrian professors of law.[35] However, the most significant of the entitlements of the sovereign power from the standpoint of this volume seems to be what Vojnović labelled as the *pravo verhovnog nadziranija* (supreme power of supervision).

The power of supreme control was identified with the notion of police, or in German *Polizei*, which might be equated with the idea of welfare in a broader sense of the term. Such a power of control had its source in the sovereign's duty to be a watchdog of public good (*da čuva od vreda opšte stvari*).[36] This goes along with Vojnović's opinion on the substance of laws. Notably, despite the

32 A. Gavrilović, *Beogradska Velika škola*, 52–58.
33 ibid. 53.
34 ibid. 55.
35 Teaching of law in Pest University was under the strong impact of Martini's doctrines. Cf. J. Szabadfalvi, 'Natural Law Tradition in Hungary from the End of the Middle Ages to 19th Century', http://L'ircocervo.it/ 2011-1.
36 A. Gavrilović, *Beogradska Velika škola*, 54.

fact that enacting laws is an entitlement of the sovereign authority, our writer explained to his students that there were several requirements which the monarch had to fulfil when acting as legislator. Among those was that the enacted laws had to be in conformity with the rights of the people (*da su zakoni prema pravima narodnim*).[37] This is the main reason why Vojnović's attitude towards the rule of law should be considered as a core feature of his course held in the Grand School. He did not mention the rule of law, but he was nevertheless in favour of the idea of a monarch who reigns in such a way as to bring welfare to his subjects. The monarch was therefore limited, despite the fact that he was the holder of all three branches of power within the state. Even if not properly checked in the modern sense of the term, the monarch should be limited by the positive law, the creation of which required following certain precepts.[38] This is what made Vojnović stand close to Dositej as regards the rule of law.

Both Vojnović and Dositej Obradović adhered to the intellectual lines of thought of their time. They were dedicated followers of the absolute monarchy, which they considered to be the best form of government. However, in line with the ideas of rationalism and the attitudes of the school of natural law, they did not find it unsuitable to sustain the idea of putting certain rather philosophical commandments upon the absolute monarch. Those were based on their view that the monarch, although absolute, i.e. exercising all branches of state powers, had to use those powers in a rational way so as to achieve some noble goals. The latter could be described in the broadest sense as welfare in general. The monarch would therefore appear to be ethically constrained to rule in accordance with the law, or in other words he would have to be faithful to the rule of law, something which neither of the two Serbian authors explicitly stated. Its substance was nevertheless present in their attitudes, especially given the fact that the two authors came very close to the idea of protection of human rights as well. Dositej Obradović achieved that stance in his *Ethics*, and Vojnović – albeit somewhat timidly – mentioned the rights of the people in his lectures. The absolute monarch, who reigns in such a way as to achieve welfare of his subjects, was the sovereign in the views of both Serbian authors. The monarch's rule aimed at accomplishing welfare was in their opinion the rule of law, or at least a phenomenon fairly comparable to what we understand as such nowadays.

---

37 ibid. 53.
38 cf. S. Savić, *Počeci teorije*, 123.

5.5 Constitutional Supremacy

Vojnović's teaching was an episode which did not last long. However, before the teaching of law was eventually introduced in Serbia the evolution of the concepts that are of interest to us in this chapter took another, somewhat peculiar direction. The idea of constitutional supremacy emerged in Serbian legal thought. It was developed in two stages, which were not connected to each other. The concept first found expression in the attitudes of Božidar Grujović in 1805, and then in completely different circumstances in the views of Vuk Karadžić in the 1830s.

In his 'A Word on Freedom' of 1805, Božidar Grujović connected the issues of sovereignty and the rule of law in a specific manner. He treated three topics of interest for this volume. The first was the notion of the sovereign, the second was the substance of sovereignty and the third was the notion and substance of the constitution.

The notion of the sovereign stood at the very beginning of the short text of the speech that was never delivered in public. It read: 'The law is the will of the country, which commands to the whole of the country and to everyone to perform good and to prevent evil. Therefore is the law the overlord and judge in the country.' The law (in Serbian: *zakon*) may seem to be unclear as an expression, for in the Serbian language it refers to laws in general, in an abstract sense, as well as to particular statutes. The dilemma, however, becomes resolved in the following sentence, which reads: 'The lords, the masters and the government, the clergy and the military, as well as the people as a whole, must be under the law, notably under the one and the same law.' That is how we learn the proper meaning of the expression *law* in Grujović's 'A Word on Freedom'. Grujović's law is unique, and can by no means be identified with a single statute of any kind. It is rather the *idea* of the law, which was one and the same for each and every person in the country. That law, unique, idealised, equal for all, was in the author's view the overlord and judge in the country. In other words, the *law* was omnipotent, supreme and therefore sovereign.

Grujović idealised the law in a way similar to how Dositej Obradović and Vojnović idealised the monarch. He seemed to be substantially close to Dositej's view, but he nevertheless switched from the specific to an abstract principle in the atmosphere of the crucial moment of forming the revolutionary government in 1805. It is significant that Grujović made a shift from the physical person of a monarch to an abstract principle, a fact which was in accordance with the circumstances existing in the turbulent time of the national revolution. He could not put forward the idea of the absolute monarchy, not even in the form of an enlightened government. Revolutions are rooted in values and principles, and Grujović was guided by those. In his thoughts, he perceived the law to be, as he put it, the overlord and judge in the country, i.e. the sovereign.

Grujović praised the law as the ultimate authority in the human sphere. That is why it would probably be more appropriate, when considering his opinion, to write that word with a capital letter at its beginning. The Law was the sovereign; the ultimate power was not vested in any person or body, but indeed in a principle which was paramount and omnipotent. Understanding the notion of sovereignty in such a way made Grujović take another step, namely to determine the substance of the sovereign power. The Law, says Grujović, 'must be rational and just'. This is so because the purpose of the Law is to 'reward the good who merit, and punish the evil, disobedient and lazy'. In his view, the task of the society was to create such a Law, in which the ultimate authority would reside. The lever of its creation was reason, which relied on justice. Grujović considered the two – reason and justice – to be inseparable and indeed represent two halves of welfare. At this point, the author of 'A Word on Freedom' seemed to have identified the welfare of the members of the society with reason and justice, taken together. His thought was nevertheless uncertain in that respect, for he immediately returned to his ideal, stating in the next sentence of the text: 'Where there is no reason and justice, there is no law.' The Law was essential; the notion of welfare encompassing both reason and justice could not prevail over the most important concept that Grujović adhered to. That concept was the Law – idealised, unique, reasonable and just. The Law was the sovereign, the ultimate authority, and the welfare consisting in reason and justice was its substance.

The Law, although sovereign and consisting of the substance that has just been explained, was primarily a philosophical concept. Grujović had prepared to address the leaders of a revolution, and he was probably guided, at least to some extent, by practical motives when exposing his ideas. The Law had to be effective to be implemented in the everyday life of the society, to be enforced. That righteous law, as he put it, had to preserve freedom. To explain the connection between freedom and the Law, as he perceived it, Grujović identified the Law with another notion. That notion was the constitution. He shaped his opinion in the following way: 'Where there is a good constitution, that is where the law is well established, and the authority is well set up under the law, there is freedom.' At this point it becomes clear that the author of 'A Word on Freedom' abandoned the purely philosophical stance in defining the ultimate authority. That authority was indeed the Law, but in reality the Law, which is just, righteous, reasonable, unique, found its expression in the constitution. The constitution was supreme in his view, because it was the emanation of the idea and the concept of Law.

Grujović also considered the conditions the constitution must exist in, finding that two elements were necessary. Firstly, the authority of those holding power had to be under the law, and secondly, freedom had to be preserved. 'A legitimate government must provide for the freedom of the citizens' might be the expression we would use today to explain the author's view on the subject. Grujović was a liberal, and his mind was focused on freedom. He wanted to deliver a speech on freedom, and to praise it, because, to borrow his words, '*it is freedom, freedom that makes us men*'.

Freedom can be achieved exclusively if there is a constitution which is superposed to all other acts and statutes. Enforcing the constitution necessarily meant the rule of law, for the constitution was the law, perceived as absolute and supreme. At this point it is remarkable that for Dositej Obradović the rule of law was a consequence of the sovereign's conduct. The sovereign brought the rule of law into being by the way in which he ran the country. For Grujović, on the other hand, the rule of law was by no means a consequence of the conduct of persons holding power. It was an attribute of the sovereign, as it was immanently attached to its being. Namely, only one who obeyed the rule of law could be considered legitimate and, in turn, a holder of the sovereign power. Considering the case of a power holder who deviates from the rule of law, producing evil for the citizens, Grujović made his point in the following words: 'he would by no means merit to be the judge and the chief'. The author's stance was clear at this point: a decision maker who acts *ultra vires* becomes illegitimate, and he can no more exercise the powers conferred to him. That is so because it is the constitution that is supreme, and not the ruler of the country.

The course of nation building in the Principality of Serbia was cumbersome and had a peculiar evolution. Home-rule had actually been introduced in 1815, and the Serbs had immediately started striving for recognition of the status in view of introducing autonomy in the country, which was achieved in the 1830s. In that period the leader of the Second Serbian Uprising against the Ottoman rule, Miloš Obrenović, elected by the people to become Prince of Serbia, instituted his personal regime.[39] The character of the system of governance that Prince Miloš practised in the country more or less confirmed the fears of Dositej Obradović. His prediction that the new nations, once liberated, might become 'their own Turks and tormentors' found evidence in the conduct of Prince Miloš. It was in 1832 that Vuk Karadžić, in his famous letter to the Serbian Prince, to which we shall return later in this chapter, wrote the

39 Miloš Obrenović was elected in an informal way to lead the people. The election was formalised by adopting an Act on the Prince's Dignity at the popular assembly, held in 1817. Cf. M. Stefanovski, *Srednjovekovna shvatanja uzorne vladavine*, 183–206.

words that sounded like the evidence of Dositej's prediction. Vuk's wording was as follows: 'nego se ovde govori … da Beograđanima našega zakona nije bio veći zulum ni pod kakom vladom Turskom, nego što je u današnje vreme' (The Belgrade people of our faith claim that there has never been under any Turkish government a greater terror than the one existing in our time).[40]

Among the best sources for researching the regime that existed at that time in Serbia is the *Historical Material for Serbian History of Our Time*, which Vuk Karadžić left in his legacy with a special order not to be revealed until the year 1900.[41] Vuk displayed the main features of the regime under three headings. The first was 'Mockery', which explained how the primitive and illiterate Prince was making fun of his compatriots. The second was 'Self-Love and Disdain of All Others' and the third was 'Arbitrary and Unlimited Government'. The second and third headings also portrayed the Prince and his autocratic behaviour.

To illustrate the mockery, it suffices to point to one of the short notes attached to the main text of the historical material.[42] The short note describes an event concerning a person that has already been mentioned in this volume. It was Stefan Radičević, the Prince's secretary. Vuk Karadžić relates that the Prince once travelled from Kragujevac to a monastery near Belgrade. To humiliate his secretary for an unknown reason and make fun of him, the Prince ordered that Radičević be transported in a wagon, together with a calf. An accident occurred during the journey, so that there was no longer a horse to pull the wagon. The Prince's servants then forced both the calf and the Prince's secretary to hit the road on foot. Vuk Karadžić has remarked that the Prince laughed more watching his secretary walk on foot on a muddy road than when he ordered him to be transported in the same wagon as the calf. Stories of this kind were numerous.

To illustrate Miloš Obrenović's self-love and contempt for others, there is a wide choice of examples from the second section of the *Historical Material*, of which one is fairly illustrative. A Serbian diplomat, sent by Miloš to Istanbul in the 1820s was taken hostage there, and spent six years in prison. On his release in 1827 the Ottoman Porte presented the diplomat with a sabre, before allowing him to return to Serbia. It was probably the gift that made Miloš jealous and almost furious, so that he started prosecuting the diplomat at once on his return. Needless to say that the prosecution had no foundation in law. The diplomat already thought his life was at an end, but then Miloš changed his mind,

---

40 V. S. Karadžić, *Istorijski spisi*, 216.

41 See all material in: V. S. Karadžić, *Istorijski spisi*, 159–211.

42 ibid. 207. The title of the short text is 'A Note on Stefan Radičević'.

took the sabre from him and sent the poor man home with a threat not to interfere in public issues any more.[43]

In the third heading of the text, entitled 'Arbitrary and Unlimited Government', at the beginning Vuk Karadžić summarised the character of the Prince's style of governance in the country in the following words: 'Miloš is the unlimited lord of the life, estate, the mode of living and dignity of all men who live in Serbia under his rule.' He went further to report on the secret murders of nine people, including a metropolitan bishop of the Orthodox Church and a Prince's secretary.[44] Indeed, the whole text of this heading of the *Historical Material* is abundant with references to murders which were committed following the Prince's orders. Apart from those most horrible and outrageous acts, Vuk Karadžić also referred to Miloš's attitude towards public servants and officials. His statement in that respect was significant. It read: 'I am not surprised by the fact that Miloš can fire or downgrade any official, without any grounds; I am more surprised because the one who is chosen <u>must</u> accept the service and can under no excuse whatsoever leave it at will.'[45] According to Vuk Karadžić, there were people ready to pay the amount of their salary to someone else so as to avoid the public service, because in practice it amounted to little more than the role of domestic servant to the Prince. Aware of the hardships of the primitive public service, some would try to slip away and avoid taking a post, alleging they lacked the appropriate skills and could not properly serve. Prince Miloš was so insolent on such occasions that, according to Vuk's report, he would say, 'Had that been possible, I wouldn't have served either'. This was followed by Vuk's comments that the people at large were fully aware of the fact that Miloš lived the life of an emperor, while allegedly serving his people. The Prince's conduct towards the state officials was the same in respect of clergymen, whom Miloš used to move from one place of service to another, although lacking the proper authority to do so. The disrespect he showed towards the estates of individuals in Serbia completed the image. Vuk Karadžić wrote that 'Miloš disposed at his own will of the possessions of all people in Serbia, so that no one was indeed the owner of anything'.[46] In brief, it was an arbitrary government. To borrow the words of Alex Dragnich, 'Miloš's terror may have been greater and more cruel than that found in some mid-twentieth century

43 ibid. 179–80.
44 ibid. 184.
45 ibid. 193 (underlining in the original).
46 ibid. 194.

states, but there were few or no newsmen or radio or television correspondents to tell about it.'[47]

Vuk Karadžić did not participate in the warfare during the First Serbian Uprising against the Ottoman rule. As he walked limping and had a wooden peg leg, he assumed the role of a scribe in the headquarters of one of the insurgent leaders. When Belgrade was liberated and the Grand School was founded in 1808, he attended it from 1810. After the defeat of the insurgent troops in 1813 he escaped to Vienna, but returned to Serbia in the time of home-rule. He joined the public service and in 1831 he held the post equivalent to the mayor of Belgrade. He confessed in the prologue of his legacy, the *Historical Material*, that he had been the Prince's favourite, but nevertheless decided to put in writing the truth about Prince Miloš's rule in the country.[48] It was in December 1831 that he started writing the *Historical Material*, having meanwhile left the Serbian territory and escaped to the Habsburg monarchy. In April next year he addressed his famous letter to the Serbian Prince, stating his disagreement with the Prince's conduct and his mode of exercising power. Vuk hesitated for months before mailing the letter and only expedited it in August 1832.[49]

In the introductory part of the letter Vuk described the state of affairs in Serbia, using on several occasions the data that he also put in the *Historical Material*. The conclusion of that part was simple – there was huge dissatisfaction in the country; in Vuk's own words, 'no one in Serbia was satisfied' with the Prince's rule. The introduction was followed by Vuk's proposals for improving the poor state of governance in Serbia in the 1830s. Some of those concerned liberalisation of the economy, predominantly monopolised by Miloš himself and his partners in commerce, or the abolition of quasi-feudal bonds consisting of unpaid work for state officials, or reforming the schools. However, the outstanding proposal was 'To give the people their rights, or as it has currently been the expression in Europe – the constitution.'[50] At that point, as we have already realised in Chapter 1 of this volume, Vuk referred to both principal areas of constitutional law as the substance of a constitution: human rights and the organisation of power. Vuk's explanation of why a constitution should be adopted in Serbia was founded on a reason which is reminiscent of the words of Montesquieu. The constitution would lead to such a state of affairs in the country 'that everyone knows what he is supposed to do, and that he fears neither you nor any other man', he wrote to the Prince. Another liberal note

47 A. Dragnich, *The Development*, 17.

48 V. S. Karadžić, *Istorijski spisi*, 159.

49 ibid. 213–47 for the text of the letter and Vuk's own comments on it.

50 ibid. 217.

accompanied the main stance. The constitution would enable each and every person to 'pursue his work, as well as live at his own will'.[51]

Vuk tried to persuade the Prince that a constitutional regime in Serbia was preferable to the Prince's primitive autocracy. He realised that the latter stemmed from the lack of checks and balances, which were indispensable as tools of a constitutional government. At the same time, Vuk was of the opinion that the proper checks and balances were to be found in the protection of human rights, as well as in the legislation. That is why he suggested introducing the protection of the most fundamental human rights, which in his view were life, estate and dignity. He also insisted on the adoption of legislative acts. Introducing legislation in the modern sense of the term was a problem under Prince Miloš's rule. In one of his comments in the letter of 1832 Vuk displayed the Prince's attitude towards the adoption of legislation. He said that Miloš often admitted in conversations that laws were indispensable for Serbia, but was also inclined to say that it was better to govern without laws. Vuk reported the Prince's words in that respect. A government submitted to laws would in the Prince's opinion mean 'onako se čovek veže za artiju, pa ne može da čini ni zla ni dobra' (that a man is bound by a piece of paper so that he can produce neither evil nor good). Vuk added a remark in the comment that this was the Prince's proper and intimate opinion on the subject.[52] The autocratic and illiterate Prince was in favour of arbitrary power.

Vuk's insisting on the introduction of legislation in Serbia went hand in hand with his endeavour to convince the Prince to adopt a constitution and make Serbia a constitutional state. It relied on the same idea, which tackles the issue of sovereignty, which Vuk Karadžić nevertheless did not elaborate upon in detail. Adoption of laws is in essence the same as adopting a constitution. Once those acts are introduced the decision maker, or the power holder, is under constraint. There is something above the decision maker's will and superposed to it. The ultimate authority and the supreme will in the country should not be based on the attributes of a person, whoever that person is. On the contrary, the supreme authority should be vested in the constitution, i.e. in an act consisting of abstract norms or commands addressed to all the people in the country, including the Prince. Therefore, Vuk Karadžić tried to explain to the Prince the function of the constitution in the following words: 'The rights of the people and the laws should not only be promised to the people, but indeed promulgated in a constitutional assembly, taking the oath that they will

51 ibid. 217 for both citations.

52 ibid. 236.

be obeyed, so that the one who transgresses them shall be the enemy of the people and of the fatherland, and persecuted as such.'[53]

Vuk Karadžić saw no alternative to constitutional supremacy to move the country beyond the autocracy and arbitrariness to which the Prince was accustomed. He required checks and balances and found them exactly in a piece of paper, as the Prince put it, that would limit the decision maker's power. The Prince would have to comply with the rules of conduct imposed by the constitution, and the constitution would stand above the Prince. One could say that Vuk envisaged an intrinsic limit of the Prince's power in the very notion of a constitution. The power holder, in his perception, could not decide himself on whether his conduct was proper, but instead had to comply with certain rules of conduct when exercising his power. These should be articles of the constitution, providing for checks and balances. Therefore the constitution enables the rule of law. The constitution, together with the laws, represented in Vuk's view the foundations of the rule of law. To achieve it the constitution had to become the ultimate authority; in other words, the constitution should be the sovereign.

Vuk Karadžić and Božidar Grujović, each in their own way and in different historical circumstances, were both in favour of the supremacy of the constitution. Grujović was definitely more philosophical in his approach to the issue, and also more idealistic, whereas Karadžić sounded more realistic, requiring checks and balances to put a constraint on the Prince's arbitrariness. The latter, of course, is true only if we disregard the fact that the personality of the Serbian Prince, his spiritual countenance and character were by no means adaptable to a constitutional regime. However, the two authors were basically unanimous in advocating constitutional supremacy, and in that respect they stand alone in Serbian constitutional history.

5.6 Conclusions

As in many other nations that had been subjugated to a foreign rule, achieving sovereignty was one of the main goals of Serbian nation building. The sovereignty can be linked to two concepts – human rights and the rule of law. In other words, the sovereign may be the one who provides protection of human rights or the rule of law, or eventually both. In Serbian constitutional developments, the rule of law had more weight in determining the sovereign than was

53 ibid. 218.

the case with human rights, which were mostly put aside and played a modest role.

It was by no means easy to display the connection between the concepts of sovereignty and the rule of law. A chronological approach had to cede and leave room for a thematic order, which was governed by ideas and their developments. Three ideas emerged in times of Serbian nation building as regards the relationship between the rule of law and sovereignty. On the one hand, there was the concept of popular sovereignty. It was combined to some extent with the monarch's sovereignty on the occasion of the adoption of the 1835 Constitution. On the other hand, the concept of the monarch's sovereignty had been developed among Serbian intellectuals decades before the adoption of the first constitution in 1835. It had been shaped as an element of absolute monarchy, although enriched by features of the Enlightenment. Apart from that, there was also a clear idea of constitutional supremacy. It emerged in 1805 and reappeared in 1832.

Sovereignty of the people was a vague idea which found a place in the popular poetry. It was neither developed, so as to attain the shape of a proper intellectual concept, nor could it connect with the concept of the rule of law. Moreover, Dositej Obradović expressed fears that the switch from foreign to domestic rule in the case of the Balkan people might serve no purpose because the compatriots, once in power, may continue terrorising people and pursue arbitrariness as a style of governance developed under the foreign rule. As a matter of fact, that was exactly what happened in Serbia, according to Vuk's report from the 1830s. The inhabitants of Belgrade complained of the arbitrariness of the Serbian Prince.

The rule of law timidly appeared on the occasion of the adoption of 1835 Constitution, albeit unrelated to the notion of sovereignty. Dimitrije Davidović, the Prince's secretary who drafted the Constitution text, was a supporter of the concept of limited monarchy and the representative form of government. He therefore stood half-way between the sovereignty of the people and the monarch's sovereignty, naively hoping that Prince Miloš might agree to the introduction of a somewhat constitutional regime. The latter would encompass the rule of law. In Serbia in the 1830s, the pattern of sovereignty shared between the monarch and the people was more the dream of a convinced liberal such as Davidović, than a feasible concept.

The concept of the monarch's sovereignty was developed among Serbian intellectuals decades before the adoption of the 1835 Constitution. It was attached to absolute monarchy as a form of government. Dositej Obradović, in a philosophical approach to the issue, idealised both the sovereign and the law in general. The former had to pursue the law in running his realm, whereas the latter had to be equitable and just. In other words, the rule of law was for Dositej Obradović a consequence of the monarch's decision on the manner in which he would exercise his power. The first Serbian professor of public law, Lazar Vojnović, followed similar ideas, but he supported the opinion that the state power was paramount to all civil powers, thus adhering to the theory of state sovereignty. The decisive feature of sovereignty was in his view the ultimate authority vested in the absolute monarch.

Two Serbian intellectuals were in favour of constitutional supremacy: Božidar Grujović, who had formative training in law, and Vuk Karadžić, a historian and linguist. Grujović idealised the notion of law in general, identified it with the constitution and expressed the view that it should be, as he put it, the overlord and judge in the country. Vuk was more realistic. He required checks and balances to put effective constraints on the authoritarian rule of the Serbian Prince in the 1830s, and perceived the constitution as a tool to achieve such a task.

CHAPTER 6

Two Outstanding Professors of Law and Their Views on the Rule of Law and Human Rights

6.1 Introduction

Two professors of law, Jovan Sterija Popović (1806–56) and Dimitrije Matić (1821–84), marked a milestone regarding the development of ideas on the rule of law and human rights towards the mid-nineteenth century, i.e. in the advanced phase of Serbian nation building. The academic careers of the two professors were short for similar reasons. They both left their roles as teachers of law in order to be appointed to the posts in government, where their careers in the administrative branch were successful.

Both professors left their lectures in writing, but only Matić published his works. Matić studied under Popović, following his course in 1840. However, he wasn't much influenced by his Serbian professor. Most of the intellectual influences he received stemmed from his German professors, whose courses he had followed while preparing his PhD thesis in Leipzig, Berlin and Heidelberg. Sterija Popović was also intellectually influenced by the Germans. German scholarship thus played a decisive role in Serbian constitutionalism and its developments in the 1840s and the 1850s. The two outstanding professors transmitted the achievements of German scholarship to their Serbian students, thus spreading the German influence on the developments of Serbian law.

6.2 Jovan Sterija Popović

The teaching of law, which had been launched in Serbia for the first time in the modern era at the Grand School in Belgrade in 1808, did not properly take roots in the country for a long time. Serbian rule in the city of Belgrade – and across the whole country – was short-lived, and its fruits were annihilated with the Turkish return to power in 1813. The Grand School then ceased its activity. When a new political settlement was introduced as an outcome of the Second Serbian Uprising in 1815, the political circumstances had considerably changed. In those years the issue of replacing the home-rule of the Serbs – which was in a way a *gouvernement de fait* – with the formally recognised autonomy of a

 | DOI:10.30965/9783657791026_007

semi-independent state, became paramount. It took the Serbs fifteen years of complex diplomatic efforts and negotiations to convince the Sultan to grant autonomy by a formal act.

Throughout the home-rule period, political and constitutional issues prevailed over those concerning education in public life. It was only after the settling of the autonomous status of the country that matters of education were once again added to the agenda of Serbian authorities. Higher education was re-launched in Serbia, and this encompassed the teaching of law. *Licej* was founded in Kragujevac in 1838. Jovan Sterija Popović, a prominent Serbian intellectual from Austria, was invited to teach law at *Licej*.

Jovan Sterija Popović was born in Vršac, nowadays in north-east Serbia, which in the nineteenth century was in the territory of the Habsburg monarchy. He studied in Vršac, Timisoara and Pest and later graduated in law from the university in Kežmarok, which is today in Slovakia. He started a career as an attorney at law in his native city, but this was soon interrupted when he was invited to come to Serbia. From 1840 to 1842 he had been teaching law at *Licej*, before he was committed to a post in Serbian government. He was appointed as head of department for the Ministry of Education, where he remained until 1848. Sterija was enormously successful as a civil servant. He initiated the foundation of the National Library, the National Museum and the *Društvo srbske slovesnosti* (Society of Learned Men), which was the predecessor of the Serbian Academy of Sciences and Arts. The first theatre in Belgrade was opened in 1841, and played one of Sterija's tragedies at the opening. Following certain disagreements with some of the politicians in power, he resigned from his post in 1848 and left Serbia to return to his native city, where he passed away in 1856. Despite his accomplishments as a civil servant, he is best remembered as a comedy writer, with his works still performed in Serbian theatres.

The outcome of Sterija's work as a professor, however, passed almost unnoticed for a long time; his academic career had been stunted when he took up his position in the government administration, and the course materials he had generated were not used. Sterija's principal university course was in the area of Natural Law, and for this he had prepared a manuscript of quite a considerable volume. Unfortunately he did not live to see this published. It had almost fallen into oblivion, when the Belgrade University School of Law decided in 1956 to commemorate one hundred years of the author's death. For that occasion, Professor Radomir Lukić gave a lecture on the manuscript, assessing Sterija's academic contribution to Serbian legal developments.[1]

1 R. Lukić, 'Jovan Sterija Popović – professor prirodnog prava na Liceju' [Jovan Sterija Popović – professor of natural law at the Lyceum], *Anali Pravnog fakulteta u Beogradu*, 1957/V, 1–13.

Although this lecture indeed revived some interest in Sterija's academic work, it would be several decades before his manuscript was lifted out of obscurity through publication.[2]

Sterija had written his manuscript before the language reform took place and also before the Serbian legal vocabulary was fixed. In his lecture, Lukić described Sterija's language as the 'usual official language of those times, distinct from the vernacular, insufficiently understandable'. As for the style, he found it to be based 'on long sentences of German composition with verbs at the end and hardly comprehensible'. Despite such language, the formulations were accurate, and the legal notions sharply defined, which made the substance of the manuscript brilliant from a juristic point of view.[3] Sterija was a lawyer who had received his formative legal training in German and was highly influenced by the German legal doctrine.[4] In numerous footnotes in the manuscript of his lectures, he referred to the works of German authors as well as to classical ones, the latter being either the philosophers of antiquity or those from the period of renaissance. The footnote text was in Serbian, German and Latin. As far as the language and legal terms were concerned, Sterija had a dispute with the Serbian language reformer, Vuk Karadžić. Their views on legal terms were opposed to one another. In 1841, the authorities entrusted the Society of Learned Men with forming the official language in Serbia, by way of editing a dictionary. At a decisive meeting of its board in May 1845, two attitudes on the issue were confronted. Sterija and Vuk were on opposite sides. Vuk favoured the vernacular and rejected the method of creating new words on the basis of agreement among the board members. To borrow the expression from Professor Žika Bujuklić, the dictionary consisted of 'clumsy new phrases … proclaimed as Serbian words'. Vuk's opinion prevailed, the project was abandoned and the modern language experts consider the outcome of the dispute over legal terms as a triumph of the vernacular, which echoed the democratic spirit of the popular poetry, being Western-oriented and European.[5]

The notion of State, as a polity, was the main point in the development of Sterija's ideas. Sterija perceived the State as a union of free men, i.e. a society, as he put it, which was distinguished from other societies by its special goal. The State's goal was to provide security to the independent persons forming it. That

2 The edition used in this volume is M. Stojanov (ed.) *Prirodno pravo Jovana Sterije Popovića* [Natural law of Jovan Sterija Popović], Novi Sad 1995. (Hereinafter referred to as J. S. Popović, *Prirodno pravo*).

3 R. Lukić, 'Jovan Sterija Popović', 1.

4 Cf. J. S. Popović, *Prirodno pravo*, 103–04. Sterija presented a special appendix to his lectures referring to the relevant scholarship in public law, mentioning mostly German authors.

5 Cf. Ž. Bujuklić, 'Nation-building', 544–46.

was also the origin of the State, which made our author declare, 'pričina dakle postanja države jest obezbedije prava' (the cause of the origin of the state is to secure rights).[6] Notably, Sterija indicates at the same point that the persons who compose the State are *građani* (citizens). He also used the expression subject (*podajnik*, in the old version of the noun), but he gave priority to the former expression when explaining to his students the theory of social contract. It was by virtue of the latter that the State was founded. The professor, however, insisted on the fact that the philosophical origin of the State did not correspond to historical facts, putting a remark in Latin in a footnote, which reads, *Jurista non scribit historiam*.[7]

Having defined the notion of State as a community of free citizens relying on a contract in order to preserve their rights, Sterija proceeded in his lectures to the notions of sovereign and sovereignty. In the ultimate analysis, the two notions appear to be linked to the concept of State by way of the goal the latter has to accomplish.

Sterija used the term *vladatelj* (literally: ruler) to denote the sovereign. He also pointed to two other terms – *državni načalnik* and *poglavica* – putting in brackets the French term *le souverain* as a translation.[8] On analysing the manuscript, Lukić rightly remarked that the term *vladatelj* applied to the sovereign organ of the state and not necessarily to a monarch.[9] In this regard, Sterija stands close to Lazar Vojnović, whose work has already been discussed in this volume. Vojnović used the term *načalstvujušti* to denote the sovereign. This word, which is grammatically masculine, also refers to a ruler, i.e. the head of state. There are some more points of convergence between the two authors, which are most likely due to their education in German and the use of German doctrine to prepare their lectures for the Serbian students. Notably, both Vojnović and Sterija were of the opinion that the sovereign had certain entitlements, which were accompanied by his duties. The two authors used the same term to denote the sovereign power. That term was *veličestvo*, a word that has since disappeared from the Serbian language. It was the old form of the word *veličanstvo*, meaning *majesty* in modern Serbian. Vojnović was of the opinion that there were six features of sovereign power. Sterija, on the other hand, expressed the view that there were four.[10] For Sterija, the sovereign was vested with the ultimate authority, his acts were not subject to approval, he

6 J. S. Popović, *Prirodno pravo*, 98.
7 ibid. 100.
8 ibid. 105.
9 R. Lukić, 'Jovan Sterija Popović', 8.
10 Cf. A. Gavrilović, *Beogradska Velika škola*, 52 (for Vojnović's attitude) and J. S. Popović, *Prirodno pravo*, 106.

was not accountable to anyone and could not be put under constraint. At the same place in his manuscript, Sterija discussed the notion of sovereignty with a reference to Rotteck, which brought his ideas close to those of Vojnović. In fact, some of the content in Sterija's footnote was identical to that covered in the six features of sovereignty in Vojnović's course. It is not at all likely that Karl von Rotteck (1775–1840) could have inspired Vojnović as he clearly did with Sterija: Rotteck published his main works after Vojnović had passed away.[11] However, the origins of such attitudes were probably rooted in the same source in the German scholarship, which cannot be identified today. Vojnović and Sterija did not belong to the same generation; there was in fact a gap of three decades between their respective law teaching careers in Serbia. However, the characteristic features of sovereign power were similarly explained in the courses of the two professors.

Another point in common for both authors was the idea that the sovereign was vested with certain entitlements. As to the enumeration of entitlements, Sterija's opinion was a bit more complex than Vojnović's. However, the most significant sovereign entitlement for both professors was the power to legislate. They also agreed that the sovereign enjoyed the power of supervision, as well as executive power. Sterija compressed the two and wrote 'o nadziratelnom i izvršitelnom pravu veličestva' (about the supervision and executive powers of the sovereign). Speaking of the executive power, Sterija expressed the opinion that the judiciary was a part of it.[12] Notably, what brings complexity to Sterija's lectures is the fact that he broadly referred to some particular entitlements of the sovereign which would nowadays be considered as sectors of the executive branch. Those were, for example, military power, power to appoint to offices, power to regulate church matters, etc.[13]

In line with the attitudes marked by the rationalistic approach to the concept of sovereignty, Sterija was of the opinion that the *vladatelj* (holder of the sovereign power) had certain duties, along with his vast entitlements encompassing all three branches of state power. In other words, the sovereign was limited, despite the fact that he was the holder of all branches of power. Sterija did not find the supremacy and the limitations of the sovereign power to be in contradiction. He conveyed this clearly in a footnote in Latin, referring to Hobbes: 'non est contradictio: suprema potestas et limitata, prout Hobbes

11 On Karl von Rotteck and his works, in brief, cf. G. Kleynheyer and J. Schröder, *Deutsche Juristen aus fünf Jahrhunderten*, Heidelberg 1989, 236–38.

12 J. S. Popović, *Prirodno pravo*, 112–13.

13 ibid. 114–33.

dicit'.[14] Sterija also invoked in this respect the example of Frederick the Great, who expressed the view that the Prince was the first servant of the state, so as to put his main stance in a footnote in German: '… die Erhaltung der Gesetze die einzige Ursache war, welche die Menschen vermochte sich Oberherren zu geben; denn dies ist die wahre Ursprung der Souveränität' (maintaining laws was the only reason why men wanted to give themselves overlords; that is the real origin of sovereignty). This idea was clearly rooted in the theory of social contract. Powers were instituted among men to enable obedience to laws, so preserving the legal order was the first and most important of the sovereign's duties. Therefore the sovereign was under obligation to 'maintain the constitution of the country in all points and conditions, and particularly in respect of personal freedom of the citizens and their security, equality before the law, freedom of thought and religion, and also in respect of the free enjoyment of their estate' (Ustav zemlje u svim točkama i uslovijama, poimence pak u smotreniju lične građana slobode i bezbednosti, jednakosti pred zakonom, slobode uma i veroispovedanija, a najposle u smotreniju slobodnog uživanja dobara podržavati). Apart from this evidently overriding duty of the sovereign, Sterija mentioned three others, namely an ethical approach to the exercise of power, equitable distribution of titles and appointments to office and an overall obligation to provide for the public good. The latter included *red sudova ne uznemiravati* (independence of the judiciary).[15]

Sterija's opinion on the fundamental duty of the sovereign is of the utmost importance for understanding his attitudes in general. What was announced by Dositej Obradović and Lazar Vojnović in Serbian legal thought found a clear-cut expression in Sterija's lectures, despite the fact that the latter was not influenced by the two older authors. The three Serbian writers stood in line with the rationalistic philosophy of their time and were prevailingly influenced by the Germans. Dositej was the exception, because he was the only one of the three to spend some time in England, becoming a supporter of English social ideas. It is perfectly clear, when reading Sterija's lectures of 1840, that he considered the protection of human rights to be the sovereign's most important duty towards the citizens. In other words, the protection of human rights represented the substance of the order the sovereign had to maintain, i.e. the rule of law. Sterija indeed enumerated a whole catalogue of human rights, placing an obligation on the sovereign to preserve those. Human rights, in his opinion, preceded the foundation of the state, which was commonplace in the theory of social contract. Sterija was a follower of this theory. His ideal

14 ibid. 146.
15 ibid. 134–35.

was, nevertheless, absolute monarchy, and where he elaborated on the duties of the sovereign he gave priority to the practice of absolutism over Rousseau's opinion on social contract. Noting that Friedrich the Great considered himself to be the first servant of the state, Sterija put in a footnote that 'long before Rousseau's social contract the ruler's dignity was considered to emerge from a contract' (consideravit igitur [longe ante Rousseau Contrat Social] regiam dignitatem e contractu emergentem).[16]

Sterija's opinion on the notion of constitution completes the stance just mentioned. He considered the constitution to be one of the three fundamental contracts that were indispensable for maintaining a state. The first is the one labelled as the contract of the union of citizens (*ugovor građanskog jedinstva*), the second contract is the constitution (*ustav*) and the third is the contract of submission (*ugovor podvergatelni*).[17] It appears that the first and the third of the three contracts taken together cover substance that mostly corresponds to the concept of social contract as perceived by the theory. However, our main interest here is in the notion of constitution. For Sterija it was a contract by virtue of which the citizens determined the form of government. To borrow the author's words, the constitution was the contract 'by which [the citizens] mutually agree to recognise a certain form of government' ('kojim se uzajamno obvezuju određeni način pravlenija priznati').[18]

Sterija was aware of the fact that constitutions in their original form could not last forever. The people had to adapt the constitution of a polity according to the developments and changes in the society. The changes intervene because 'with the improvement of a man in time, changes occur not only in a man's character but also in his nature, spirit and accomplishment, which lead to the alterations of the needs of certain peoples' ('po usoveršatelnosti čoveka i po vremenu menja se ne samo prirodni čoveka karakter, no i naravi, i duh, podvig, a po ovom i potrebe pojedini naroda'). For such reasons, constitutions must be susceptible to amendments. Sterija added in a footnote that a bad constitutional law was the mother of thousands and thousands of other bad laws ('Ein schlechtes Constitutions-Gesetz ist Mutter von tausend und tausend anderen schlechten Gesetzen').[19] Notably, he remarked in the same footnote, following Rotteck, that the motion to amend the constitution should never originate in the executive power.

16 ibid. 134, footnote 1.
17 ibid. 100.
18 ibid. 100.
19 ibid. 138.

Having thus established that constitutional amendments were indispensable from time to time, Sterija raised another question, namely the one of the momentum and opportunity of constitutional amendments. They were indeed not necessary 'where the right of personal freedom and equality before the law exists, where the freedom of thought relies on conscience, where the security of persons and estate is particularly confirmed' ('gdi se pravo lične slobode i jednakosti pred zakonom nalazi, gdi je sloboda mišljenja delo sovesti, gdi je bezbednost lica i imanja podrobno utvrđena').[20] A constitution containing such guarantees could not, in the author's view, become substantially outdated ('ne može ... veštestveno ostariti'). At that point, Sterija displayed his attitude on the substance of a constitution: fundamental rights are guaranteed in a constitution and they indeed represent the main element of the constitution's substance. This is a valid conclusion, despite the fact that our author defined the notion of constitution as an act that merely determines the form of government. Sterija neither used the expression 'rule of law', nor 'human rights', but both concepts were present in his understanding of the notion of constitution. Human rights were guaranteed by the constitution, and its provisions on the form of government should enable their protection. The proper outcome of the implementation of a constitution would therefore be the realisation of the rule of law. The two concepts that are of interest for the study in this volume were inseparable in the author's view.

Turning to forms of government, Sterija did not show an original attitude. On the contrary, following the Aristotelian tradition, he stood close to Lazar Vojnović and Dimitrije Davidović. Notably, there was an evolution in the Serbian language as regards legal terms, which becomes evident if we compare Davidović's writing on the forms of government in *Novine Srbske* in 1834 with the terms Sterija used in his lectures of 1840. Davidović was inclined to excessive translation of foreign words, such as republic or monarchy.[21] He used the expression *narodoobščestvo* for the former and *samodržavstvo* for the latter. Neither of the two has survived in modern Serbian. Sterija, for his part, used the terms *republika* and *monarhija*, which are still in use today, as the adaptations of the foreign expressions almost universally accepted in many languages.

Sterija's concepts of the forms of government were, however, more complex than those of Vojnović and Davidović. He endeavoured to explain to his students that, in the original sense of the term, each and every polity was a republic. This was so because of the origin of the state, i.e. a polity based on the

---

20 ibid. 139.

21 On his language, D. Popović, *Prapočetak*, 41–43.

social contract. Our author was, however, aware of the fact that such a concept had not been accepted in the course of history. That is what made him take a realistic stand, defining monarchy as relying on the personal dignity of a monarch, i.e. a physical person. In a republic, on the other hand, the sovereign's dignity was vested in an office and could be performed by many people, who were removable and responsible for their acts. Sterija at the same time insisted on the fact that *građanska sloboda* (civil liberty) could find its place both in republic and in monarchy.[22]

Further on, Sterija explained that there were three forms of government, namely monarchy, democracy and aristocracy. The distinguishing criterion for the three was the holder of the sovereign power. In monarchy, the sovereign power was vested in the monarch, in democracy in the people and in aristocracy in a body. Sterija did not mention the nobility, which created the impression that his notion of aristocracy could be identified as an oligarchy.[23] He nevertheless remained within the Aristotelian framework when explaining the forms of government. Towards the end of the relevant part of his lectures devoted to the forms of government, Sterija tackled the issue of the best of governments. He put forward the opinion that there was no system of government that would be applicable in all states and at all times. Another general remark he made was that the form of government should be in accordance with the spirit of the people and time, as well as with the circumstances existing in a society. However, he opted for a monarchy with a national representation in which the monarch retained the executive power as the most justified form of government.[24]

In an overall assessment of Sterija's ideas as part of his milestone lecture on the author, Lukić insisted on combating the stance that he had merely been a supporter of absolutism.[25] Lukić considered Sterija to be a liberal, especially because of the latter's opinion in favour of a monarchy with national representation. In such a form of government, Lukić explained, the legislative power is vested in the people, and the executive with the monarch.[26] Lukić nevertheless seems to have narrowed the scope of Sterija's liberalism. The explanations on the substance of the constitution in Sterija's lectures confirm his liberal views. They evidence his attitude on the rule of law and human rights, two concepts that were linked and intermingled so as to form a specific unity. The protection

22 J. S. Popović, *Prirodno pravo*, 142–43.

23 ibid. 143–48.

24 ibid. 149–50.

25 R. Lukić, 'Jovan Sterija Popović', 13. He did not make any reference at this point. We do not know to whom Lukić addressed his criticism.

26 ibid. 13.

of human rights was the object of the enforcement of the rule of law. Its realisation was indeed the main goal of the State.

6.3 Dimitrije Matić

Dimitrije Matić (1821–84) was born in Ruma, which at the time of his birth was in Habsburg territory. He came to Serbia as a boy to study at the *Licej* in Kragujevac. Having completed his higher education he was granted a Serbian governmental scholarship to prepare for his PhD in Germany, and received his doctorate from Leipzig University in 1847. On his return to Serbia he was appointed professor at the *Licej*, which had meanwhile moved to Belgrade. He taught law for only three years. Due to the political circumstances, which were unfavourable to his liberalism, he was removed from the university's teaching staff, but nevertheless made a career in the government administration and in politics. In the former capacity he performed various duties, e.g. as secretary of the Court of Appeals, as well as of the Prince's Chancery. Later he was a judge at the Court of Cassation and a member of the Council of State. In terms of politics, Matić was one of the founders of the Liberal Party, a minister of education and justice, a representative in the National Assembly, and indeed was its speaker many years later in 1878 when the independence of Serbia was proclaimed at the session in Kragujevac.[27] Matić was also present in 1848 at the May Assembly in Sremski Karlovci, on the Austrian territory, when the Serbian Dukedom was proclaimed within the Habsburg Monarchy. He had been appointed as a member of the steering committee of the May Assembly, but nevertheless returned to Serbia and lived there.

Unlike Sterija, whose work in the field of law remained unnoticed for a long time, probably because he occupied a place in the memory of the people as a writer, Matić attracted more attention in the scholarship. This was also due to the fact that the manuscript of Sterija's lectures fell into obscurity, while Matić published his works. The most outstanding among these were *Objasnenje Građanskog zakonika* (*Commentary of the Civil Code*, Belgrade 1850–51), *Javno pravo Knjažestva Srbije* (*Public Law of the Principality of Serbia*, Belgrade 1851) and *Načela umnog državnog prava* (*Principles of Rational State Law*, Belgrade

27 For Matić's biography in brief, B. S. Marković, 'Foreword', in D. Matić, *Načela umnog državnog prava, Kratki pregled istorijskog razvitka načela prava, morala i države od najstarijih vremena do naših dana* [Principles of Rational State Law; A brief overview of the historical development of the principles of law, morality and the state from ancient times to the present day], Belgrade 1995, 7.

1851). To those should be added 'Kratki pregled istorijskog razvitka načela prava, morala i države od najstarijih vremena do naših dana' ('A Short Review of Historical Development of Principles of Law, Ethics and State from the Earliest Times to Our Days'), as well as his diary – *Đački dnevnik* (*A Student's Diary*).[28]

As regards his work in the field of law, Matić has his intellectual biographer. Professor Božidar S. Marković published a monograph, thoroughly explaining and critically assessing Matić's attitudes and achievements.[29] Matić's views on philosophical issues were also subject to comments in Serbian scholarship in the nineteenth and twentieth centuries.[30]

The analysis of Matić's attitudes on the rule of law and human rights begins with his opinion on the notion of State.[31] He was the follower of the idea that the state was a union of men under law. The notions of *state* and *law* were in his view inseparable. Therefore, he wrote, 'without state as a condition of a human being, the notion of law is inconceivable' ('bez države kao uslova ljudskog bića, ne može se pojam prava ni zamisliti').[32] In the footnote on the same page, Matić *inter alia* referred to Kant and his opinion that the State was based upon the law. On the next page, our author quoted Hegel in a footnote, namely his opinion that 'the state was a materialised and realised moral idea' ('ostvarena i realizovana moralna ideja').[33]

Matić's opinion on the notion of State parallels his understanding of the State's goal. Discussing different attitudes on the issue existing among academics, Matić expressed the opinion that 'the state should be the guarantee and not the failure of the individual freedom' ('garantija, a ne propast slobode pojedinca'). The State's task was to develop institutions that were able

---

28 'Kratki pregled istorijskog razvitka načela prava, morala i države od najstarijih vremena do naših dana', in: *Glasnik Društva srpske slovesnosti* [A brief overview of the historical development of the principles of law, morality and the state from ancient times to the present day], Belgrade 1851, 63–130; *Đački dnevnik* (1845–48), Belgrade 1974. *Načela umnog državnog prava* and 'Kratki pregled …' have a new edition in one single volume: D. Matić, *Načela umnog državnog prava, Kratki pregled istorijskog razvitka načela prava, morala i države od najstarijih vremena do naših dana*, Belgrade 1995. They will be referred to as D. Matić, *Načela* and D. Matić, *Pregled.*

29 B. S. Marković, *Dimitrije Matić – lik jednog pravnika* [Dimitrije Matić – The character of a lawyer], Belgrade 1977.

30 B. S. Marković, 'Foreword', 9–10.

31 D. Matić, *Načela*, 23.

32 ibid. 23 (for all translations DP).

33 On Matić's fidelity to Hegel's philosophy, cf. B. Milosavljević, 'Dimitrije Matić. Navodni prelaz s hegelovstva na naturalizam' [Dimitrije Matić. The alleged transition from Hegelianism to naturalism], *Theoria* 1 (2015), 103–51.

to provide for the enforcement of law. Matić believed that the state had to enhance all benefits for a man, which in his opinion consisted in its threefold mission: 'the rule of law, enhancing the public morals among people and supporting general welfare' ('da zakoni vladaju, da se podiže javni moral u narodu i da se potpomaže opšte blagostanje').[34]

Matić remarked that if considered from the standpoint of their goal, the states could be classified in two different types. One was the State based upon the law, to which the German term of *Rechtsstaat* applied, and the other was the state that put its citizens under guardianship; this was known as *policijska država*, which would be *Polizeistaat* in German. The author explained in a footnote that it would be better to use the term *starateljska država*, instead of *policijska*. The former equals the German expression *Bevormundungsstaat*. At the same point in his volume, Matić remarked that the ideas of communism and socialism indeed relied on the concept of a guardianship state dressed in a democratic outfit.[35]

To denote the notion of sovereignty, Matić used the old term, *veličestvo*, but described it as sovereignty in the text. He considered the sovereign power to be paramount within the State, and therefore, as he put it, *potestas suprema*, which he defined as the ultimate power as regards its foundations. The latter means that the sovereign power neither finds its origin in any other power, nor can it depend on another. As it is unique, the sovereign power is also indivisible. Notably, the ultimate power is in Matić's view by no means unchecked. Its scope is limited by its fairness and legitimate character, so that Matić creates an image to explain its proper reach. In his opinion, 'gde je kraj državnoj vlasti, tamo počinju narodna prava' ('where the state's power ends, the rights of the people find their beginning').[36] Having thus defined the sovereign power as ultimate but nevertheless limited by fairness and legitimacy, and turning to the issue of the sovereign, whom he describes as the *vladalac države* (ruler of the state), Matić insists on the idea that the notions of sovereign and state are interdependent. He explained that the concept of state indeed represented a unity of the sovereign and the governed. The sovereign, in Matić's view, personified the State, despite the fact that the sovereign could be either a physical person or a body.[37]

When discussing the issue of sovereignty from the standpoint of its powers, Matić reviewed the attitudes of French and German scholars, accepting

---

34 D. Matić, *Načela*, 41.
35 ibid. 43.
36 ibid. 63.
37 ibid. 64–65.

the arguments of both groups.[38] Turning to the enumeration of the sovereign's powers, he explained that the legislation and administration were two modes of operation by which the state power intervened in human relations in public life. This showed his inclination towards some sort of confusion between legislation and the executive. At the same time, Matić underlined the fact that it had been almost universally accepted among scholars that it was necessary to institute the judicial power as a separate one within the state. However, he added that some scholars understood the judiciary as a part of the administration, i.e. the executive power. Apart from the three powers just mentioned, Matić also classified the power of supreme control as among the entitlements of the State.[39]

In this context, our author also considered the issue of the separation of powers. He noted that the theory was introduced by Montesquieu and John Locke. However, Matić expressed a critical stance towards the theory, based on the attitude that the separation of powers did not properly consist in the division of the state power as such. The separation of powers only meant conferring the state power to different organs of the State. In the author's view, the state power remained, nevertheless, undivided. At this point Matić invoked the example of the United States of America, so as to put forward the opinion that even there the sovereign power as such was vested in the people as a whole.[40] This exaggerated opinion clearly displays Matić's discordance with the concept of separation of powers. As regards the topic, Matić remained somewhat conservative and could not match the more liberal attitudes of his contemporary Stefan Radičević, who was a supporter of the theory of separation of powers.[41]

One of the core issues in the whole course that Matić presented to his students was the concept of the constitution. At first glance, Matić was in agreement with his Serbian professor, Sterija Popović. The concept of the constitution was for both of them linked with the form of government, so as to determine the form of government in a given state. However, the *genus proximum* was not the same for the two professors. As we have learned above in this chapter, for Sterija the constitution was one of three contracts which the citizens should conclude among them in order to institute a government. For Matić, the constitution was above all *zbir pravnih načela* (an aggregate of legal principles) that are in force in a State as regards the form of government. Another

38 ibid. 69–70.

39 ibid. 72–74.

40 ibid. 74–75. Matić expressed his principal criticism of Montesquieu in his 'Short Review'. Cf. D. Matić, *Pregled*, 131–32.

41 On Radičević's view on the issue, cf. D. Popović, *Prapočetak*, 106–14.

point of difference between the concepts of the two professors consisted in the fact that Matić believed that the principles applied to the relationship between the organisation of the State and the rights of the people. Moreover, Matić insisted on the stance that the 'constitution guaranteed the fairness of administration, because it was a hindrence to bad governance' ('jemči da će administracija biti dobra, pošto on rđavoj vladavini države staje na put').[42] This was a clear-cut expression of constitutionalism in its usual form.

Matić lectured on what he labelled as a constitutionally limited state. Such a state was founded on the rights of the people, the consequences of which were the equality of citizens before the law, as well as the independence of the judiciary. He noted that in that type of state there was inevitably political contestation in the form of opposition to the government. The opposition activity, performed within a legal framework, was in his view highly valuable from the standpoint of the general interests of the society as a whole. Therefore, Matić concluded that 'a state governed by constitution is founded on the public recognition that the power holders derive their powers from their unity with the people' ('Ustavna država osniva se dakle na javnom priznanju da moć vlasti zavisi od njenog jedinstva i spajanja s narodom').[43] Opinions of this kind were probably what put an end to Matić's academic career. In 1851, when his book on *Principles of Rational State Law* was published, the oligarchs were in power in Serbia. Their views on the organisation of state were considerably different from those which Matić presented to his students. In the time when Matić lectured from the academic chair on the benefits of the opposition, one of the outstanding oligarchs formulated a completely opposite view on the relationship between the state power and the people. He declared that the people are like 'a minor', with the 'state power [as] his guardian'.[44]

As regards the forms of government, Matić was within the framework of the Aristotelian formula, distinguishing monarchy, aristocracy and democracy.[45] Matić was a partisan of the mixed form of government. The one he considered best was what he called the syncratic form of government. It was a monarchy in which the monarch was limited by the representation of the people in such a way that the latter was entitled to give its approval in matters of taxation.[46] In this respect Matić stood in agreement with his Serbian professor, although

42 For the notion and the role of constitution, cf. D. Matić, *Načela*, 87–88.
43 ibid. 91.
44 It was Jeremija Stanojević who expressed the opinion; cf. S. Jovanović, *Ustavobranitelji*, 53.
45 D. Matić, *Načela*, 85.
46 ibid. 87.

without making any reference to Sterija; he also favoured the monarchy with national representation.

The rights of the people played one of the key roles in Matić's lectures. The rights of the people were, in his view, the fundamental human rights. In his teaching on human rights, Matić departed from the simple idea that a society was composed of individuals. Therefore, the state, i.e. the polity, was based on the rights of the people, who were considered both as individuals and as the whole of the society: 'Narodna prava jesu ona koja pripadaju građanima delom kao pojedinima, a delom svima zajedno prema državnoj vlasti'.[47] Matić developed this starting definition of rights, explaining to his students that (a) the substantial rights of the people serve to determine the notion and the goal of the State, and (b) that these were primordial human rights of each and every person. The state had a mission to protect those rights. Matić went into details, as regards the fundamental human rights. First he noted that the fundamental rights were twofold. In the broadest sense, those rights, according to Matić, were liberty and estate.

At this point, although not influenced by him, Matić seems to have come close to Grujović in his undelivered speech of 1805, 'A Word on Freedom', which was the subject of interest in Chapter 1 of this volume. The formula on the most essential human rights coined by Matić was extremely short and reduced to only two elements. Instead of Grujović's triad of life/estate/dignity, Matić simply posited liberty/estate. One could perhaps think of the 'life' and 'dignity' of the older author's concept being compressed into the 'liberty' used by the younger author, and the similar attitudes of the two authors would make the two formulas match. There is, however, no trace of influence, and it is hard to believe that Grujović inspired Matić. Rejecting the idea of influence is corroborated if we follow the development of the concept put forward by Matić. He developed his main stance on human rights by extending their number to cover four concepts that he cited as the most important.[48]

First was the right to an independent judge. The right to a natural judge came next. Those two rights appear to be mostly procedural, and are very closely linked to one another. In parallel to this, the remaining two were also linked. This connection between the third and the fourth most fundamental human rights was provided by the notion of equality. Matić placed equality before

47 ibid. 81.
48 ibid. 83.

the law third in his enumeration of the paramount human rights. However, the human right that comes fourth, concluding the list, calls for comments. Matić styled it as the 'equality of rights and duties as regards political participation and taxes'. The wording does not remind us of the declarations of rights known in history, but the substance of the right nevertheless needs explanation and deserves comparison. The mostly procedural human rights listed first and second in the enumeration above, and equality before the law in general (the third concept) were somehow an introduction to the most fundamental of the four mentioned in the professor's theoretic scheme. Matić insisted on the equality of the rights and duties of each and every citizen in two areas of law that are indeed decisive in a polity. These are political participation in the decision-making process and taxation.

Political rights remained, for the most part, outside the scope of work of Serbian constitution drafters in the time of nation building, i.e. in the first half of the nineteenth century. The only exception was Stefan Radičević, who included freedom of the press in his draft constitution for *Vojvodovina Srbska* in 1848. In this respect, Matić stood relatively close to Radičević; however, this was in contrast to the mainstream of the evolution of ideas which preceded his work. His approach to the issue of political rights was wide-ranging. Matić did not enumerate political rights, but rather considered them aggregated as a comprehensive whole, which was encompassed by the concept of political participation and even contestation. That was a qualitatively different approach from the technique of enumeration. Notably, Matić's general comprehensive approach to the concept came to light while, with one exception, there had still been no provisions on particular political rights in the Serbian constitutions, either promulgated or drafted. Matić was the first Serbian professor of constitutional law and it should be emphasised that he was of the opinion that the State relied on human rights. Moreover, he laid the foundation for the State enjoying human rights through the political participation of citizens. Matić took the bold step of supporting the thesis that protection of human rights was the task of the modern State's mission in the human sphere, and that human rights indeed encompassed political rights.

Dimitrije Matić was removed from the university because of his liberalism. He forged a successful career in other branches of public service and also participated in political events. He was one of the founders of the Liberal Party. Notably, in a historical perspective his academic legacy appears to outweigh all other aspects of his work and career. Although only a professor for a short time, he nevertheless managed to leave a significant contribution to the legal developments in Serbia – above all, in legal thinking on constitutionalism.

6.4 Comparison

The activity of these two professors represented a milestone in Serbian legal thought in many ways. Jovan Sterija Popović and Dimitrije Matić were learned lawyers, educated in German, who were able to present to the students the most accurate and up-to-date information as regards constitutionalism and its principles. They referred to foreign authorities in their lectures, which provided for the development of critical attitudes among their students towards the issues treated in their academic courses. The fact that they were both removed from the university chairs clearly speaks for itself. The two professors, being outstanding intellectuals, supported liberal ideas. However, despite the fact that their liberal attitudes did not properly fit into the political atmosphere of the oligarchs' regime in Serbia, the liberal opinions they confessed were mild and moderated, if considered from a global perspective. For instance, Matić was not willing to accept the idea of separation of powers, and Sterija preferred the example of an absolute monarch as an authority, over Rousseau's social contract.

The professors' views on the topics of the rule of law and human rights were not identical, but they converged on many aspects. Thus, for instance, Sterija was of the opinion that the goal of the State was to preserve individual rights, whereas Matić viewed the State as the guarantor of individual freedom. Matić supported the stance that the whole of the law consisted in suppressing arbitrariness in a rational way in order to achieve freedom. He concluded his 'Short Review' by identifying the law with freedom. What he called the supreme definition of law and freedom read: 'Hence the law is freedom and inversely the freedom is law.'[49]

Significant features of constitutionalism found their place in the lectures and were highlighted by both professors. On the one hand, for both professors the sovereign power was limited by the rule of law. On the other hand, the rule of law was impossible without the protection of fundamental human rights. Sterija expressed the view that the substance of the constitution was to provide security of persons and estate, while Matić supported the idea that the sovereign power was limited by fairness and legitimacy. What the latter labelled as a constitutional state, or a state governed by constitution, was the form of state in which the power was derived from the people and the people's fundamental rights.

---

49 D. Matić, *Pregled*, 150.

In respect of fundamental rights, the two professors differed in their approaches to the issue, but nevertheless came to similar conclusions. Sterija was of the opinion that there was no need to amend the constitution of a state in which personal freedom and equality before the law existed. Matić, for his part, explained to the students that equality of rights and the duties of citizens as regards political participation and taxes were fundamental in a state governed by the constitution. Protecting the fundamental rights of the citizens was indeed essential for both professors. They understood the protection of fundamental human rights as the most important feature of the rule of law. The latter was in turn the core element of the modern state constituted as a polity.

Matić influenced Serbian legal developments more than Sterija, whose work in law teaching almost fell into oblivion. However, Matić could not play a decisive role in the evolution of Serbian constitutionalism as far as we consider the practice. The developments of governance in everyday life in Serbia did not correspond with the opinions shared by the learned lawyers and university professors. The government's practice slowly evolved towards modern patterns of governance, cautiously approaching the ideas coming from the West.

CHAPTER 7

Rule of Law – Practical Aspects

7.1 Earlier Developments

The fact that the Serbs were to be governed by themselves when the home-rule was introduced in Serbia did not mean immediately breaking off from traditions, whether the oriental customs brought along by the Ottoman Turks, or the more ancient medieval Serbian mores. It has been remarked upon by scholars that 'the survival of the strong sense of national identity was the most important' in the process of Serbian nation building.[1] Therefore, although a basic idea of order existed in both traditions mentioned, it was mostly due to the influence of the Orthodox Church that the Serbs embraced the concept of order that had existed once upon a time in the Middle Ages. The idea was simple: the governance of the country had to be performed in an orderly manner. That could by no means match the modern concept of the rule of law, but nevertheless included the beginnings of this. The idea of proper governance, or rather of the outcome of such governance, was expressed in a formula stemming from the Serbian medieval sources. The formula was 'peace and quietness'. It referred to the state of affairs in the country, which was allegedly run in a proper manner, and also allegedly to the satisfaction of the governed.

The formula existed in the acts of popular assemblies, which were traditional institutions of 'a primitive form of democratic decision-making'.[2] It also found a place in the Prince's speeches, when addressing the assemblies. As to the former sources, it suffices to note that it was present in the Act on the Prince's Dignity, adopted by the traditional popular assembly in 1817, through which Miloš Obrenović was confirmed to be the Prince of Serbia.[3] Peace and quietness were mentioned in the Act on the Prince's Dignity in a peculiar manner. Namely, it was stated in the Act that peace and quietness were given to the Serbian people by the Almighty Himself. That, however, occurred via the intermediary of the Serbian Prince, whom the Almighty commissioned to rule the country.[4]

---

1 Cf. A. Dragnich, *The Development*, 5.

2 ibid. 5.

3 On the Act on the Prince's Dignity, cf. M. Stefanovski, *Srednjovekovna shvatanja uzorne vladavine* [Medieval conceptions of exemplary rule], Belgrade 2018, 183–206. The author considers the period of home-rule in Serbia to be an aftermath of the medieval times.

4 ibid. 199.

 | DOI:10.30965/9783657791026_008

The formula of peace and quietness was often present in the Prince's speches. That was, for instance, the case in January 1827, then in May 1828, if we are only quoting the use of the proper and genuine formula.[5] The wording of the speech of January 1827 was significant. Prince Miloš declared, 'By justful severity I managed to maintain in this country the peace and quietness, as well as the order'. In the same speech, the Prince insisted on the idea of order, saying, 'We cannot sustain ourselves otherwise than by a strict administration of justice among us'. The Prince certainly meant order by these words, but to understand his ideas on the subject, one should bear in mind what has been displayed in previous chapters of this volume as regards his conduct when exercising power. Therefore, despite the narrative, the Prince's concept of order could by no means be seen to align with the rule of law. Moreover, in the course of time, Prince Miloš tended to rephrase the formula, reshaping its substance considerably and putting forward some other values alongside the peace and quietness. That is how the notion labelled with the Serbian word of *sloga* emerged in the Prince's speeches. Several translations of that word into English can stand, such as concord, harmony or even unanimity. The Prince expected the masses to approve of his policies, portraying them as being best for the Serbian national cause, of which the Prince himself claimed to be the most skillful defender.

By the 1830s the formula of peace and quietness was fading away, leaving room for concord (*sloga*) as a principal value, and towards the end of that decade the formula practically disappeared.[6] The formula, which denoted the concept of order, was subject to a slow transformation, at first merely including the notion of concord, before eventually being replaced by it. Towards the end of Prince Miloš's rule in the late 1830s, the wording of the old formula stemming from the Middle Ages disappeared completely. By that time the notion of order was no more identified with peace and quietness.

The order that was installed under Miloš's rule was seriously disturbed by rebellions on several occasions. Explaining the cause of rebellions, Vuk Karadžić wrote that it was somehow normal for this to happen in a country which was on its way to introducing social order in the proper meaning of the term. Vuk found that the profound reason for dissatisfaction among the people was that the Serbian society was in a phase of evolution during which the masses still remembered the social equality they had had before.[7]

5 ibid. 180–81.
6 ibid. 181–82.
7 V. S. Karadžić, *Istorijski spisi*, 143.

The rebellions were relatively frequent. The first occurred in 1815 at the beginning of Miloš's rule; there was another one in 1817, and one more in 1821. These rebellions were based on the growing discontent of some outstanding persons belonging to the ruling class that was being established in Serbia. From time to time, ambitious individuals attempted to threaten the Prince's position, aiming to replace him.[8] In some of the rebellions important questions were raised, resulting in the demands formulated by the rebels and their leaders. That was the case with the rebellion of Miloje Đak, which took place in January 1825. At that time, complaints were made about excessive taxes, the terror of local governors (*zulum od knezova*), as well as about injustice in general. The Prince managed to suppress the rebellion. Its leader was executed, but the Prince nevertheless replaced the local governors that the masses had complained of.[9] The rebellions were incidents that could not put an end to the Prince's arbitrariness in the long run.

Miloš Obrenović did not want to rule in a way that would limit his power via checks and balances. Therefore, we should be prudent in our efforts to properly understand his declarations when mentioning the introduction of laws in Serbia, which was the shape in which the concept of the rule of law first appeared. It was in the second half of the 1820s that Vuk Karadžić suggested to the Serbian Prince to launch activities aimed at drafting laws for the country. The general idea was that written laws should apply, so as to avoid arbitrariness. The fundamental concept was nevertheless simplified, because governing the country according to the law was for the most part identified with the passing of statutes. The problems concerning the implementation of those were by no means within the scope of the ruler's considerations.

It was indeed the Prince himself who, despite his inclination towards arbitrary power, mentioned laws that should be introduced in the country on different occasions. That was the case in the time in which the drafting of laws was already underway.[10] When Vuk Karadžić returned to Serbia from exile in the spring of 1829, the activities concerning drafting of laws were intensified. There had indeed been attempts to translate foreign laws in advance of Vuk's return to Serbia. They were mostly related to the aim of adopting a civil code for the country.[11]

---

8 ibid. 143–45.

9 On the events of Đak's rebellion, cf. ibid. 146–47.

10 Cf. S. Avramović, 'The Serbian Civil Code of 1844: A Battleground of Legal Traditions', in: Th. Simon (ed.), *Konflikt und Koexistenz*, 379–483.

11 ibid. 394–95. The author critically revisited the scholarship on the beginning of legislation in modern Serbia, especially the works of Aleksa Jovanović and Slobodan Jovanović, from the first decades of the 20th century. On Vuk's role, cf. D. Nikolić, 'Prvi pokušaj izrade

The turning point in the developments came with the formation of two legislative committees to pursue the task of drafting legislation. One worked under Vuk's chairmanship. Its mission was to prepare a translation of the French civil code. Another committee, chaired by the Prince's secretary, Dimitrije Davidović, would then be charged with making a selection and suggesting what should actually be enacted as a statute in Serbia. Davidović was fairly optimistic about the task and thought it could be accomplished in six months, whereas Vuk was more prudent about the outcome in such a short time.[12] Soon after the formation of the committee tasked with drafting legislation for the country, Prince Miloš declared at an assembly session that the laws were being drafted. His words revealed the method applied to the whole enterprise, for he said, 'I ordered drafting laws for our people to apply in courts. I chose from all laws what was good and useful and what could be used among us, so that we do not render justice arbitrarily, but according to laws.'[13] The activity of the committees faded away when Vuk left Serbia in 1831. The work on preparing the first legislation in Serbia remained unaccomplished, so that Miloš repeated his stance before the assembly in 1835 on the occasion of the adoption of the First Serbian Constitution. The Prince then declared that the laws had been in preparation for four years.[14] The Serbian law had to wait for the adoption of codes for more than a decade after the launch of work on their drafting. Nevertheless, one issue was entrenched. The Serbian legislation was supposed to follow Western patterns and rely on translations of foreign legislation. On one occasion that was called into question, and some doubts were raised in respect of the method of introduction of the rule of law in Serbia.

It was in May 1837 that a British diplomat, while visiting Serbia, suggested to his Serbian interlocutor an alternative path for the development of legislation in the vassal principality of Serbia. The question of adopting laws in the country was still open when Dimitrije Davidović, one of Miloš's collaborators, met with David Urquhart (1805–77), secretary of the British embassy in Istanbul, who visited Serbia on his route westwards. Davidović informed the Prince on

---

građanskih zakona u Srbiji' [The first attempt to draft civil laws in Serbia], *Zbornik radova Pravnog fakulteta u Nišu*, Niš 1981, 403.

12 Cf. D. Popović, 'Dva oprečna shvatanja o vladavini prava u obnovljenoj Srbiji' [Two conflicting views on the rule of law in a renewed Serbia], in: V. Vasilijević (ed.), *Pravna država*, Belgrade 1991, 30. Cf. references on that page.

13 A. Jovanović, 'Rad na "Toržestvenim zakonima" II, Doterivanje prevoda', *Arhiv za pravne i društvene nauke*, 1911, XI/1, 11–12.

14 S. Avramović, 'The Serbian Civil Code', 397.

the conversation he had had with the British official in a special letter.[15] The conversation was around the drafts of Serbian legislation that had been prepared. Davidović had presented the draft legislation to the British diplomat on several occasions: it transpires from the beginning of the letter that they met more than once.[16] We do not know exactly what material was presented to the British visitor, but it is evident from the text of the letter that its main contents must have been the translations of foreign laws that had been made, with a view to converting them into pieces of Serbian legislation.

Davidović summarised Urquhart's comments on the drafts in several points. One of these claimed that Napoleon's code was indeed one of the causes of his political collapse. The visitor's first general remark was that Serbia should not be governed on the basis of written laws. It was followed by another, which claimed that written laws would jeopardise the nation building. They were, in Urquhart's view, perilous for the national identity. In brief, the most important ideas that the British diplomat put forward as regards introducing the rule of law in Serbia were the following.[17] The judiciary in Serbia should be conferred to the village elders. The judiciary must be independent, for the central government of the country should by no means interfere with the administration of justice performed by the elders in villages. This was supported by the diplomat's stance that the governance of different peoples within the Ottoman Empire should be founded on their customs and not on written law.

Urquhart was hostile to the written law and favoured legal developments through case law. Such a stance was echoed in Davidović's explanation to the Serbian Prince, reproducing his interlocutor's words, which read, 'a code ties everyone's hands, because it reflects in advance on all cases that may happen among the people'. This was the usual reproach of a person coming from a Common Law country to the attitude of lawyers educated in the European continental law tradition. A remark should be made at this point that neither of the two interlocutors who exchanged their views on the future of Serbian law in May 1837 had formal legal training. Davidović had accomplished his study of philosophy in Kezmark, whereas Urquhart had a specific education under his mother's supervision.[18] They nevertheless reflected the characteristic attitudes of the two legal systems, or families. To this it should be added that Urquhart did not mention, or maybe Davidović failed to note and report

15 The original of the letter is preserved in the Archives of Serbia in the fund of the Prince's Chancery (Kneževa kancelarija) (KK) under the number VI-929.

16 On the letter and the whole conversation, cf. D. Popović, 'Two contradictory attitudes', 29–36.

17 ibid. 32.

18 cf. V. S. Karadžić, *Istorijski spisi*, 203.

to the Prince, an important requirement for the evolution of a legal system through the case law. That was keeping records of judgments that were to be rendered by the judiciary organised as one of the village elders. Urquhart probably did not go that far due to the fact that his remarks were a weak echo of his interlocutor's.[19] There is no trace that any of Urquhart's ideas have ever been seriously taken into account by the Serbian authorities, and especially not by the Prince himself. They had in germ an alternative for Serbian legal developments in progress, and a view to shifting to the modern notion of order. The concept of the rule of law that they wished to introduce was different from the one that eventually occurred.

A shift towards the modern notion of order, i.e. rule of law, had already been evident in Vuk's famous letter to the Prince of 1832.[20] Introducing the rule of law was indeed one of his suggestions to the Serbian Prince. Moreover, Vuk Karadžić was aware of the potential problems of implementing these laws once they become adopted in Serbia. Therefore, he wrote to the Prince, 'The rights and laws should not only be promised to the people ... What is established and laid down by those must be maintained and preserved as the greatest sanctity'.[21] While exiled in Austria, Vuk Karadžić addressed the Prince and suggested laying down the foundations of the rule of law and constitutionalism in the Serbian principality. He nevertheless consented, although without mentioning it in express terms to the mode or pattern of legal developments in Serbia. The emerging modern nation was to follow European continental patterns. That is what eventually happened when the rule of law found its place in a sequence of constitutional settlements in Serbia.

7.2 Rule of Law in Constitutional Settlements

Surprisingly enough, the adoption of a constitution in Serbia preceded proper legislation. It is therefore noteworthy that the rule of law was provided for in the short-lived 1835 Constitution. The provisions were mostly programmatic but were nevertheless contained in the text, in articles 46 to 49 of the Constitution. Their position in the Constitution text was in its Chapter 6, regulating the activity of the Council of State. The provisions of articles 46 and 47 have something in common. They somehow seem to repeat one and the same idea that the country should be governed by law and constitution. In

19 D. Popović, 'Two contradictory attitudes', 34.
20 V. S. Karadžić, *Istorijski spisi*, 215–29.
21 ibid. 218.

an idealistic way, Article 46 states that it is the duty of the Council of State to prevent anyone from violating the Constitution. The next provision mirrors the same idea – the State Council should see that no one suffers injustice, and should it realise an instance of injustice, it should quickly work with the Prince to remove this. The following pair of provisions – articles 48 and 49 – also have something in common. Article 49 reads 'The Council of State lays the foundations of all other Serbian authorities by way of statutes'. The preceding Article 48 provides that public affairs are subject to legal provisions, so that 'the law governs the whole of Serbian people'. An overall view of the four provisions does not leave much room for doubt as regards their meaning and character. They are all programmatic because there was still no legislation in Serbia at the moment of adopting the first Constitution. Besides, if the substance of the provisions is considered, they were rather vague from a purely legal standpoint. They must have been drafted in a way that would not disturb the ruling Prince, whose attitudes towards a written constitution did not match the precepts of genuine constitutionalism. The importance of the provisions mentioned is to be found in the fact that they were put in the text. Their existence seems to have paved the way for further developments.

Several articles of the 1838 Constitution, given by the sovereign Sultan to the vassal state of Serbia, were related to the rule of law in different aspects. Article 27 provided for the protection of fundamental rights of Serbian citizens as regards their estate, personality, honour and dignity. It was stipulated that any prosecution and/or punishment was to occur in accordance with the law. A similar idea was contained in Article 28 of the Constitution, providing that each and every punishment was to be pronounced by a court and in compliance with the law (*shodno glasu zakona, suđen i osuđen pred sudom*).

Articles 44 and 55 of the 1838 Constitution found inspiration in the idea of separation of powers, which is a cornerstone of the rule of law, despite the fact that the form of government under the Constitution was not properly based on the separation of powers. Article 44 prohibited civil and military authorities from interfering with the enforcement of judgments of the courts of law. In the same tone of separation of powers, Article 55 prohibited the judges from holding any service other than the one they were to fulfil as sitting judges.

Articles 47 and 66 of the 1838 Constitution were more far reaching than any other in the Constitution text as regards the rule of law. Notably Article 47 provided that a Serbian citizen could be deprived of his right exclusively by a judgment of a Serbian court, rendered in due process of law (*razvje zakonom presudom jednog od ustrojeni sudova zemaljski*). In Article 66, which closed the 1838 Constitution text, the Sultan ordered the Serbian Prince as follows: 'I hereby order Thee to respect the status, honour, rank and dignity of everyone, as well as to take care that the abovementioned paragraphs and conditions of this Constitution be executed in full and forever'.

The maintenance of the concept of the rule of law in the 1838 Constitution calls for some remarks. More than anything else, it was a sign of the influence of foreign powers on the drafting of the Constitution text. Notably, some of the foreign governments wanted to limit the Prince in his exercise of power. At the same time, however, it was also a vestige of modernity in a constitution that was given to the vassal state of Serbia by the Sultan. The introduction of provisions prescribing the rule of law in the 1838 Constitution were in a peculiar way connected to the introduction of oligarchy as a form of government. Both aimed to achieve the same goal of introducing checks and balances to the Prince's power. The oligarchs were to sit in a council of seventeen members, which was to share the power with the Prince while being responsible only to the Sultan. Through their participation in the decision-making process, the oligarchs were expected to place limits on the Prince's arbitrariness. There was, nevertheless, a substantial difference between oligarchy as a form of government and the rule of law. The introduction of provisions on the rule of law was in line with the concepts of organisation of a modern state, whereas introducing oligarchy was a pre-modern approach to the concept of checks and balances. The rule of law for the most part did not prove to be effective under the 1838 constitutional settlement. On the contrary, the oligarchy started functioning as a system of government in Serbia. The oligarchs had their own views on nation building, organisation of power and the rule of law, which they began to carry out once in power.

The oligarchs' ideas on the rule of law and on the participation of the population in the political process were indeed patriarchal and pre-modern. The oligarchs, who were opposed to the Prince's arbitrariness and therefore also to the previous autocratic regime, favoured the law, which in their view was mostly identified with statutes. Regarding the 'law' as the core notion of the legislation gives rise to a semantic dilemma: 'law' can be understood in the Serbian language as a statute and as a corpus of legal provisions. The latter can also be expressed by the word *zakonik* (code). The idea of the codification of law emerged early in Serbian legal history, already in the time of home-rule, as a concept adopted from the West. However, to start with in Serbia it did not mean collecting, i.e. putting together provisions of different statutes in a code, but rather adopting one huge statute, which is named a 'code' and contains new, previously nonexistent provisions. The oligarchs were of the opinion that the Serbian principality would modernise if it were governed under the rules of written law, i.e. the statutes; several codes were therefore adopted during their rule. The fairly well-developed legislative activity under the oligarchs' regime followed foreign patterns in many aspects. The legal concepts that inspired the legislators sitting in the Council of seventeen members were mostly conservative.

The oligarchs' leading and outstanding idea was to enable the peaceful enjoyment of property for each and every citizen. Such a task could only be achieved in the presence of a governance based on obeying the provisions of statutes. Adopting statutes meant, at the same time, overcoming the Prince's arbitrary government.[22] That was a novelty, inspired by liberal attitudes, but the oligarchs nevertheless did not wish to go too far down the liberal road. Apart from protecting property, they did not care much for human rights. The rule of law, in their view, was not to include political rights. Their policies aimed at reforms were nevertheless noble in character. For instance, they managed to create the national intelligentsia. This was achieved both by improving the education system of the country and by sending eligible young men to study in Central and Western Europe at the government's expense. Well-educated young people brought new and fresh ideas to Serbia when they returned from abroad. These new ideas created a gulf between the older and younger generations.[23] Serbian young lions, educated in foreign universities, were of the opinion that the oligarchs were conservative, but there was no way to bridge the generational gap. The oligarchs prevailed and set the tone of the society and politics. Those educated abroad were still few and could not influence the public scene decisively.[24] The rule of law in its proper sense was not introduced, despite the many achievements of reforms, such as the adoption of the Serbian civil code in 1844, laws adopted in different sectors of public life, founding of schools and cultural institutions, etc.[25]

One of the most important steps towards the introduction of the rule of law consisted in the organisation of the judiciary. The oligarchs laid down the foundations of the modern judiciary in Serbia, although this suffered from a considerable number of deficiencies. The plan was to introduce in an underdeveloped country, as Serbia then was, the pattern of judiciary organisation of European nations, which followed the modern concept of the rule of law. Codes of procedure were adopted in civil and criminal law, the courts were set

---

22 S. Jovanović, *Ustavobranitelji*, 27. The first edition of this book, which is still the greatest authority on the subject, was published in 1912.

23 ibid. 74–75.

24 A. Dragnich, *The Development*, 27: 'by 1858 some 200 men were educated abroad'.

25 S. Jovanović, *Ustavobranitelji*, 35 (civil code); 55 (police regulations); 72 (educational and cultural institutions). For legislation in different areas, cf. also D. Nikolić, 'The 1860 Criminal Code of the Principality of Serbia', in: Th. Simon (ed.) *Konflikt und Koexistenz*, 486–88.

up and judges were appointed to administer justice. However, despite the considerable improvements of the judiciary, many shortcomings appeared in the course of time. For instance, in many courts the sitting judges were not trained in law, the formalism in the courts' proceedings was overwhelming and the courts became flooded by trivial lawsuits.[26]

An overall assessment of the oligarchs' regime as regards the rule of law should start from the fact that the rule of law was not properly introduced. At the same time, many important elements of its construction were posed between 1842, when the oligarchs, labelled as defenders of the Constitution, consolidated their power, and 1858, when their regime was over. The changes and reforms took place in a country that in many ways lacked the prerequisites for a transformation into a modern polity. The outcome was a paradox – the conservative oligarchs modernised Serbia.[27] It was a compromise which reflected the oligarchs' pre-modern social roots, as well as their wish to make the country go hand in hand with the developed European nations.

The constitutional settlement that replaced the oligarchs' rule was introduced when Prince Mihailo came to the throne in 1860. The institutions were reformed, despite the fact that the 1838 Constitution was still in force. By passing new legislation, Prince Mihailo put an end to the oligarchy. The council, which had had too much power in the previous regime, remained competent to legislate but was transformed into a body for which the Prince was empowered to appoint members and dismiss them at will. The will of the Prince thus became paramount. With the help of such structural changes, Mihailo introduced a personal regime of his own. As well as the legislators, the ministers were dependent on the Prince's will alone. At the same time, political contestation was barred due to the absence of freedom of the press. It was Slobodan Jovanović who remarked in the scholarship that Mihailo's regime was a political settlement unmitigated by the institutions of ministerial responsibility and free press.[28] Another expression borrowed from the same author can complete the image. The Prince stated firmly when ascending the throne that he was by no means 'a monarch who reigns but does not govern'.[29]

The Prince wished to govern the country following a programme in which two goals were prominent. The first consisted of planning a war on the Ottoman Empire with the aim of liberating the Serbian population still subjugated to

26 S. Jovanović, ibid. 47–48. On judiciary reforms, also cf. U. Stanković, 'Historische Entwicklung des Strafprozesses in Serbien' [Historical development of the criminal process in Serbia], in: Th. Simon (ed.) *Konflikt und Koexistenz*, 296–97.

27 Alex Dragnich labels the modernisation rudimentary; cf. A. Dragnich, *The Development*, 23.

28 S. Jovanović, *Druga vlada*, 403.

29 ibid. 394.

the Ottoman rule, while the second envisaged raising the material welfare of the people.[30] However, the Prince wanted to carry out his policies within the framework of legality. His intention was not to overstep the law, and he expressed this in his proclamation when he first ascended the throne. Its wording was solemn and promising: 'Let each and everyone know that while Prince Mihailo is in power, the law is the supreme will in Serbia' was the core stance of the monarch's proclamation. The phrase calls for a semantic analysis. The word *zakon* (law) has several meanings. In this context, its meaning is in fact equal to the English word *statute*. If compared, for instance, to the meaning it had half a century before, in Grujović's 'A Word on Freedom', one can see the difference. Grujović idealised the notion of law, understanding it in a broad, philosophical way as 'law in general', whereas in Prince Mihailo's proclamation it had the meaning of an enacted statute. The enacted statutes emanated from the legislators sitting in the State Council, which had been reformed in line with the Prince's ideas. The legislators were appointed by the Prince.

A contemporary author, writing in French, can help with understanding Prince Mihailo's ideas. Ubicini, a French journalist and historian of Italian origin, published his book on the Serbian constitution in 1871 in Paris. To denote the main goal of Mihailo's policy, he used the French word *légalité*, explaining that notion in the following way: 'une légalité, claire, réelle, basée sur un texte positif, entourée de garantie sérieuses'. This could be translated into English as 'clear and effective legality, based on the text of the law and surrounded by serious guarantees'. As to the form of government, the French author mentioned at the same place in his book 'état régulier ... et légal'.[31] It seems that Ubicini stood between two concepts in his explanation. One was mere legality, while the other tended towards what we would label today as the rule of law. The latter was supported by the enumeration of serious guarantees, which were to serve the implementation of Mihailo's political programme. Those were indeed, according to the French author, ministerial responsibility, independence of the judiciary with judges immovable in office, regular convocations of the National Assembly and freedom of the press.[32] Those guarantees were not introduced during Prince Mihailo's reign, except for the regular sessions of the National Assembly convoked once every three years.

Mihailo substantially transformed the political settlement set up by the 1838 Constitution and firmly defended by the oligarchs. The oligarchs created the

30 On the programme and the proclamation, cf. S. Jovanović, *Druga vlada*, 347–49; A. Dragnich, *The Development*, 40.

31 A. Ubicini, *Constitution de la Principauté de Serbie*, Paris 1871, 22–23.

32 ibid. 23.

Serbian bureaucracy in an effort to overcome the patriarchal rule of the first Serbian Prince, Mihailo's father, Miloš. In the oligarchs' view, the public servants were to be superposed upon the masses, because the masses were inclined to follow Miloš's populist policies. Mihailo put the public servants under his own supervision, thus creating a system of bureaucratic despotism.[33] In a political settlement of that kind, there was indeed no room for the rule of law in the proper sense of the term. The regime that was put in place was not excessively oppressive, but it could not provide fair treatment of citizens in respect of protection of their rights. Behind the screen of legality, i.e. the network of enacted statutes, there was not much room for freedom. Slobodan Jovanović may have exaggerated in his statement that Serbia under Mihailo's regime resembled a 'German bureaucratic despoty of the 18th century'.[34] It would nevertheless be justified to compare Serbia in the 1860s with some small German principalities of the 19th century. Even in such a comparison, Serbia could not fully match what the Germans label as an earlier form of constitutional monarchy.[35] That form emerged in German lands at the beginning of the 19th century. In some examples it only accepted the participation of certain constitutional factors in the monarch's personal rule, and was by no means characterised by the limitation of the monarch's power.[36] That form of government, nevertheless, was a constitutional monarchy, or at least the beginnings of one, because the monarchs were to enforce their personal will, while respecting some legal procedures. Such procedures could not achieve the stage that would qualify them to attain the level of the rule of law.

Although proper political contestation was forbidden in Serbia in the 1860s, it emerged little by little, so as to make the Prince and his regime unpopular to a considerable extent. The main issue of the contestation focused on the rule of law and constitutionalism. The enlightened Prince, as Mihailo undoubtedly was, could not make himself popular among the masses. His father knew how to address peasants, which was not the case for Prince Mihailo, who had spent sixteen years in exile in Europe, received education, and as a consequence somehow became separated from the people. Those he governed respected him from a distance. The initial sympathy towards the Prince slowly evaporated because of the widely spread practice of suppressing any sort of political

33 S. Jovanović, *Druga vlada*, 509.

34 ibid. 412.

35 On earlier forms of constitutional monarchy in German lands, cf. C. F. Menger, *Deutsche Verfassungsgeschichte*, 122–24.

36 ibid. 124.

contestation. The dissatisfaction increased due to the choice of ministers who remained in office for a long time.[37]

The Prince, stern, rigid and reserved in communication, distinct from his environment and unable to get support from the masses, was at the same time very much inclined to make use of his prerogative. He enjoyed his princely power to the full, and sometimes even overstepped the law. When the judges of the Supreme Court did not want to condemn several persons involved in a mutiny, he clashed with the judges. By doing so, the Prince, who in 1860 'began his regime with the emphasis on the rule of law found himself jailing five judges of the Supreme Court' in 1864.[38] The criticism of the Prince's rule was becoming more hostile as time went on. The famous poet, Jovan Jovanović Zmaj, who was a citizen of the Habsburg monarchy and lived there out of Mihailo's reach, published an allegorical poem in 1865, calling it a national anthem of an imaginary tribe of Jututunians, and mentioned the tribal chief in the poem. The allusions were clearly to the Serbs and their Prince. The anthem more or less echoed the opinion of the masses on the Prince's personality and his behaviour. The introductory stance of the poem read:

Bože mili podrži nam Knjaza, Zdrava, krepka, ohola i slavna, Jer na zemlji nit je kadgod bilo, Niti će Mu ikad biti ravna.	God Almighty save our Prince, Solid, haughty, looking so fair, For on Earth there has never been, Nor will ever be one to compare.[39]

The Serbian Prince, distinguished, melancholic and stern, was excellently portrayed in Zmaj's words. He was the one who ruled alone, with his ministers as levers, and with the help of statutes enacted by an obedient legislative council. The national goal he had put forward as the main policy made him neglect many other issues and detest opposition, as an unnecessary obstacle to carrying out his ideas and policies. He was intolerant towards the opinions of others, which made his rule difficult to bear.

Constitutionalism was therefore at stake during Prince Mihailo's rule, despite the fact that he was the one to introduce constitutional monarchy as the form of government in Serbia. On the one hand, the Prince was considering the adoption of a new and properly domestic constitution, which would replace the Sultan's act (i.e. the 1838 Constitution), officially still in force. On the other hand, those who criticised the monarch were in favour of constitutionalism, and by no means content with a new constitutional text, which may

37 S. Jovanović, *Druga vlada*, 403.

38 A. Dragnich, *The Development*, 43.

39 J. J. Zmaj, *Jututunska narodna himna*, 1865.

fail to provide for institutions based on the principles of constitutionalism. The Prince was indeed preparing a new constitution when he was assassinated in 1868. In the spring of that year he had committed the chief justice of the Court of Appeals to draft a constitution which would provide for a bicameral system of national representation, entitled to approve the budget and to take on ministerial responsibility.[40] It was not only too late – it was insufficient. The contents of the draft undoubtedly gave preponderance to the Prince's prerogative. The draft was completely within the framework of the earlier form of constitutional monarchy. As an illustration, it suffices to mention that the ministerial responsibility was based on the allegation of a transgression or violation of the constitution. It would lead to a trial against the minister before a court of law, and would by no means function as a motion of censure. Ministerial responsibility in the modern sense of the term was not provided for in the draft.[41]

Such provisions were drafted in an atmosphere of accentuated criticism against the Prince and his unhampered rule that had been developing for years. Zmaj was mocking the Prince and his endeavours to pass a constitution deprived of proper substance and neglecting the rule of law. The imaginary tribe of the *Jututunians* was to receive a *juhahaha*, an onomatopoeic word which imitates the sound of laughter. The poet made a joke of the Prince's efforts, which were deprived of substance as far as the rule of law was concerned. Such a ridiculous constitution was promised to the Jututunians by their monarch, the imaginary Balakaha 13th. Another poem made fun of the Serbian Prince. The whole of the story of promising a false constitution reached its peak in the last stanza of the poem. The poet's burlesque was complete. The monarch was joyful because he had deceived the Jututunians, who for their part appeared naive, having had confidence in the monarch. The last lines of the poem read:

Srećni su ti Jututunci,	Merry are the Jututunians
Srećan li je Balakaha,	Merry is also Balakaha
Kad ih tako razveseli	Unbelievably cheered by
Prazna rečca juhahaha.	The void word of juhahaha.[42]

With Prince Mihailo in power, the constitutional monarchy in Serbia was at its beginning. The constitution which was adopted in 1869, after the assassination of the Prince, had been drafted starting from the primordial draft committed by Mihailo in 1867. The 1869 Constitution did not provide for parliamentary

40 J. Prodanović, *Ustavni razvitak*, 150–63; M. Stefanovski, *Postanak Namesničkog ustava*, 13–31.

41 M. Stefanovski, *Postanak Namesničkog ustava*, 30.

42 J. J. Zmaj, *Jututunska juhahaha*, 1865.

government, but this nevertheless emerged while that constitution was in force.[43] Further developments went towards introducing more constitutionalism and the rule of law. The latter was never implemented in full, but it became a relevant issue in political debates and a topic that can be traced in the scholarship.

7.3 A Closing Word

The practice of the rule of law faced arduous developments in Serbia. At the very beginning, it was the notion of order, originating in medieval times, which served as a model of acceptable social behaviour. This slowly disappeared, so as to leave room for the concepts belonging to the treasury of modern political institutions, such as the rule of law. The latter notion was generally perceived as the opposite of arbitrariness. However, it was reduced to mere legality through the evolution of constitutional settlements, which meant, in a somewhat simplified expression, enacting statutes and following those in practice, irrespective of their contents.

The crucial concepts of constitutionalism, such as, for instance, the protection of human rights, the equality of citizens before the law and the independence of the judiciary, were not emphasised in practice and had to wait for the last decades of the nineteenth century. They could not find proper regulation in the times of constitutional monarchy and were to come to the agenda with the introduction of parliamentary government. Regretfully, the rule of law was not introduced in full even then, although the Serbian political settlements came closer to constitutionalism in the 1870s. The developments were reflected in the evolution of the doctrine of the rule of law.

43 A. Dragnich, *The Development*, 53–56.

CHAPTER 8

The Doctrine of Rule of Law

8.1 Receiving Foreign Influence

Rule of law is a notion that developed in modern Serbian language mostly after World War II. It has a skillful translation from the English original: *vladavina prava*. The substance covered by the expression is almost identical to a German notion that had been in use among the Serbs since the mid-nineteenth century, before the English expression prevailed. The German word *Rechtsstaat* was translated into the Serbian expression *pravna država*, the English translation being a state based on law. Nowadays it is commonplace to say that the two notions are not fully identical, but it is because of their strong similarities that we can trace their unique evolution in Serbian legal thought.

Serbian intellectuals who lived at the end of the eighteenth and beginning of the 19th century did not use either of the two terms mentioned. They nevertheless put forward an idea that belonged to the treasury of natural law, which made room for further developments of the concept of the rule of law. The idea was connected to the exercise of sovereign power in the times of absolute monarchy in Europe. The absolute and enlightened monarch was, according to this school of thought, under obligation to obey the law. In other words, although the absolute monarch was the legislator himself, he was bound by the law he had created and was not entitled to overstep the legal order, of which he was the origin. Dositej Obradović, in his works, and Lazar Vojnović, in his Grand School lectures, were in favour of such a stance at the very beginning of the nineteenth century.[1]

Jovan Sterija Popović, in his lectures on natural law at the Grand School at the beginning of the 1840s, continued along the same path, but also contributed to the advancement of the idea. It is therefore with Sterija that the true story of the doctrine of rule of law in Serbian legal thought began. Sterija stood in line with Dositej and Vojnović, supporting the concept of the sovereign's duties. Among those duties, two stood out. The sovereign, i.e. the enlightened monarch, had to comply with the constitution to safeguard the personal freedom and security of the citizens, their equality before the law, freedom of conscience and religion, as well as the peaceful enjoyment of their possessions.

1 Cf. Part Two, Chapter 5.

 DOI:10.30965/9783657791026_009

Another duty was *inter alia* to obey the law and not to interfere with the activity of the judiciary.[2]

Sterija neither mentioned the Rechtsstaat nor the rule of law. However, the substance of both concepts was contained in the attitudes he presented to his students. The rule of law indeed requires that everyone belonging to a polity is subject to the law. This applies to judges and public servants, as well as to the lawmakers in modern society. In brief, those who hold power of any kind are constrained by the law. Therefore, if we compare Sterija's view with the modern expression of an American professor, a striking parallel emerges. Thus, for instance, Almon Leroy Way Jr, in his *The American System of Government*, insists that the rule of law implies 'limits to the power of any governing elite to rule the society, no matter how that elite acquired governing authority'.[3] There is an arch towards the past, providing a link between the Serbian professor of the nineteenth century and the modern scholarly opinion just quoted.

Sterija was primarily influenced by Kant. He started the chapter of his book devoted to the sovereign's duties by quoting the famous German philosopher, albeit without a proper reference. Kant was at the origin of the doctrine of the rule of law, or Rechtsstaat. The Serbian professor reproduced the idea of his German role model. He put in a footnote the words in Latin attributed to Kant, *regem habere mera iura nulla officia*, and then discussed the issue in German language in the same footnote. Sterija expressed the view that the maintenance of laws (*Erhaltung der Gesetze*) was the only reason why men wanted to have an overlord, and underlined that it was the real origin of sovereignty (*wahre Ursprung der Souveränität*).[4] The substance of the concept of the rule of law was present in Sterija's university lectures. The term, however, was missing. He did not use the similar German term of Rechtsstaat, either.

Teaching a university course a decade after Sterija, Dimitrije Matić was the first to introduce the term of Rechtsstaat to the Serbian legal scholarship.[5] He did so in his textbook, in a passage dealing with theories that explained the State's goal or mission. From the standpoint of this goal, Matić classified the states into two groups. One was *policijska država* (*Polizeistaat*) and the other *pravna država*/Rechtsstaat. In Matić's view, in the latter form of state the freedom of an individual was guaranteed, whereas the former imposed its guardianship on individuals using police enforcement.[6] Matić was supportive of the

2 J. S. Popović, *Prirodno pravo*, 134–35.
3 https ://www. proconservative. net (visited 17.3.2020).
4 J. S. Popović, *Prirodno pravo*, 134, footnote 1.
5 D. Popović, 'Begriff des Rechtsstaates', 18–20.
6 D. Matić, *Načela*, 43.

concept of a welfare state. His view on the subject was strongly influenced by the German academics and their opinions, and he followed and reproduced the attitudes of professors whose classes he had attended while preparing his doctoral thesis in Germany.[7] The German influence continued in Serbian scholarship, and the above-mentioned classification went undisputed. The two types of states were considered to be clearly distinguished, and the State's goal served as a criterion for the distinction.

The scholarly attitude presented by Matić remained salient for a long time. That was evident in 1893 when a young professor held his inaugural lecture at the Grand School in Belgrade. His name was Jakov M. Nenadović, and he was a member of the famous Nenadović family that enriched the history of Serbia with several prominent personalities. Jakov M. Nenadović received his PhD in law from Leipzig University, and later became a diplomat and professor of law. He taught the subject, which was in that time still named, after the German tradition, *državno pravo* (*Staatsrecht*). He chose the State's goal or mission as the topic of his inaugural lecture.[8] The notion of the *pravna država*/Rechtsstaat was the starting point in his lecture, in which he pointed to J. J. Rousseau as the author of the concept. Nenadović explained that the French philosopher showed how the State enabled the substitution of natural equality by legal equality. This was brought about by the intermediary of the social contract, which laid the foundations for submitting the wills of individuals to the general will. By entering into the contract on which the State is founded, an individual lost their natural freedom, in order to acquire the civil freedom and protection of their possessions.[9] However, as regards the State's mission, Nenadović mostly followed Adam Smith. In his view, the State's mission was to provide justice to the individuals and protect them from foreign enemies, but also to develop public establishments that private interests were unable to develop. The State's goal could not be reduced to the first requirement, and it was only if the three of those were simultaneously fulfilled that the State's mission was accomplished. The form of state accomplishing the mission in full was, according to Nenadović, the *pravna država*/Rechtsstaat.[10]

Further on in his inaugural lecture, the young professor expressed his view, following the Swiss jurist Bluntschli, that the form of state which the Germans called *Kulturstaat* was his preference. That form of state has the goal of

7 D.Popović, 'Begriff des Rechtsstaates', 20.

8 J. Nenadović, 'O zadatku države' [On the State's mission], *Pravnik 3* (1893), 720 ff. Also published as a separate volume under the same title. The separate volume will follow in footnotes.

9 ibid. 5.

10 ibid. 7.

maintaining a stable legal order, not impeding individuals in their free activity, and also helping substantially where private forces were unable to fulfil certain goals without the State's aid.[11]

In an overall review of the inaugural lecture, and comparing Nenadović to Matić, it should be highlighted that they both sought definition of the Rechtsstaat, taking the goal or mission of the State as the starting point. Another feature in common was that they were supporters of the welfare state. Although Nenadović was also mainly influenced by the German scholarship, he somehow widened the scope of adoption of foreign ideas, being receptive to the concepts developed by Smith and Rousseau. He nevertheless remained in line with Matić as far as the understanding of the Rechtsstaat was concerned.[12]

8.2 Introduction of New Topics

The turning point in Serbian scholarship on the rule of law/Rechtsstaat had already been announced years before Nenadović's inaugural lecture. It appeared in a law review and was inspired by comparative law. The author who introduced a novelty remained unknown. New ideas were presented in the form of a literature review published by an anonymous critic in the law review *Porota*, in September 1881. The book was German, and its author was K. J. Schmidt. It had been published in Stuttgart in 1878 under the title *Die Grundlagen der Verwaltuntungspflege im konstitutionell-monarchischen Staate*. The title in English would be: *Foundations of Judicial Review of Administrative Action in Constitutional Monarchy*.[13]

An issue largely discussed in comparative law in the 1870s was the supervision of administration; within that framework, there was a particular emphasis on the judicial review of administrative action. Constitutional monarchies on the European continent were organised so as to make use of the monarch's administrative apparatus that had been developed of old, and their staff were traditionally faithful to the monarch. In the second half of the nineteenth century, with the rise of the ideas and practice of parliamentary government, the issue of the responsibility of the executive emerged. Its consequence was to raise the issue of judicial review of administrative acts among lawyers. The French law developed the concept of settling disputes between an individual and the administration by creating a special body within the administration

11 ibid. 14.

12 D. Popović, 'Begriff des Rechtsstaates', 24–25.

13 *Porota*, I–III, September 1881, 385 ff.

itself. That body was competent to deal with cases arising from disputes between individuals and the administration. In France the competent body was the Council of State (*Conseil d'Etat*), which was also vested with other powers, e.g. discussing draft laws and the like.[14]

The German law took another angle on the issue of judicial review of administrative action. There was a movement among academics and practitioners in German lands that was in favour of introducing special administrative tribunals that would be competent to review administrative decisions. The anonymous critic mentioned above was a supporter of such a concept, considering it to be liberal and able to carry out the precepts of the Rechtsstaat at the same time.[15] He considered the trend of introducing administrative tribunals to be in line with the guarantees of freedom of the citizens, because it would overcome the omnipotent character of the administration and the executive power. At the beginning of his article, the critic referred to respective legislation adopted in German lands between 1863 and 1878, which introduced administrative tribunals. Such legislation was passed in Baden, Prussia, Würtemberg and Austria. In some of these countries the legislation to determine the scope of jurisdiction of administrative tribunals was based on a system of enumeration, while in others it was based on a general clause.[16]

In the interest the anonymous critic showed in German academic writing and his comments on the book reviewed, he displayed two major points. Firstly, he showed his attachment to the concept of Rechtsstaat, which he considered crucial for the freedom of citizens; secondly, by his interest in the organisation of administrative tribunals and judicial review of the administrative action, he highlighted the scope of interest for comparative law in Serbia. A small nation was looking for foreign models, searching for inspiration in the course of its own legal developments. Looking back to the evolution of the doctrine, one realises a connection between the ideas of Dimitrije Matić and this anonymous critic. The link was established by their faith in freedom and the rule of law, the latter of course in the form of Rechtsstaat. However, a new element emerged in the article of the anonymous reviewer at the beginning of the 1880s. He switched from Matić's mostly theoretical attitude to practical issues, which to some extent altered his major stance on the topic of Rechtsstaat. He abandoned pure theory, because his main interest lay in the way in which executive power was exercised. By searching for remedies and reviewing the

14 *Porota* II, 386.
15 ibid. 387.
16 ibid. 385–87.

administrative action, the anonymous reviewer was in favour of checking the executive on the basis of a particular issue, materialised in a case or lawsuit.[17]

8.3 Further Developments

The main approach towards the concept of rule of law, as developed in the doctrine, was subject to evolution. The topic of judicial review of administrative action was prevalent, and it decisively influenced legal thought, shifting the focus of the approach to the concept. A vestige of this can be found in the work of a Grand School scholar, Vojislav Veljković (1865–1931), who was professor of administrative law between 1886 and 1889. He had received his PhD in law from the University of Paris. On his return to Serbia he got involved in politics, being a minister in several cabinets and the mayor of Belgrade. Veljković published a treatise under the title *Odnos sudske i administrativne vlasti u državi* (Relations between judicial and administrative powers).

Despite the fact that Veljković did not use the term *pravna država*/Rechtsstaat, his attitude finds a place in the evolution of the doctrine of rule of law/Rechtsstaat, for valid reasons. It remains inexplicable why instead of *pravna država* he used the expression *pravno organizovana zemlja*. The translation of his expression into English, 'legally organised land', clearly shows its unusual character, somehow escaping the legal vocabulary in Serbian language too.[18] Veljković's starting point was the theory of separation of powers. His problem was whether the two branches of government – the judiciary and the executive – would remain separated if the judiciary were competent to review the acts of the executive. His main topic was indeed the organisation of the judicial review of administrative acts, which he treated with a view to the recent developments in comparative law. Veljković declared himself as an opponent of the extreme interpretation of the doctrine of separation of powers, and suggested the introduction of administrative tribunals in Serbia after the German model.[19] The opinions expressed in the volume brought Veljković close to the anonymous critic whose article we have already discussed.

The topic of the day in Serbian public law towards the end of the nineteenth century was the judicial review of administrative action. Its nature was one of the reasons for alteration of the approach to the broader issue of rule of law/

17 D. Popović, 'Begriff des Rechtsstaates', 27–28.

18 V. Veljković, *Odnos sudske i administrativne vlasti u državi* [The relationship of judicial and administrative power in the state], Belgrade 1896, 21.

19 ibid. 23–26.

Rechtsstaat. Practical aspects of the topic were decisive, because the scholars considered the problem to be crucial for the functioning of a modern state. It was one of the outstanding goals of a modern state to provide legal certainty, but that appeared to be insufficient. The mode in which the state power was exercised became paramount, because the question of individual freedom was closely connected to it. Issues like how to preserve the separation of powers in case the courts were to perform a review of administrative action were therefore on the agenda. The Serbian authors followed developments in comparative law and gave precedence to the adoption of the German system regarding judicial review of administrative acts. The fundamental approach to the rule of law was altered; what became important in legal thought was the exercise of state power, in the sense of introducing checks to the executive in order to avoid arbitrariness.[20]

Serbian scholars were for the most part in agreement about the necessity of introducing a judicial review of administrative action into Serbian law. Gligorije Geršić, one of the outstanding professors of law at the turn of the twentieth century, was one of those who took part in the discussion. He dealt with the broader topic of the rule of law/Rechtsstaat from the perspective of the theory of modern state. Geršić expressed his views on the subject in his *Encyclopedia of Law* (*Enciklopedija prava*). The volume was published in 1908–09, but contained the professor's attitudes exposed to his students in lectures for many years.[21] Geršić was a radical who did not properly fit into the party's orthodoxy. He had studied law in Budapest and Vienna, and had been professor of law at the Grand School of Belgrade since 1866. He was also a justice minister and a member of parliament. Geršić was heavily influenced by German legal scholars, especially Gneist and von Stahl, who promoted the formal notion of Rechtsstaat.[22] The way he expressed his view was somewhat complicated, albeit rooted in the concept of checks and balances. The leading idea was that the entitlements of state power must be carried out within determined limits and in proper forms according to the law. Geršić insisted on what he labelled as the 'limits (of power) and forms envisaged by public law'.[23]

Geršić followed Gneist, who opposed the concept of defining Rechtsstaat by the intermediary of the State's goal or mission. The Serbian professor supported the authors who believed that the legally framed mode of exercising

20 D. Popović, 'Begriff des Rechtsstaates', 29.

21 G. Geršić, *Enciklopedija prava*, Belgrade s.a. In this volume the most recent edition of 2012 will be followed for quotations.

22 D. Popović, 'Begriff des Rechtsstaates', 30 and the scholarship referred to.

23 G. Geršić, *Enciklopedija prava*, 247.

the State's power was indispensable for the existence of Rechtsstaat. It should materialise in safeguards and guarantees that the power holders would conduct themselves in this way. The guarantees for their part were to be found in the existence of bodies or committees to which an individual could appeal whenever power holders acted *ultra vires* and overstepped the law.[24]

Pravna država was adopted among Serbian academics as a concept and a version of rule of law. The latter expression was not used as a term, despite the similarities between the two notions. The German influence still generally prevailed in Serbian law, and it persisted in this regard into the beginning of the 20th century. Slobodan Jovanović used the term *pravna država* in his book on the theory of State, a subject which equalled the German notion of *Allgemeine Staatslehre*. He followed the German academic traditions in this respect. Jovanović's book was a university manual for his course in what was called *Opšte državno pravo*, which is almost a direct translation of the German expression just mentioned. The subtitle of Jovanović's book *On the State* was 'Foundations of a Legal Theory of State', meaning that the subject of the book was the concept of the State, discussed on the basis of the theory of law. Slobodan Jovanović was a prolific author in law and history and also the President of the Academy of Science. Without having been involved in politics before, he became deputy prime minister in his old age, in the government of the coup d'état on 27 March 1941, then went into exile. He was one of the prime ministers of Yugoslavia in exile and never returned to his country, having been sentenced *in absentia* by a communist court. Today the little square in front of the Belgrade University Law School building is named after him. His remains were returned to Serbia in 2011.

Slobodan Jovanović first explained the origins of *pravna država*/Rechtsstaat. Its birthplace was in Western Europe, where it was shaped in the period in which the absolute monarchy was transformed into a constitutional one. In those times *policijska država*, in which the executive was guided by the *raison d'état* had to give up arbitrariness and cede before the concept of a State governed by law. It was essential in the beginning that the administration had to act within the legal framework to provide security to the citizens. The State was initially limited to what Jovanović labelled as its legal mission; however, an increased understanding of the Rechtsstaat came later. Its more developed concept allowed the State to broaden its mission beyond security safeguards, provided it remains within the framework of law.[25]

---

24 ibid. 248.

25 S. Jovanović, *O državi*, 118–19.

At another point in his course, Jovanović treated the issue of *pravna država* again. It was in the passages dealing with the separation of powers. The author's main stance was that without the separation of powers the Rechtsstaat was impossible to achieve. In order to reach the level of Rechtsstaat, the executive had to be separated on one hand from the legislative power, and on the other from the judiciary. He paraphrased Rousseau by saying that he who commands the laws should not command the men, adding that the laws, in order to make all personal interests equal, were not to be governed by human passions.[26]

Slobodan Jovanović thus situated the topic of Rechtsstaat in a key position within the ambit of the theory of separation of powers. At the beginning of the 20th century the discussion of the issue of judicial review of administration was no longer on the agenda. Like Geršić before him, Slobodan Jovanović was of the opinion that the branches of government, and especially the executive, had to be constrained within checks and balances. The separation of powers was traditionally perceived as the origin of safeguarding of individual freedom in the modern state. The mode in which the separation of powers was carried out was decisive for the existence of the rule of law, or Rechtsstaat, to use the term familiar among the Serbian academics.

It was on the eve of World War II that an academic summed up the evolution of the concept of Rechtsstaat in Serbian scholarship, which had been in development over the course of almost a century. Milivoje Marković, a young professor of law, published a treatise in 1939, under the title *Pravna država*.[27] His short volume presented to readers the attitude prevailing in Serbian law on the issue of the rule of law as it was understood under the concept of Rechtsstaat, which was then in use. Milivoje Marković (1908–86) received his PhD in law in France, in the University of Lyon. He started his career in Belgrade University, but was removed to Niš after World War II, where he continued teaching in the Law School of the University of Niš.[28]

Marković underlined one of the issues that had appeared in the evolution of Serbian legal thought as regards the rule of law. In his view, the Rechtsstaat acquires its full meaning only in the presence of a judicial review of administrative action.[29] It is, however, of utmost importance here to reproduce Marković's general definition of the notion of *pravna država*/Rechtsstaat, because it crystallised a century-long evolution. The author's expression on the subject read: 'When the provisions on the exercise of the State power are

26 ibid. 259–61.
27 M. Marković, *Pravna država*, Belgrade 1939.
28 www.prafak.ni.ac.rs/files/zbornik.
29 M. Marković, 10.

laid down by substantial law, and when safeguards of the lawful exercise of that power are provided in the substantial law, that means that the State is founded on the principles of the rule of law (Rechtsstaat).'[30] This was in line with the attitudes of Geršić and Slobodan Jovanović, and in a certain way was a reproduction made by a young lawyer of the views of the renowned Serbian professors of law. Marković did not have to make quotations and references to previous authorities in Serbian law, which demonstrates the wide reception of the views of those authorities on the subject among Serbian lawyers.

After World War II, Serbian lawyers and political scientists turned to the expression *vladavina prava* (rule of law) instead of *pravna država*/Rechtsstaat. The shift was not difficult to make, owing to the substantial similarities between the two notions. With the change of cultural environment, marked by the preponderance of the English language, the term 'rule of law' became accepted in academia and to a large extent replaced the older term of Rechtsstaat.

Decades of evolution of Serbian legal thought on the subject had elapsed when a young academic published an article, which gave a thorough review of the developments of the concept of the rule of law. Dragutin Avramović, when summarising the developments of the concept of rule of law, was of the same age as Milivoje Marković, who had summarised the evolution of the concept of Rechtsstaat in 1939. Avramović, professor of law at the University of Novi Sad, made a comparison of the two concepts and raised the crucial question already in the title of his article: were they identical or divergent? His remark was that the Serbian academic literature often used the two terms as synonyms.[31] The author's general conclusion was nevertheless that the two notions under discussion were substantially different. As the main distinction, he put forward the fact that the concepts had different approaches towards the issue of human rights. In the author's view, the concept of the rule of law perceived human rights as antecedent to the State, which was not the case with the concept of Rechtsstaat.[32] Notably, Avramović underlined the fact that the term *vladavina prava*/rule of law had an assimilating capacity which led to Serbian authors merging that expression with the rival term of *pravna država*/ Rechtsstaat.[33]

Two observations appear to be necessary to close this chapter. First, the Serbian scholars altered their sources of inspiration, which were inevitably

30 ibid. 5.

31 D. Avramović, 'Vladavina prava i pravna država – istost ili različitost' [*Vladavina prava* and *pravna država* – sameness or difference], *Zbornik radova Pravnog fakulteta u Novom Sadu* 3/2010.

32 ibid. 433.

33 ibid. 434.

coming from the foreign law. The prevailing German influence ceded before the one coming from the Common Law countries, mostly because of the fact that Serbian lawyers were more inclined to read in English after World War II. The influence was so strong and widespread that a concept developed in Common Law managed to overcome the concept formerly accepted by the academics, which came from the same legal family as the one to which Serbian law belonged. Indeed, it still represents a part of the European continental law, so that this can be viewed as an example of an overarching predominance in our time of legal concepts stemming from the Common Law. Second, while influenced by different sources from the one that previous generations of lawyers had adopted, the Serbian scholarship mixed up and to a considerable extent confused the concepts of the rule of law and Rechtsstaat.

CHAPTER 9

A Century of Teaching Constitutional Law

9.1 Introduction

The study of constitutional law is a specific topic, which constitutes a part of the broader theme of the evolution of constitutionalism. Two elements are paramount for those who want to research the study of constitutional law in Serbia. The first is the university curriculum, and the second is the schoolbooks or university manuals in constitutional law. The latter were few until recently. Thus, throughout the long nineteenth century, i.e. from its beginning until World War I, only three Serbian professors left their lectures in constitutional law in writing: two of them published their schoolbooks, and the third left his work in a manuscript which was published only towards the end of the twentieth century. The three professors were Dimitrije Matić (1821–84), Milovan Milovanović (1863–1912) and Slobodan Jovanović (1869–1958). Milovanović passed away young and did not have time to publish his lectures. They remained in manuscript form, and were published in 1997 in one single volume, together with some of his other works. There were two separate editions in the same year.[1] Matić and Jovanović have already been mentioned in this volume, and their biographical records have been presented above. Milovanović was much younger than Matić, and he was indeed Jovanović's predecessor in the university chair of public law in the Belgrade University School of Law.

Milovanović graduated in law from the University of Paris. He received his PhD from the same university and returned to Serbia at the beginning of 1888, where he immediately ascended to the chair of public law. In the same year, the King appointed him to the post of secretary of the drafting committee for the new Serbian constitution. That position enabled him to contribute considerably to the drafting of the 1888 Constitution. Milovanović launched into politics, joining the Radical Party. He was a member of Parliament, cabinet minister, diplomat and he ultimately became prime minister of Serbia in 1911/12, passing away while in office.[2]

1 Cf. M. Milovanović, *Državno pravo i Načela spoljne politike* [State Law and Principles of Foreign Policy], Belgrade 1997, edited by Radoslav and Dubravka Stojanović, and M. Đ. Milovanović, *Državno pravo i druge ustavnopravne studije* [State law and other constitutional studies], Belgrade 1997, edited by Ratko Marković.

2 For a biography, cf. V. Grol, *Pravna misao Milovana Milovanovića* [Legal thought of Milovan Milovanović], Belgrade 1989, 5–17.

 | DOI:10.30965/9783657791026_010

9.2 Dimitrije Matić

Dimitrije Matić can be considered the first Serbian professor of constitutional law in the uninterrupted tradition of the first university in Serbia. However, when Matić was appointed professor his title was literally Professor of the Law of the Fatherland (in Serbian: *Otečestveno pravo*). The law of the fatherland, which as an expression was abandoned later on, encompassed several areas of law, such as the civil code and civil procedure, but also the public law of Serbia.[3]

The term *državno pravo* was adopted in the legislation concerning the Grand School and remained the expression which covered the area of law that we usually call constitutional law nowadays. *Državno pravo* is a translation of the German term *Staatsrecht*. Adopting the term from the German language was a sign of the high influence of German academic literature on Serbian intellectuals, which was preeminent for a long time. Despite some weakening of the impact of German legal science in Serbia in the 1860s, the term *državno pravo* persisted until World War II.[4] The prevailing foreign intellectual influence in Serbia and the legislation which followed it created a tradition of handling the constitutional law in general. That was especially the case of dealing with the positive constitutional law.

Dimitrije Matić worked in the early days of the *Licej*. He had received excellent formative training in law, but also in philosophy in Germany. While lecturing he understood his task to be to thoroughly transmit the most recent achievements in law and legal scholarship from abroad to the Serbian students. The pattern he chose for the course was simple. Among many schoolbooks of German professors, he picked up the one he considered the most appropriate to explain the substance of his course to the students in Belgrade. Notably, his choice was the book of a professor whom, for unknown reasons, he did not mention in his student diary.[5] It was for pedagogical reasons that Matić took Professor Zoepfl's schoolbook as a paradigm. The book, entitled *Grundsaetze des allgemeinen und des constitutionnel-monarchischen*

3 D. Popović, 'Strani uticaji na našu udžbeničku književnost ustavnoga prava (Matić i Milovanović)' [Foreign influences on our textbook literature on constitutional law (Matić i Milovanović)], in: K. Čavoški (ed.), *Ustavnost i vladavina prava* [Constitutionality and the rule of law], Belgrade 2000, 83, 85 and the references made there.

4 The French influence on Serbian law showed up in the second half of the 1860s and started in private law; cf. D. Popović, *Uvod u uporedno pravo* [Introduction to comparative law], Belgrade 2005, 103.

5 Cf. D. Matić, *Đački dnevnik*, 30–96, which tells of the time of his studies in German universities.

Staatsrechts (*Foundations of General and Constitutional-Monarchical Law of State Organisation*), has already been mentioned in this volume. It was published in Heidelberg in 1846. Matić thoroughly followed his German model book while lecturing. He nevertheless shortened several passages, left out others and basically made a shortened translation of the German book for his Serbian students. He explained the method he adhered to in the foreword to his own schoolbook. Two points mentioned in the foreword are of relevance for our topic in this chapter. The first is the fact that Matić revealed the way in which he proceeded to shape his own volume. Matić wrote: 'I had (the works of) several authors at hand, but when I analysed and compared those it turned out that for my purpose the most appropriate was the work of my professor of Staatsrecht (*državno pravo*) in Heidelberg University, Mr. Heinrich Zoepfl, a moderate and persistent man who wholeheartedly cherishes the progress of his discipline. Therefore I mostly followed his system, omitting only what was not fit for us and our understanding.'[6]

The fact that Matić followed his role model's system can be evidenced if we compare the contents of the two works. His discussions on the subject matter in its various aspects run somewhat in parallel to the works of the two authors.[7] Matić acted as almost a translator of the German schoolbook, to which he nevertheless added his own personal touches. These consisted in some references and shortenings of the text, as well as in the choice of topics, which the Serbian professor left out wherever they were not 'fit for us and our understanding'. What did not fit into the Serbian social *mileu* in the late 1840s were the chapters devoted to human rights, e.g. freedom of expression, right of petition or freedom of association. Matić showed some conformism, complying with the attitudes of the ruling oligarchs who were hostile to the protection of the political rights of the citizens. It was to no avail, and he was removed from the Licej.

Matić published a whole separate volume, mostly reproducing constitutional documents and international treaties relevant to Serbia in order to discuss the positive public law of the country. He did that in comments concerning the documents contained in a book of 165 pages, which appeared in a small format.[8] For the volume treating the positive law of Serbia, Matić did not use the term *državno pravo*. He used *javno pravo* (public law) instead. One of the reasons for that consisted in the fact that Serbia at the time the book was published was a vassal state, under the sovereignty of the Sultan.

---

6 D. Matić, *Načela*, 21.

7 For a thorough analysis of the two works in parallel, cf. D. Popović, 'Strani uticaji', 92–96.

8 D. Matić, *Javno pravo Knjažestva Srbije* [Public law of the Principality of Serbia], Belgrade 1851.

Some of the documents contained in the volume were indeed legal acts of the Ottoman Empire, while others were international treaties. Besides, there were regulations. The public law was mentioned in the Serbian legislation on the curriculum.

Another point that stood out in Matić's foreword to his own book concerned the teaching method in public law. Matić appeared to be the founder of a tradition. The Serbian professor, under the impact of his German sources of inspiration, started a line in Serbian law and legal scholarship. He transferred to Serbia the mode of teaching in constitutional law, which has remained dominant ever since. The beginning of the foreword of his theoretical volume read: 'When lecturing on public law of the Principality of Serbia in our Licej I thought it was purposeful to explain to the students first the theory of rational Staatsrecht (teorija umnog državnog prava), before turning to the positive public law, which the students will better understand having got acquainted scientifically with the State and its organisation.'[9]

That was the announcement of the deductive method of teaching constitutional law, which became a firm rule. The professors teaching after Matić followed it, and generations of Serbian lawyers received their formal training following the precepts of this mode of teaching, which penetrated the Serbian law from Germany. First comes the theory, and only then the positive law; this became a golden rule in the university teaching. The logical method of induction, where texts regarding the national law are used initially to teach the law, has never been accepted in Serbia. The traditional method is deductive: it has its specific features, but it also has shortcomings that are still present, marking our way of thinking and reasoning in constitutional law.

9.3 Milovan Milovanović

Several professors lectured on constitutional law in the Grand School of Belgrade after Matić started and before Milovanović ascended to the chair. In his monograph on Milovanović, Vojislav Grol mentioned four professors.[10] They did not leave any traces of their lectures, so that we do not know today what their teaching method was. It is nevertheless highly doubtful that they deviated from the traditional deductive method instituted in Serbian constitutional law by Matić. This seems even more likely considering the fact that

9 D. Matić, *Načela*, 21.

10 V. Grol, *Pravna misao*, 101. The professors mentioned were Čumić, Ugričić, Geršić and Nastas Petrović.

Milovanović, who was in the university chair towards the end of the 1880s, followed the same method.

The application of the traditional teaching method by Milovanović is evident if we consider the posthumously published manuscript of his lectures. Out of less than 200 pages of the whole volume, the author devoted some thirty pages at the end of the book to positive constitutional law.[11] The fact is probably due to the basically embryonic stage of Milovanović's manuscript if considered from the standpoint of understanding the final shape of his university course. The kernel of the teaching mode was nevertheless present. The professor first exposed on the theory of State and then on positive law, although the two parts of the course remained in one unfinished volume of the manuscript. The way in which Matić approached the teaching method in constitutional law had become a rule. Towards the end of the nineteenth century, Milovanović did not escape the rule despite the fact that in some aspects his attitudes were quite different from those of the first Serbian professor of constitutional law.

Milovanović was under the impact of the French academic scholarship. He was more inclined towards sociology than philosophy, and had a strong background in evolutionist sociology. His manuscript does not reveal any French contemporary professors of constitutional law as role models, which makes him different from Matić, who chose a model from abroad for his course. Unlike Matić, Milovanović looked to synthesise the influences he had received, and therefore showed a more original approach to the composition of his schoolbook. We can not conclude today that Milovanović followed any of the French authors of treatises in constitutional law of his time. The composition of Milovanović's lectures has traits in common with the schoolbooks of Duguit and Esmein, but the former could not have influenced the Serbian professor, because his schoolbook was published after Milovanović had written his manuscript.[12] Another fact makes him different from Matić. The latter had published a whole volume devoted to positive public law. Milovanović did not have time to achieve the final stage of his course, and we cannot speculate today as to whether his intention was to publish a separate volume on positive law, or to put the whole course in a single volume.

Matić mentioned the term 'constitutional law' in his theoretical book, understanding it as the law on the form of state and its organisation. *Administrative law* was for him the law that regulated the proceedings of the administration. Those two, taken together, constitute *državno pravo*, which was explained in

11 M. Đ. Milovanović, *Državno pravo*, 145–79.

12 Cf. D. Popović, 'Strani uticaji', 96–98.

detail earlier in this volume.[13] Milovanović went beyond that stance. In the introductory part of his lectures he presented the terms *državno, ustavno* and *konstitucionalno pravo* as identical.[14] The identification of the three terms that we meet in Milovanović's volume calls for comments. Milovanović did not prepare the manuscript for publishing himself. Therefore the reason for identification of the three terms remains unclear, and at odds with the rules of university legislation.

9.4 Slobodan Jovanović

Slobodan Jovanović succeeded Milovanović in the university chair in the Belgrade University School of Law. He had received his formative training in law in Germany, France and Switzerland. Jovanović was, for the most part, a dedicated follower of German academic writing, mostly following the concepts of Jellinek and Laband. Notably, Jovanović published a theoretical textbook, under the title *O državi,* on the subject he was teaching in 1906. Its second edition appeared in 1914, and the third in 1922. The subject matter of the book was defined in the university curriculum as *opšte državno pravo,* which corresponds to the German expression *Allgemeines Staatsrecht* (General Law on State Organisation). The theoretical volume was the first part of the whole course. Its second part was devoted to the public law of the Kingdom of Serbia.

We have seen above that Jovanović's textbook, which appeared in 1906, had the title *O državi – osnovi jedne pravne teorije,* which would be in English *On the State – Foundations of a Legal Theory of State.* That may have been inspired by Jellinek, whose renowned volume on *Allgemeine Staatslehre* (General theory of State) had the title of *Allgemeine Sttatsrechtslehre* (*General Legal Theory of State*) for its third part.[15] The subtitle of Jovanović's book matches part of Jellinek's in name. The volume which Slobodan Jovanović published represented a landmark in Serbian scholarship on constitutional law. His work consisted of a creative synthesis of contemporary academic writing on the subject at an international level. It has been remarked that in his theoretical book Jovanović laid down the foundations of his attitudes towards the modern state, which was a prerequisite for his future fruitful work in the area of

13 D. Matić, *Načela*, 30.

14 M. Đ. Milovanović, *Državno pravo*, 14.

15 Cf. G. Jellinek, *Allgemeine Staatslehre*, Berlin 1914, 383–796. Jellinek's book was first published in 1900 in Heidelberg.

constitutional law.[16] As of the second edition of his volume, Jovanović added references at the end of respective paragraphs instructing students to consult relevant books and articles in various languages.[17] The references show the author's inclination towards German academics and their writing, but also the wide spectrum of his intellectual interest as well as his profound scholarly approach to the issues discussed in the book. Some examples taken at random appear to be illustrative. Thus, for instance, when dealing with the topic of the separation of powers Jovanović referred to five works in German language, seven in French, two in Italian and six in English. After the paragraph, which dealt with the parliamentary and presidential forms of government, he referred to twelve works in German, ten in French, one in Italian and nine in English, etc.[18]

Jovanović's theoretical book in constitutional law, devoted to the theory of the modern state, marked an advanced stage in the evolution of Serbian scholarship on the subject. Matić translated a foreign model book as the basis for his course. Milovanović was mostly influenced by one national school of thought in constitutional law: the French school of thought. Jovanović went further: he was influenced by German academic writing, but nevertheless integrated in his work a wide range of influences from comparative law and the various national schools of thought. Jovanović was not original at any cost; on the contrary, dependent on the issue, he often agreed with the mainstream doctrine or with the views of other schools. What made him original, and indeed great, as an academic, was his capacity for synthesis, which was unknown in Serbian scholarly writing at the time and has been unsurpassed to date.

The composition of Jovanović's schoolbook can in the broadest sense be compared to those of his foreign counterparts, but the volume as a whole remained distinctive from others and indeed original. For instance, if compared to Jellinek's crucial volume, the composition of Jovanović's book has one feature in common: it also encompasses three sections. In Jovanović's work these parts are less voluminous, so he called them 'parts', whereas Jellinek labelled his as 'books'. Jellinek's first book, entitled *Introductory Research*, does not find a parallel in Jovanović's work. The parallel begins, however, with Jellinek's second book, which has the title *Allgemeine Soziallehre des Staates*. After a short chapter consisting of several pages only, Jellinek turns to the topic

16 Thus, S. Vračar, 'Prethodni pogled na ustavnopravni sistem Slobodana Jovanovića' [A first glance at Slobodan Jovanovic's constitutional system], published as a Foreword to S. Jovanović, *Ustavno pravo Kraljevine Srba, Hrvata i Slovenaca* [Constitutional law of the Kingdom of Serbs, Croats and Slovenes], Belgrade 1995 (first published in 1924), 9–10.

17 S. Jovanović, *O državi*, Predgovor ka drugom izdanju (Foreword to the second edition).

18 Cf. S. Jovanović, *O državi*, 264, 412.

of the concept of State in the next chapter.[19] Jovanović, having made a short introduction to the whole of his volume in ten pages only, opens the lectures in Part One, which has the title 'Pojam države' ('The Concept of State'). There is also a parallel in composition in terms of dealing with certain important issues, e.g. *zadatak države/ Zweck des Staates* (the purpose of State), which could also be translated into English using the words 'goal', 'mission' or 'aim'. Jellinek deals with this topic in his second book, while Jovanović placed it in Part One of his volume. What Jovanović treated in Parts Two and Three of his volume mostly found their place in the third book of Jellinek's volume. That explains to some extent the second part of the title of Jovanović's book. He borrowed the expression *Allgemeine Staatsrechtslehre*. This survey of the two works, although just on the surface level, nevertheless displays the Serbian professor's propensity to focus on foreign influences, as well as the degree of originality of his approach towards the issues of theory of State and constitutional law.

At one particular point, Jovanović maintained the tradition stemming from Matić. He was professor of public law, and that discipline of the university curriculum encompassed two areas: the general theory of State and the positive law of Serbia. Like Matić before him, Jovanović published a separate volume for the positive law part of his course. Since the positive public law encompassed constitutional law and administrative law, Jovanović published a volume as a co-author with his university colleague, Kosta Kumanudi, professor of administrative law.[20] Matić was in favour of the bipartite composition of the area of public law just mentioned, and examined the public law of Serbia from both the constitutional and administrative aspects. Hence his book on positive law bore the title of *Public Law of the Principality of Serbia*. This was also partly due to the fact that Serbia was a vassal state in the 1840s, and some of its public law was indeed either international or even Ottoman Turkish. At the time when Jovanović wrote his book on public law, Serbia was an independent state, with its own domestic constitutional law. That is why he gave his book the title *Constitutional Law of the Kingdom of Serbia*. To this should be added that by the beginning of the twentieth century the sources and documents in both constitutional and administrative law had made considerable leaps and could not be dealt with in one single volume. Moreover, there were two professors in

---

19 G. Jellinek, 136–74. The title of the relevant chapter is 'Das Wesen des Staates', which would equal in English 'The Nature (or Essence) of State'.

20 S. Jovanović–K. Kumanudi, *Osnovi javnog prava Kraljevine Srbije* [Fundamentals of public law of the Kingdom of Serbia], Belgrade 1907–09, of which the first book was: S. Jovanović, *Osnovi javnog prava Kraljevine Srbije (Knj 1) Ustavno pravo* [Book 1: Constitutional law], Belgrade 1907.

the Belgrade University School of Law to teach the two areas – constitutional law on the one hand, and administrative law on the other.

Jovanović presented the positive constitutional law of Serbia in three parts, examining three organs of the State. The first part was devoted to the Grand National Assembly, which was the organ of constituent power, the second to the National Assembly and the third to the King.[21] A modern reader will remark that the author of the book did not consider the cabinet and the ministers. The force of tradition and German influence was decisive. In the old-fashioned style of teaching, the study of such topics was mostly considered to fall within the ambit of administrative law. The very last paragraph of the book, however, dealt with the position of ministers. The paragraph found its place in Chapter III of Part Three of the book. The chapter as a whole treated the King's prerogative.[22] Apart from that, in some of the paragraphs of Chapter XII of Part Two of the volume, dealing with the competence of the National Assembly, Jovanović treated the issues of questioning and interpellation, as well as of accusing the ministers.[23]

Jovanović's book on the constitutional law of Serbia had much less success than his theoretical work on the theory of State. The latter saw three editions published in some fifteen years, whereas the former has never been republished.[24] Except for the author's highly positivistic approach to the subject, one explanation for the book's destiny lies in the fact that World War I broke out only seven years after its publication. After the war, there was no more Kingdom of Serbia because of the unification of the Southern Slavs into a new, enlarged state. However, the method of teaching constitutional law persisted in the new country; this led Slobodan Jovanović to publish the third edition of his theoretical work in 1922, and soon after that he published another schoolbook in constitutional law. It was devoted to the constitutional law of the new country and appeared under the title *Constitutional Law of the Kingdom of the Serbs, Croats and Slovenes*.[25] The positivistic method that was predominant in the book on the constitutional law of Serbia that was published before World War I was preserved in the book treating the constitutional law of the new kingdom. The composition of the volume was, however, altered. The book consisted of five parts. The first was a long introduction of some sixty pages, which explained the emergence of the new state and the drafting and adoption of

21 ibid. Part One, 13–21; Part Two, 21–261; Part Three, 261–315.

22 ibid. 306–15.

23 ibid. 232–56.

24 S. Vračar, 'Prethodni pogled', 11.

25 S. Jovanović, *Ustavno pravo Kraljevine SHS*. A new edition of the volume, which appeared in 1995, will serve for quotations.

its constitution in 1921. It was followed by a part that dealt with the fundamental principles of the 1921 Constitution of the Kingdom of Serbs, Croats and Slovenes. The next three parts corresponded to those of the volume of 1907 on the constitutional law of the Kingdom of Serbia. They were devoted to the Constituent Assembly, the National Assembly and the King. The last part of the book dealt with the status of citizens, i.e. their fundamental rights.[26]

Pursuing the positivistic method, Jovanović referred to the sources in brackets after the title of each paragraph of his book. He made an exception, however, when dealing with ministerial responsibility. In Chapter 13 of Part Three, where he treated the competence of the National Assembly, paragraph VII had the title 'Ministerial responsibility', but it remained without a reference in brackets. Jovanović split the text of the paragraph into two sub-paragraphs. One was 'Political responsibility', and the other 'Criminal responsibility'. The latter sub-paragraph nevertheless had a reference to sources in brackets. It was only the text on what was labelled as 'political responsibility of ministers' that remained without a reference to sources.[27] In one and a half pages of text concerning ministerial political responsibility, Jovanović skillfully and clearly explained the mechanism of parliamentary government. Jovanović's approach to the issue of ministerial responsibility at this point displays his predominantly continental European attitude. He was an excellent connoisseur of the British system of government, which he compared with the French in his theoretical schoolbook.[28] However, when treating the issue of parliamentary government in his country, he gave precedence to the ideas and precepts of European continental law and distinguished two types of ministerial responsibility.

9.5 Comparison

The three Serbian professors of constitutional law had different academic backgrounds. Matić received his formal training in law in the tradition of German academic liberalism, which preceded the 1848 revolution. Milovanović studied in Paris in the time of the liberal regime of the Third Republic. Jovanović was mostly influenced by the German academics active at the turn of the twentieth century, despite the fact that his journey took him also to Switzerland and France to receive his legal training.

---

26 ibid. Introduction, 33–85; Part One, 87–98; Part Two, 99–110; Part Three, 111–366; Part Four, 367–500; Part Five, 501–43.

27 ibid. 355–57.

28 S. Jovanović, *O državi*, 394–402.

Another point of difference between the three professors was their attitudes towards the models which they chose for their lectures. Matić clearly stated that he followed one of the German academics and practically adapted his professor's schoolbook for Serbian students. It was different with Milovanović. A thorough analysis of his posthumously published schoolbook does not lead to the identification of a model based on the French legal scholarship. It seems that Milovanović did not make use of any of the relevant French schoolbooks as an immediate role model for his lectures. He was, nevertheless, mostly under the influence of French authors. Jovanović went a step further. Although for the most part following the renowned German academics of his time, he managed to avoid the influence of one single national school of constitutional law. His approach was rooted in comparative law, the influences of which he skillfully shaped into a fruitful and – to a considerable extent – original synthesis. That is what made him the champion among Serbian legal scholars to date.

Despite all the differences which distinguish the three professors of constitutional law, there was a point in common for all of them. It consists in the line of stability which existed in respect of teaching and curricula, encompassing the concept and understanding of constitutional law. That area of law was perceived as a part of public law. This particular attitude lasted for almost a century, if we consider Matić's ascent to the university chair in 1848 as the starting point and the moment of retirement of Slobodan Jovanović in 1940 as its end.

PART THREE

Serbia and Yugoslavia

CHAPTER 10

A Long Episode and Beyond

10.1 Absorption

Formation of Yugoslavia

After World War I, Serbia was absorbed by the newly formed state of Southern Slavs, which at first took the name of the Kingdom of Serbs, Croats and Slovenes. It was only as of 1929 that the country was officially given the name of the Kingdom of Yugoslavia. However, the name Yugoslavia became known worldwide, and will be used here for reasons of brevity. The new kingdom emerged in December 1918 and, as is the case for many other issues, the Serbs and the Croats disagreed on the interpretation of facts concerning the foundation of the new state. Therefore, let us first consider the facts.

At the beginning of the war, which Austria-Hungary declared on Serbia in July 1914, the Serbian government initially declared that the goal of Serbian warfare was the defence of the country. However, the Serbian cabinet's stance altered in December of the same year. This was due to the circumstances that had meanwhile transformed the war between Austria-Hungary and Serbia into World War I. The National Assembly held its session in Niš and adopted the so-called Niš Declaration, in which it stated that Serbia was struggling for liberation and unification of the Serbs, Croats and Slovenes. Along with Croats and Slovenes, many Serbs lived in Austria-Hungary and were citizens of that country.[1]

A group of prominent Serbs, Croats and Slovenes from Austria-Hungary, exiled from that country and siding with the Entente Powers, formed a Yugoslav Committee in 1915 in London tasked with advocating the unification of all Southern Slavs in one independent state. The founding members were seven: four Croats, one Slovene and two Serbs. One of the Croats, Ante Trumbić, was chosen to chair the committee, which grew in number in the course of time. Serbian constitutional factors, the King, the Regent and the cabinet were in exile as of 1915, when the territory of Serbia was occupied by the Central Powers. After a conference held in Corfu in July 1917, the Yugoslav Committee and the Serbian government issued a joint declaration, known as the *Corfu Declaration*, in favour of Yugoslav unity. Its main idea was to invoke the principle of self-determination of nations that would speak in favour

1 S. Jovanović, *Ustavno pravo Kraljevine SHS*, 31.

 | DOI:10.30965/9783657791026_011

of the creation of one free and independent nation-state of all Serbs, Croats and Slovenes after the war. The declaration envisaged constitutional, democratic and parliamentary monarchy under the Karađorđević dynasty as the form of government.[2]

Towards the end of World War I, it became clear that the Austro-Hungarian monarchy was unlikely to survive. The situation on its territory worsened and approached chaos. In these circumstances, political representatives of the Slovenes, Croats and Serbs from the Austro-Hungarian lands inhabited by those three ethnicities formed the National Council in September 1918, with its seat in Zagreb. The National Council proclaimed itself to stand for political representation of all the Yugoslavs in Austria-Hungary. Its chair was a Slovene and his two deputies were a Croat and a Serb. The council required unification of the 'whole of our people, Slovenes, Croats and Serbs, on all of its ethnic territory … in one sovereign state'.[3]

The next step on the path to the formation of Yugoslavia was taken by the Croatian Diet. Croatia had held a special status within the complex constitutional settlement of the Habsburg monarchy since the Austro-Hungarian Compromise (*Ausgleich*) of 1867. Following the example of that constituent act, the Hungarians and the Croats made the Croato-Hungarian Compromise of 1868, by which Croatia obtained self-government and had its own government organs. Those were the head of government – *ban* – and the Croatian Diet, which was a representative body.[4] On 28 October 1918, Austria-Hungary asked for peace. The next day, the Croatian Diet proclaimed, invoking the principle of self-determination, that all public law relationships between Croatia on one side and Hungary and Austria on the other be resolved. The Diet proclaimed Croatia to be a completely free state, which 'according to the modern nationality principle, and on the grounds of national unity of the Slovenes, Croats and Serbs accedes to the common national and sovereign state … on the whole ethnic territory of that nation'.[5]

The National Council in Zagreb then started acting as a legitimate government of a new state of Slovenes, Croats and Serbs. It empowered the Yugoslav Committee in London to act in its stead in international relations. The Serbian government recognised the National Council as legitimate. However, that was the only recognition obtained. Other countries, including great powers,

2 ibid. 32.
3 ibid. 33.
4 On the organisation of Croatian self-government under the 1868 Compromise, cf. D. Popović, "Hrvatska" in: D. Jevtić and D. Popović, *Narodna pravna istorija*, 226–32.
5 S. Jovanović, *Ustavno pravo Kraljevine SHS*, 34.

refrained from recognition. That is how, in November 1918, three states existed on the territory that was to become known as Yugoslavia. Those were the State of Slovenes, Croats and Serbs just mentioned, the Kingdom of Montenegro and the Kingdom of Serbia.[6] The next stage in the formation of Yugoslavia was marked by the conference in Geneva at the beginning of November 1918, which had an agreement as its outcome. This was given the name of the *Geneva Declaration.* The deputies of the National Council and the Serbian government agreed on the creation of a new state in which the Serbs, Croats and Slovenes were to live united.

Several important events took place towards the end of November 1918. On 25 November the National Assembly elected for the territory of Vojvodina, convened in Novi Sad, proclaimed the unification of Vojvodina with the Kingdom of Serbia. On 26 November the Grand National Assembly of Montenegro in Podgorica proclaimed the unification of Montenegro with Serbia. On 27 November the National Council sent a delegation to Belgrade with the task of addressing the Serbian regent and declaring the wish of all Yugoslavs from Austria-Hungary to join a unified state that would encompass the whole territory inhabited by Southern Slavs.

Prince Regent Aleksandar Karađorđević (1888–1934) received the delegation of the National Council on 1 December 1918. In response to the address of the delegation, the regent proclaimed, in his father's name, 'the unification of Serbia with the lands of the independent state of Slovenes, Croats and Serbs into the unique Kingdom of Serbs, Croats and Slovenes'.[7] This was the foundation of the country which became known as Yugoslavia.

Different interpretations of the above-mentioned facts were given from the standpoint of public international law, as well as constitutional law. As for the first standpoint, it was clear that the new state, the Kingdom of Serbs, Croats and Slovenes, was a continuation of the Kingdom of Serbia. The second standpoint is, however, of interest for this volume. In that respect, one prevailingly Serbian thesis was that the new kingdom created on 1 December 1918 was a continuation of Serbia. The thesis met criticism for numerous reasons, e.g. the new state had a new name, its creation was communicated by way of diplomatic communication to all other countries, the new state launched the process of adopting a new constitution, etc.

---

6 ibid. 35.

7 On the address and the regent's proclamation, cf. Lj. Dimić, 'Uzroci Velikog rata, Srbija i jugoslovensko ujedinjenje' [Causes of the Great War, Serbia and Yugoslav unification], in: B. Begović and Z. Mirković (ed.), *Sto godina od ujedinjenja: stvaranje države i prava* [One hundred years since unification: creation of the state and rights], Belgrade 2020, 31–32; S. Jovanović, *Ustavno pravo Kraljevine SHS*, 37.

Another thesis, prevailingly Croatian, was that the constituent acts aimed at the formation of a new state had at their beginning an act of the Croatian Diet. By virtue of that act, the links concerning statehood between Croatia on the one side and Austria and Hungary on the other were resolved. The Croatian Diet issued the act in question invoking the old, traditional right of the Croats to have their own state. This stance was criticised from a procedural standpoint. Notably, it somehow construed the event and the regent's act of 1 December as an international act, i.e. a treaty. There was no ratification of such a treaty.

Still another thesis relied on the assumptions that were widely spread in the time of formation of Yugoslavia. According to this, the Serbs, Croats and Slovenes were one nation, and that nation was entitled to enjoy the right to self-determination. The idea, as presented in the language of the day, was that the unique nation of Southern Slavs had three different tribes, which nevertheless formed the nation. This was the stance adopted by the drafters of the first constitution of the new state. In brief, from the constitutional standpoint the state created on 1 December 1918 was a new state.[8] Its constitutional settlements had a characteristic evolution mostly rooted in the discussion of the third thesis mentioned in this text.

The 1921 Constitution – Adoption

The first constitution of the new state was adopted in June 1921 by the Constitutional Convention. That body was elected via universal male suffrage provided for by special legislation under the provisional government. The elections were held on 28 November 1920. There were four main political parties represented. Out of 419 deputies to the Constitutional Convention, the Democratic Party won ninety-two seats. The democrats were the successors of former independent radicals in pre-war Serbia. They had a thoroughly Yugoslav stance on the issue of national identity and considered the Serbs, Croats and Slovenes to be three tribes of one and the same nation. The Popular Radical Party, which was dominant in pre-war times in Serbia, won ninety-one seats in the Constitutional Convention, and the recently formed Communist Party won fifty-eight seats. The fourth-ranking party as regards the distribution of seats was the strongest political party among the Croats, the Croatian Peasant Party, with fifty seats. However, deputies belonging to that party refused to sit, because the party started advocating separatism as of 1920. Some smaller parties followed the example, so that eventually only

8 S. Jovanović, *Ustavno pravo Kraljevine SHS*, 39–51.

258 deputies participated in the work of the Constitutional Convention.[9] It opened sessions in mid-December 1920. The process of drafting a new constitution started in January 1921, when a drafting committee was appointed by the plenary to discuss draft constitutions stemming from various political parties, as well as from the provisional government.[10]

The government draft received the majority of votes in the drafting committee, so that first the committee and then the plenary of the Constitutional Convention proceeded on the basis of that draft. There were, nevertheless, several other drafts which did not pass to the plenary. The government's draft was the only one subject to debate. The final proposal was put to vote on 28 June 1921 and received 223 votes in favour and thirty-five against. However, 161 deputies did not take part in the ballot.[11] The date of voting for the 1921 Constitution was St Vitus' Day for the Serbian Orthodox Church. That is why the Constitution is usually known, including in academic writing, as the St Vitus Constitution.

The 1921 Constitution – Organisation of Power

According to Article 1 of the 1921 Constitution, the State of Serbs, Croats and Slovenes was a constitutional, parliamentary and hereditary monarchy. The Constitution text had a catalogue of human rights in its Section II (articles 4–21), under the title 'Fundamental Rights and Duties of Citizens'. It was followed by Section III (articles 22–44), which had the title 'Social and Economic Provisions'. Some of the fundamental rights were given protection in the latter section. An example can be found in Article 23 of the Constitution providing protection of women and minors at work.

The legislative power was vested in the King and National Assembly, according to Article 46 of the Constitution. By virtue of Article 47, the King was vested with executive power, performing it through responsible ministers. Article 48 conferred judicial power to the courts.

The National Assembly (articles 69–89) was a single-chamber body. One deputy was elected for 40,000 inhabitants in a universal, equal and direct male suffrage in a secret ballot. Article 78 of the Constitution empowered both

9 On the distribution of seats in the Constitutional Convention and the attitudes of political parties, cf. M. Zdravković, 'Formiranje države bez konsenzusa' [Forming a state without consensus], in: B. Begović and Z. Mirković, *Sto godina*, 63; D. Janković and M. Mirković, *Državnopravna istorija Jugoslavije* [State law history of Yugoslavia], Belgrade 1997, 344.

10 D. Jevtić, 'Najnovije doba (XX vek)' [The latest age: 20th century], in: D. Jevtić and D. Popović, *Narodna pravna istorija*, 258–260.

11 S. Jovanović, *Ustavno pravo Kraljevine SHS*, 65–71 (debates and ballot); 72–85 (other constitution drafts).

ministers and deputies to the National Assembly to introduce bills. The mandate of deputies was four years.[12] Article 91 of the Constitution provided that ministers were answerable both to the King and the National Assembly. The system of parliamentary government was envisaged, and it started functioning accordingly.

The King was the head of state, vested with promulgation of laws, and was also the commander in chief of the army. Article 56 of the Constitution provided for the rule of the Karađorđević dynasty. The King could grant amnesty, but if he were to use his power to pardon a minister he would need the approval of the National Assembly, as provided for by Article 50 of the Constitution. The King was empowered to convene and dissolve the National Assembly, but his act of dissolution had to contain a call for new parliamentary elections within three months. That was the provision of Article 52 of the Constitution. The King was also empowered to appoint responsible ministers to exercise executive power in his name. The King was not a decision maker.[13]

The ministers appointed by the King formed the council of ministers. That body was chaired by the President of the council of ministers, as provided for by Article 90 of the Constitution. The ministers were responsible before the National Assembly and could be challenged on any policy issue.[14]

The Council of State was, by virtue of Article 103 of the Constitution, the Supreme Administrative Court. For the appointments of councillors the old system existing in Serbian constitutions was preserved. The King was competent to appoint councillors based on the proposals coming from the National Assembly and the council of ministers.

The judiciary was regulated in only four Constitution articles (109–12). Judicial independence was guaranteed, and the Constitution provided for one Court of Cassation for the whole kingdom, with the seat in Zagreb. That was an idea that was never carried out, and the same was the case for the unification of the courts' system in general. The court systems existing in different parts of the country at the moment of unification were maintained. Due to the international obligations of the country, Sharia law applied in family law and the law of succession applied to citizens of the Muslim faith. The Sharia courts were organised following a pattern inherited from the Austro-Hungarian legislation for Bosnia and Herzegovina. In sum, the unification of law in the kingdom was not achieved under the 1921 Constitution, despite many efforts. The court

---

12 On the National Assembly *in extenso*, cf. S. Jovanović, *Ustavno pravo Kraljevine SHS*, 111–365.

13 ibid. 367–424.

14 ibid. 355–356.

system of the country remained complex even when the 1921 Constitution was no more in force. Its peculiar trait was the existence of multiple supreme jurisdictions for different parts of the country. Those instances were the Court of Cassation in Belgrade, the Table of Seven in Zagreb, the Supreme Court in Sarajevo and the High Court in Podgorica.[15]

The parliamentary government functioned as a multi-party system. It was characterised by instability of cabinets, despite the fact that most of the cabinets under the 1921 Constitution were headed by Serbian radicals. Pašić was the prime minister from the adoption of the Constitution until 1924, although he reshuffled his cabinets several times and formed different coalitions. The only exceptions to the radical prime ministers were Ljubomir Davidović (1863–1940), chief and founder of Democratic Party, whose cabinet lasted several months in 1924, and Anton Korošec (1872–1940), chief of the Slovene People's Party, who was a Roman Catholic priest. Korošec formed the cabinet in July 1928, at a moment of crisis of in the parliamentary system in the country, when that form of government collapsed.

Constitutional identity under the 1921 Constitution was to some extent linked to the issue of territorial organisation of the country. The two may appear even as facets of the same coin. The notion of constitutional identity is relatively modern and has a trend of replacing the concept of the sovereign subject, i.e. the person or body vested with sovereign power. The authors distinguish three types of constitutional identity: ethnocentric, based on citizenship and multi-cultural.[16] In his recent inspiring contribution to the discussion of the issue of constitutional identity, Tanasije Marinković claimed that the concept of integral yugoslavism, i.e. ethnocentric identity, was dominant in Yugoslavia until 1939. He nevertheless endeavoured to deviate from the thesis on ethnocentrism by finding elements of basing the state on citizenship, as well as elements of multi-culturalism in the 1921 Constitution.[17] It is true that such elements existed in the Constitution. However, taking into account the fact that there was no clear-cut expression on the issue in the Constitution text, the fundamental thesis should be upheld. The 1921 Constitution took the stand that Serbs, Croats and Slovenes were one and the same nation. For the sake of political reasons, mostly fearing Croatian separatism, the text remained silent on the issue as such. The integral yugoslavism was nevertheless the

15 cf. D. Popović, "Izjednačenje prava" in: D. Jevtić and D. Popović, *Narodna pravna istorija*, 302–05.

16 cf. T. Marinković, 'Ustavni identitet vidovdanske Jugoslavije' [The constitutional identity of Vidovdan Yugoslavia], in: B. Begović and Z. Mirković, *Sto godina*, 76–79.

17 ibid. 85–89.

founding idea of the 1921 Constitution. In some of its provisions, such a stance was clearly evident. That was the case for Article 19 of the Constitution, for example, which regulated access to public service and reserved it for nationals. Its text mentioned Serbo-Croato-Slovenian nationality.

The stance on the constitution identity issue was reflected in the territorial organisation of the State, provided for in articles 95 to 102 of the Constitution, which found their place in the text of Section VIII which was devoted to the executive power. The sub-national units were of several types, but the largest among them were *oblasti* (Serbian singular: *oblast*). They were decentralised units, which by virtue of Article 95 of the Constitution, could not have more than 800,000 inhabitants, and their delimitation was to follow natural, social and economic circumstances. Each *oblast* had its own organs, namely the *great župan* appointed by the King, as well as its assembly and council (Article 98). The *oblasti* were not enumerated in the Constitution text. They were subject to legislation. Since, due to parliamentary complications, the relevant law could not be adopted in time, the division of the state territory into *oblasti* was introduced by a government decree in 1922. There were a total of thirty-three.[18]

Collapse of Parliamentary Government and Introduction of Royal Dictatorship

The parliamentary system collapsed in 1928. A parliamentary government can function in a homogeneous society, which was for the most part the case in pre-World War I Serbia. Its political system was practically transplanted into the new Yugoslav state under the 1921 Constitution. The Constitution could not construe the structure of a society that was by no means homogeneous. Among many other issues provoking serious problems, the divergence of Croatian and Serbian views on constitutional matters was quite significant and increased tensions. The majority of Serbs were in favour of a unitary state, whereas the majority of Croats would have preferred a federation, or even some sort of confederation.

Political tensions were high. The Croats reproached Serbian hegemonism, the Serbs complained of Croatian separatism. In such circumstances, the spark which started the fire was an event that happened in the National Assembly. In a heated debate, full of verbal insults and death threats, one of the deputies, a Montenegrin Serb belonging to the Radical Party took a handgun and started shooting while the National Assembly was in session. He shot dead two Croatian deputies and mortally wounded the chief of the most influential

---

18 S. Jovanović, *Ustavno pravo Kraljevine SHS*, 452–56; cf. also D. Popović, *Osnovi ustavnog prava* [Fundamentals of constitutional law], Belgrade 2004, 141–42.

Croatian political party, who passed away several weeks later. The shooting in Parliament took place on 20 June 1928. In July the Crown invited Korošec, chief of the Slovene People's Party to form a cabinet. That move could not resolve the crisis, and the King introduced his direct rule on 6 January 1929.

The 1931 Constitution – General Approach

On 6 January 1929 the King made a coup d'état by introducing a royal dictatorship. The royal proclamation of that date presented the King's action as removing the intermediaries between the Crown and the people. The King issued new legislation, i.e. the Royal Power and Supreme State Administration Act, which defined the State as a hereditary monarchy, without any other attribute. However, since the King proclaimed himself legislator, the form of government was indeed an absolute monarchy.[19]

A royal act of October 1929 altered the name of the country, officially adopting 'Kingdom of Yugoslavia' for the first time. The same act introduced a new territorial organisation of the Kingdom. Instead of thirty-three *oblasti*, nine larger units were created. They were given the name of *banovina* (in Serbian singular; in plural: *banovine*). Outside of all of these was the administration of the City of Belgrade.[20] The *banovine* were named after local rivers. The Drava Banovina had a seat in Ljubljana. Its population practically encompassed all the Slovenes living in the country. The Croats lived in several banovinas, but had the majority in two. These were the Sava Banovina, with its seat in Zagreb, and the Littoral Banovina (Primorska) with its seat in Split. The latter was an exception, and was not named after a river. The Serbs were majoritarian in all other banovinas, and considered these to be the Serbian ethnic territory. However, the Croats contested some of the territories in the Danube, Vrbas, Drina and Zeta banovinas. The system of banovinas was preserved even after the end of royal dictatorship. The latter was transformed into a constitutional monarchy by way of the Constitution granted by the King in September 1931.

The organisation of power in the 1931 Constitution of Yugoslavia was different from the one envisaged in the 1921 Constitution. By virtue of Article 1 of the Constitution, Yugoslavia was a hereditary and constitutional monarchy. Like in the previous Constitution of 1921, sections II and III were devoted to the fundamental rights and duties of the citizens and social and economic provisions,

---

19 D. Popović, *Osnovi*, 142.
20 ibid. 143.

respectively. The constitutional guarantees in the text of 1931 were restricted in comparison to those of 1921.[21]

Articles 26 to 28 provided for the national branches of power. The legislative power was vested in the King and national representation. The latter consisted of the National Assembly and Senate. The executive power was vested in the King, who was to exercise it through responsible ministers. The courts were vested with judicial power.

According to Article 29 of the Constitution, the King was the depositary of the national unity and integrality of the state. Article 34 of the Constitution called for countersignatures, making it obligatory for all the King's acts. Nevertheless, the constitutional system was not an example of parliamentary government. Article 36 provided for the reign of the Karađorđević dynasty. Many articles of the Constitution text concerning the King and his powers were similar to those of the 1921 Constitution. However, the King influenced the decision-making process in a more accentuated way than was the case under the previous constitution.

The two houses of the national representation were not formed in the same way. Deputies to the National Assembly were elected by the people for a four-year term in universal, equal and direct ballot (Article 54). As was the case under the previous constitution, women did not have the right to vote. The Senate was elected only by one half. The senators had a six-year term of office. However, one half of the Senate was appointed by the King (articles 50 and 51).

The ministers were appointed by the King and formed a Ministerial Council (Article 77). Ministerial responsibility was provided for in principle (articles 79–80), but the whole constitutional settlement was not envisaged to function as a parliamentary government. The judiciary was given only two provisions in the Constitution text (articles 100 and 101). As regards the Council of State, it was mentioned only in Article 99 of the Constitution, which provided that the Council of State was the supreme administrative court of the kingdom. The same provision left all the issues concerning the Council of State, including the appointments of councillors, to the special legislation which should be enacted.

The 1931 Constitution – Functioning and Revision

The 1931 Constitution entered into force in September 1931, right after two years of dictatorship, i.e. the monarch's immediate rule, so that the political parties, forbidden under the dictatorship, could not easily recover and renew their

21 On restrictions of constitutional guarantees in the 1931 Constitution, cf. T. Marinković, 'Ustavni identitet', 92.

activities. As a result, the elections organised immediately after the granting of the Constitution were indeed a 'one-horse race': there was only one list presented to the electorate, and that list won all the seats. In 1934, King Aleksandar I was assassinated in Marseille while on a visit to France. The assassination was organised by the Bulgarian irredenta and Croatian separatists. The Kingdom of Yugoslavia entered into the period of regency. The most influential of the three regents was the late King's cousin, Prince Pavle Karađorđević (1893–1976).

An important feature of the 1931 constitutional settlement, important for its implementation, was to be found outside the Constitution text. It was the electoral legislation.[22] The Electoral Act of 10 September 1931 provided for public voting. The voter had to give his vote for a list *viva voce* in front of the electoral board. Apart from the provision on voting publicly, the electoral legislation had two main features. One of these concerned the candidates' lists, the other the distribution of seats after parliamentary elections. As to the lists of candidates running for office, the leader of the list was allowed to present it only if he could put forward candidates in all constituencies of the country. This requirement was difficult to meet for many political parties, especially those that were smaller or were ethnically labelled in their names. As noticed above, in the elections of 1931 there was only one list presented, and it won all the seats. Over time, this kind of electoral regulation resulted in the creation of electoral blocks sometimes composed of parties that were different in their fundamental political programs and attitudes.

Another feature of the electoral legislation produced the same outcome. Notably, the system of electoral prime was introduced. It favoured the strongest list presented in the elections. The winner of the elections at the national level received two-thirds of the seats in the National Assembly, no matter how small the margin of victory. Two parliamentary elections were held while this legislation was in force. In 1935 the government list – led by prime minister Bogoljub Jevtić (1886–1960) under the name of the Yugoslav National Party – won by 303 seats (and 60.65% of the votes) to 67 seats (37.32%) against the United Opposition, whose leader was Vladko Maček (1879–1964), chief of Croatian Peasant Party. The system was rather generously weighted towards the strongest. A list that obtained some 60% of votes gained more than 89% of the seats.[23]

22 D. Popović, *Osnovi*, 144; on the electoral legislation of Yugoslav monarchy in general, cf. B. Balkovec, 'Izborno zakonodavtsvo prve jugoslavenske države (1918–1941)' [Electoral Legislation of the First Yugoslav State (1918–1941)], *Časopis za suvremenu povijest*, 1/2016, 197–216.

23 On the 1935 parliamentary elections, cf. D. Janković and M. Mirković, *Državnopravna istorija Jugoslavije*, Belgrade 1989, 394.

This story was repeated in the 1938 parliamentary election, the last held in the Yugoslav monarchy, but with slight differences. The two blocks were more profiled. Prime Minister Milan Stojadinović (1888–1961) led the list of the Yugoslav Radical Union, composed of the Popular Radical Party, Slovene Popular Party and Yugoslav Muslim Organisation. It was opposed by a list once again led by Maček, and composed of the Croatian Peasant Party, Independent Democratic Party, Democratic Party, Agrarian Party and Montenegrin Federalist Party. The government list won, but this time by a significantly smaller ratio of 54.1% to 44.9% of votes. In terms of seats, the ratio was, however, 306 to 67.[24]

The fundamental idea of the 1931 Constitution was to uphold Yugoslav unity. The electoral system served the purpose to some extent, by way of coercing different political parties to find common grounds in order to present a joint list. That was nevertheless achieved to the detriment of electoral justice.

The constitutional identity in the 1931 Constitution was rooted in accentuated integral yugoslavism, inspired by the Crown. That was a continuation of King Aleksandar's policies during his immediate rule between 1929 and 1931. The King intended to introduce national unity by way of decree. His endeavour quite simply contradicted the facts. An illustration of the discrepancy between the royal wishes and reality was Article 3 of the 1931 Constitution, which provided for the official language. According to that provision, the official language of the Kingdom of Yugoslavia was Serbo-Croato-Slovenian. There was, however, no such language at all. It could be discussed, especially after the mid-1850s and the achievements of Austrian cultural policies, whether the language of the Serbs and the Croats was one or two.[25] The Slovenian language was clearly different, and its speakers had difficulties understanding the Croats and the Serbs. These two main ethnic groups, for their part, had different views on the foundations of the state they lived in. Most of the Serbs understood it in the last analysis, at least, as a nation-state of Yugoslavs, whereas the majority of Croats perceived the country as a multi-ethnic state.[26]

Conflicting ideas on constitutional and national identity were reflected in the text and in the implementation of the 1931 Constitution. Its text preserved the territorial organisation of the kingdom that had been introduced under the royal dictatorship (articles 83–95). Article 83 of the 1931 Constitution was by far the largest in the Constitution text. It preserved the territorial organisation of

24 ibid. 395.

25 On the language cultural policies and the so-called Vienna Agreement on the language, cf. P. Ivić and J. Kašić, 'O jeziku kod Srba u razdoblju od 1804. do 1878. godine' [About the language of the Serbs in the period from 1804 to 1878], in: *Istorija srpskog naroda V-2*, Belgrade 1981, 360–63.

26 T. Marinković, 'Ustavni identitet', 94.

the Kingdom of Yugoslavia that had been introduced in 1929. There were nine *banovinas*. They were enumerated in Article 83 in geographical order, from the west to the east, along with the cities in which their representation organs and administration had seats. The Drava Banovina had a seat in Ljubljana, the Sava Banovina in Zagreb, the Vrbas Banovina in Banja Luka, the Littoral Banovina in Split, the Drina Banovina in Sarajevo, the Zeta Banovina in Cetinje, the Danube Banovina in Novi Sad, the Morava Banovina in Niš and the Vardar Banovina in Skopje. According to Article 85 of the Constitution, the territory of the city of Belgrade, including Zemun and Pančevo, was under its own separate administration.

Two features of this territorial division of the kingdom are worth remarks. Firstly, the previous system introduced under the royal dictatorship was not only maintained, but indeed promoted to represent a part of the Constitution text and subsequently enjoy more solid protection. It could be altered only by way of constitutional amendment. Secondly, Article 83 of the 1931 Constitution in its long text went so far as to delineate the borders of the banovinas in a precise manner, which was quite unusual for Constitution texts. Not only could the system as such not be altered, but that was also the case with the borders of banovinas provided for in the Constitution. In other words, both the status of banovinas and their borders became constitutionally entrenched.

In articles 86 to 98 of the Constitution, the uniform organisation of power in the banovinas was provided for. In each banovina there was a *ban*, appointed by the King as a representative of the state executive power. Along with the ban, there were self-governing bodies in each banovina. They were *bansko veće* (Banovina Council) and *banska uprava* (Banovina Administration). The latter was appointed by the former. The Banovina Council was empowered to adopt a budget for each year. The King was competent to appoint the public servants in a banovina, but only on the proposal of the Banovina Administration.

By virtue of Article 91 of the Constitution, the Banovina Council was entitled to pass sub-legislation by way of decrees, on the proposal of the Banovina Administration. The banovina sub-legislation was subject to control of legality. Notably, the ban was competent to promulgate banovina decrees, but before promulgation he had to ask for the approval of the Council of State for each act. Should the Council of State remain silent, within a month the approval was presumed.

The constitutional system of 1931 was set up in an atmosphere of tensions between the two main ethnic groups within the State, namely the Croats and the Serbs. As mentioned above, the Slovenes were concentrated in the Drava Banovina, the Croats comprised the majority in two (Sava and Littoral) and the Serbs in the remaining six banovinas. Despite the fact that the banovinas' borders were constitutionally entrenched, the territorial division of the country was contested, which indeed put the whole system into question. The issue was linked with questions regarding the character of the state and constitutional identity.

Although it was evident in the 1930s that Yugoslavia was not a nation-state, many of the Serbs tended to perceive it exactly as such. That was, however, not the case for all political parties enjoying support in the ethnic Serbian electorate; some were ready to accept federalism. On the other side, many of the Croats were in favour of reorganising the state and introducing federalism. At least, that was the stance of the most influential Croatian political party. Such differences, and debates originating from them, obtained the label of the 'Croatian question', which required a solution by way of negotiations. It was clear and universally accepted that on the Croatian side the principal negotiator would be Vladko Maček, the leader of the Croatian Peasant Party, which was by far the strongest among Croats. On the Serbian side that would be the Yugoslav prime minister, since the post, with one exception already mentioned which occurred in 1928, was always occupied by a Serb.

The most influential regent, Prince Pavle, played a significant role in brokering a deal to be the solution to the greatest political and constitutional problem of Yugoslavia. After the parliamentary elections of 1935, Prince Pavle invited financial expert and former minister Milan Stojadinović to form a cabinet. Stojadinović became prime minister in June 1935 and remained in office until February 1939. Despite the fairly successful outcome of the prime minister's policies in the economic sphere, he was unable to resolve the Croatian question, which had been one of his most important assignments. It was the time of dictatorships in Europe. Stojadinović became a strong man in the country and was feared by some to be inclined to transform himself into a sort of authoritarian leader. Nevertheless, his crucial problem, which eventually decided his political fate, consisted in the failure to resolve the Croatian question. The undisputed Croatian leader, Maček, declared he was not ready to negotiate the issue with Stojadinović. To soothe tensions and enable negotiations, Prince Pavle dismissed Stojadinović and appointed a new prime minister in February 1939. This time, his choice was Dragiša Cvetković (1893–1969), a minister in the former cabinet. Cvetković did not have the political background of the previous prime minister, and his main task was to facilitate the approach to the solution of the Croatian question through negotiation.

An agreement between Serbian and Croatian political leaders was supposed to resolve the issue. From a legal and constitutional standpoint, the negotiations of the Croats and Serbs took the shape of negotiations between the Yugoslav government and the strongest opposition party, which represented the Croats – the Croatian Peasant Party. The subject of negotiations was inevitably the alteration of the 1931 constitutional settlement, i.e. the Constitution revision. There were only three provisions in Section XII of the 1931 Constitution (articles 114 to 116) regarding revision, i.e. on the adoption of constitutional amendments. Article 114 was explicit regarding the competence to introduce amendments. Two constitutional factors disposed of such powers – the King and the national representation. There was no mention of regency. Article 115 provided on the procedure, requiring a qualified majority in the houses of national representation for the proposal and an absolute majority in the national representation after new elections for the adoption of amendments. The procedure was difficult to pursue for many reasons. Apart from those rooted domestically, such as, for instance, possible discontent regarding constitutional amendments among voters, there was also the international situation, which was burdened by the threat of war in Europe.

Article 116 of the Constitution contained an emergency clause. It empowered the King to introduce extraordinary measures, irrespective of constitutional and legal provisions, in the case of 'war, mobilisation, disorder or revolt'. Once again, there was no mention of regency. Even leaving aside the issues of regency, replacing the King and acting in his stead and amending a constitution under a regency, for the latter had already occurred in Serbian constitutional history, Article 116 still posed a problem. Not one of the requirements envisaged by its provision was present at the moment when legal experts of both sides in the negotiations agreed that Article 116 offered the only way of amending the Constitution. The Cvetković cabinet was formed at the beginning of February 1939. At the very beginning, and standing before the National Assembly, the prime minister stated his firm commitment to resolve the most serious political problem of the country. It was towards the end of March the same year that three professors of law from the Belgrade University School of Law, invited to act as counsels to the prime minister, agreed on the best path to follow in principle. The three professors were Đorđe Tasić (1892–1943), Mihailo Ilić (1888–1944) and Mihailo Konstantinović (1897–1982). Konstantinović was at the same time the justice minister in the Cvetković cabinet.[27] The idea of an agreement that the Croats and the Serbs might conclude on the reorganisation of the Yugoslav kingdom inevitably led to giving up the concept of integral

27 cf. M. Konstantinović, *Politika sporazuma – dnevničke beleške 1939–1941; londonske beleške 1944–1945* [Agreement Policy – Diary Notes 1939–1941; London Notes 1944–1945], Novi Sad 1998, 13–20.

yugoslavism. It represented the first step towards introducing a federal constitutional settlement in the country.[28]

After several months of negotiations on sensitive issues, the Serbo-Croatian agreement was reached at the end of August 1939, bringing the revision of the 1931 Constitution as a consequence. The substance of the revision was more important than its form, albeit the latter was also significant. The Serbo-Croatian Agreement substantially altered the constitutional settlement of the Kingdom of Yugoslavia, because it served as a pretext of a decree, issued on the grounds of royal powers contained in Article 116 of the 1931 Constitution. The political agreement has become known as the *Cvetković–Maček Agreement*. The two politicians entered into cooperation in a new cabinet, headed by Cvetković, in which Maček took the office of deputy prime minister.

The Cvetković–Maček Agreement materialised in a regency decree of 26 August 1939, bearing the name of the *Decree on Croatian Banovina*. Its main features were as follows. First and foremost, the Croatian Banovina was not named after a river, but after one of the ethnic groups inhabiting the country. Its territory was composed of the territory of two banovinas with Croatian majority populations, which merged into one. Eight districts which had previously belonged to four different banovinas were added and incorporated into the Croatian Banovina. At the same time, the Croatian Banovina obtained a special status,[29] one that was different from the status that the banovinas enjoyed under the 1931 Constitution. In principle, the central government of the Kingdom retained competence in matters of foreign policy, defence, security, trade and transport. The rest was transferred to the Croatian Banovina, to fall within its competence. Article 2 of the Decree of 26 August 1939 was complex and contained a presumption of competence in favour of central government. Nevertheless, there were two enumerations of competences, one of those in favour of the Croatian Banovina and the other in favour of the central government. The text more or less reflected the sensitivity of the issue and of the political negotiations leading to the final political deal.

The organs of the Croatian Banovina were *ban* and *sabor*. The latter was a one- chamber representative body which was given the same name that similar bodies had traditionally had in Croatia. The *ban* of a Croatian Banovina was in a position somewhat different from his colleagues in other banovinas. All bans were appointed by the King, but the ban of the Croatian Banovina was entitled to countersign his own appointment (Article 8 of the Decree). By virtue of Article 5 of the Decree, the ban of the Croatian Banovina was entitled

28 T. Marinković, *Serbia*, 58.

29 D. Jevtić, 'Najnovije doba (XX vek)', 300–01.

to countersign all King's acts that had force in the banovina. Last, but not least, Article 9 provided that the Croatian ban could be put on trial by way of accusation of the Sabor and not by the National Assembly. A special tribunal was provided to try the ban. It was composed of Croatian judges.

After the creation of the Croatian Banovina, the ethnic situation in the Kingdom of Yugoslavia was peculiar. To the west of the new banovina there was the Drava Banovina, inhabited by the Slovenes. The Serbs lived as a minority in the Croatian Banovina, but they represented the majority in all banovinas lying east of it. The constitutional system was heading towards federalism and trialism. Politicians and experts required the formation of a Serbian unit within the Kingdom of Yugoslavia.[30] A draft decree was produced, aimed at creating a Serbian territorial unit composed of all the banovinas with a Serbian majority. That unit was given the name of Banovina of Serbian Lands. Its formation was supposed to be the next step in the reorganisation of the Kingdom. The issue was one of the topics during the Serbo-Croatian negotiations on amending the Constitution through the formation of the Croatian Banovina.[31] However, the question of introducing a federal structure in the Kingdom of Yugoslavia did not come to the agenda. Turbulent events overtook; there was no room for further adjustments of the constitutional settlement.

The government Cvetković–Maček, also known as the government of National Agreement, was formed on 26 August 1939. It worked in difficult circumstances, marked by the beginning of World War II only a week after its formation. The situation on the fronts, the battle of France, German plans to invade Britain and unsuccessful Italian warfare in Greece brought Yugoslavia into a complex position. The country was encircled by Nazi Germany and its allies forming the pact of the axis powers. Yugoslavia was invited to join the club. The cabinet could not decide on the issue alone. Prince Pavle convened an informal body – the Crown Council composed of the principal cabinet ministers, army generals and some others – to consult on the subject. The military estimations were that it was impossible to defend the country. The Yugoslav army would not be able to resist a possible attack of the Germans and their allies. On the other hand, there was a generous and seductive offer to join the Tripartite Pact, accompanied by a proposal to capture the port of Thessaloniki in Greece. With heavy hearts, the Prince Regent and the cabinet decided to join the pact. On 25 March 1941, in the Belvedere Palace in Vienna, Prime Minister Cvetković signed the accession document, by virtue of which Yugoslavia joined the Tripartite Pact. In the night between 26 and 27 March, a coup d'état

30 M. Konstantinović, *Politika sporazuma*, 83, 89, 94.

31 M. Konstantinović, *Politika sporazuma*, 523.

took place. A group of army officers, sympathetic to the British, overturned the government and the regency. Prince Pavle's nephew, Petar Karađorđević (1923–70), who was heir to the throne, was proclaimed to be of a suitable age to accede to the throne. A new government was formed under the leadership of one of the generals who organised the coup. A catastrophe followed. Germany and its allies attacked Yugoslavia on 6 April 1941. The royal army crashed, and after twelve days of war the whole country was occupied. King Petar II and his government went into exile.

10.2 Reappearance

Yugoslavia in World War II

Yugoslavia was occupied in 1941. Soon after the occupation, resistance showed up. It had two main factions: one was legitimistic and the other revolutionary. The first had military forces officially labelled as the Yugoslav Army in the Fatherland, usually known as *chetniks* (*četnici*). The second force was the People's Liberation Army, whose members were called *partisans* (*partizani*). The legitimist troops had General Dragoljub 'Draža' Mihailović (1893–1946) as commander in chief, whereas the partisans' commander was Tito, whose real name was Josip Broz (1892–1980). Tito was secretary general of the Communist Party of Yugoslavia, which had been banned as of the 1920s. He was also a functionary of the international communist movement.

The two factions of Yugoslav resistance cooperated in the beginning; however, their cooperation was over in 1942 and they engaged in a ferocious civil war. The great powers had a sensitive attitude towards Yugoslav resistance factions and the civil war in the country. As of the end of 1943, they were supportive of the People's Liberation Army. That army won the civil war in Yugoslavia, and at its end in 1945 instituted a communist government in the country.[32] In communist Yugoslavia, Serbia reappeared as a sub-national unit.

Communist Constitutional Settlements – Foundation

The communist constitutional settlement in Yugoslavia was forged between 1943 and 1945. Towards the end of November 1943, in Jajce, a little Bosnian city, the political representation of the partisans' movement was transformed into the germ of a government representative body. Along with that transformation, an executive body was formed under the name of the National Committee of Liberation of Yugoslavia. The royal government in exile thus obtained a rival.

32 D. Popović, *Osnovi*, 146–47.

Tito became the head of the National Committee and was proclaimed Marshal of Yugoslavia. A resolution of the representative body banned the King in exile and his cabinet from returning to the country. Post-war Yugoslavia, it was then decided, was to be founded on 'democratic principle as a union of equal peoples'.

The communists tended to pursue their policy, labelled as 'brotherhood and unity' in Yugoslavia. The political settlement they introduced was based on republicanism and federalism. In power at the end of the war, the communists organised elections for the Constitutional Convention in mid-November 1945. The elections were boycotted by the opposition, which claimed to have faced intimidation. Running in a one-horse race, the governing People's Front, dominated by the Communist Party of Yugoslavia, won more than 90% of votes cast, as well as all of the seats.[33] Towards the end of November, the Constitutional Convention proclaimed the institution of the republican form of government. The issue of federalism had been entrenched already, given the fact that the Constitutional Convention was elected as a two-house body. The Constitutional Convention adopted the first republican constitution of the country in January 1946. That was the beginning of the second Yugoslavia, dominated by the communists, which introduced a new constitutional settlement. Despite different transformations, the Yugoslav republic faced in its further developments it never abandoned three characteristic features, being republicanism, federalism and the communist rule. Notably, the foundations of the Yugoslav republic were not sufficiently clear.

The general idea of the founding fathers in 1943 seemed to be of an ethnic federation, since the equality of peoples was mentioned. The idea materialised in recognition of the fact that peoples of certain groups had not been treated as such before World War II. We have seen above that behind the idea of integral yugoslavism that was favoured in the times of monarchy there was indeed a trialistic approach to the question of ethnic identity. Three ethnic groups were recognised from the beginning of Yugoslavia: Serbs, Croats and Slovenes. During the war, two other groups achieved recognition: Montenegrins and Macedonians. Right after the war, these five groups were usually enumerated as constituent ethnicities of Yugoslavia. Notably, Article 1 of the 1946 Constitution provided that the Yugoslav state was 'a community of peoples equal in rights who, on the basis of the right to self-determination, including the right to secession, have expressed their will to live together in a federative state'.[34] It was clear, therefore, that the country was organised as an ethnic

33 D. Janković and M. Mirković, *Državnopravna istorija Jugoslavije*, 487.

34 On the nation-state character of federated republics, cf. T. Marinković, *Serbia*, 67.

federation. Article 9 of the Constitution followed the same path. It provided on the sovereignty of the peoples' republics which were the components of Yugoslavia. Each people thus had its own homeland, which was a fact reflected at a symbolic level as well. Article 3 of the 1946 Constitution regulated the coat of arms of the country, describing it in detail. It was a unique flame, made of five torches. The torches represented the five recognised peoples of Yugoslavia.

There were five peoples officially recognised, but the federation nevertheless consisted of six federated republics. These were, from west to east: Slovenia, Croatia, Bosnia and Herzegovina, Montenegro, Serbia and Macedonia. Each of the constituent peoples had a republic, but the Republic of Bosnia and Herzegovina was differently conceptualised. The Muslim population of that republic were not called Bosniaks, as it is the case today, but were referred to as Muslims, being always mentioned along with Serbs and Croats. The three groups inhabited Bosnia and Herzegovina in large numbers. As regards its constitutional identity, Bosnia and Herzegovina was considered to be a homeland of the Serbs, Croats and Muslims who lived there. The latter were not recognised at first as an ethnic group. It was in the course of time, i.e. in the 1960s, that the Muslims, still named in that way, were recognised as a people in the sense used in Yugoslav constitutional law, and not only as a religious community.[35] Therefore, properly speaking, the federation created in Yugoslavia at the end of World War II was not an ethnic federation, at least not in full. Five federated republics had ethnicity at their origin, but not the sixth, which escaped the rule. The foundations of the federation, and its founding myth, were lacking a clear principle.

Another weak point of the founding myth of the Yugoslav federation consisted in its disregard for internal minorities. On the one hand, the federated republics of Yugoslavia were construed as homelands of constituent nations: practically speaking, they were federated nation-states. On the other hand, the constituent peoples of Yugoslavia, with the exception of Slovenes and Macedonians, did not inhabit compact territories. They lived mixed, so that for instance there was a significant Serbian minority in Croatia, and vice versa a smaller Croatian minority in Serbia. There also was a Bosniak Muslim minority in Serbia and in Montenegro, etc. On top of that, one of the federated republics, as noted above, was not a nation-state.

The internal minorities in Yugoslavia, i.e. the Yugoslav ethnicities living in a large number outside of their main republics, did not enjoy minority rights. In some political declarations and Constitution texts, their authors tried to brush

---

35 cf. D. Popović, 'Le fédéralisme de l'ancienne Yougoslavie revisité; Qu'est-ce qui n'a pas fonctionné?' *Revue internationale de politique comparée* 10/2003, 44.

the problem under the carpet by introducing formulas aimed at the satisfaction of certain groups, but the problem could by no means be resolved that way.[36] The deficiencies of the original concept of the federation were grave, and along with the lack of legitimacy and democratic institutions they determined the destiny of Yugoslavia.[37] The weak points of the main concept were reflected in Constitution texts, whose number evidenced the instability of the whole state construction and the basic constitutional settlement.

Developments – Initial Phase

Several constitutions were adopted in Yugoslavia between 1945 and the dismantling of the country in the 1990s. The constitutional system was indeed marked by instability. This becomes evident when enumerating the crucial years of Yugoslavia's constitutional developments after World War II. These years were 1946, 1953, 1963 and 1974. In 1953 the constitution in force was amended in the manner of a total revision, whereas in 1946, 1963 and 1974 new constitutions were adopted. Between the last two dates mentioned, a good number of constitutional amendments had intervened, before the adoption of a completely new constitution occurred. In sum, there were three constitutions, one total revision and more than forty constitutional amendments in forty-six years.

The first constitution of Yugoslavia after World War II was the one of 1946. That constitution was in many aspects a copy-paste of the Soviet constitution of 1936. The model of organisation of power at the federal level was the same in both constitutions. There was a two-house representative body, in which one of the houses was the representation of the people and the other of the federated republics. The representative body appointed the council of ministers and another body, named the Presidency, which was the head of state.[38]

Serbia reappeared in the 1946 Constitution of Yugoslavia as one of its federal units, i.e. federated republics. As such, Serbia was given a somewhat specific position, being the only federated republic which had autonomous units within itself. These were Vojvodina in the north and Kosovo and Metohija in the south. Kosovo and Metohija was at first a district, but in the course of political and constitutional developments it was promoted to the status of autonomous province, a status that was originally granted only to Vojvodina. Apart from official, ideological explanations for such a settlement within Serbia, the issue of its origin remains unresearched to date. The usual explanation was based

36 ibid. 48.

37 ibid. 47–50 for the deficiencies of the founding myth of the Yugoslav federation and their consequences.

38 T. Marinković, *Serbia*, 62–63.

on the presence of minorities in the two territories – Albanians in Kosovo and Metohija, and Hungarians in Vojvodina. However, minorities in other federated republics were not given such autonomous status. Two circumstances may have been influential in the introduction of this system. Firstly, it imitated the position of Russia within the USSR. Secondly, at the beginning of the communist rule in Yugoslavia Tito feared to some extent the possible opposition of the royalist circles and followers of pre-World War II political parties in Serbia.[39] That fear was only partly justified. There was no opposition activity in the proper sense of the term. Tito consolidated his power firmly and easily and became at once the strong man of the regime.

Under the 1946 Constitution, the strong man of the regime and the real power holder, Tito, was the prime minister and at the same time secretary general of the Communist Party, the only Party existing in the country. If comparing to the USSR, Tito's position within the system in Yugoslavia could be said to have equalled Stalin's position in the USSR.

In the late 1940s, there was a rupture in the communist movement at an international scale. Its protagonists were Stalin and Tito. The former was the undisputed chief of all communists in the world, to whom the latter denied obedience and obtained support from the West for his dissidence. Yugoslavia became a dissident communist country, no longer faithful to the block of states that were at the time called popular democracies. The dispute of the two national leaders provoked consequences for constitutional developments in Yugoslavia.

The form of government remained unaltered immediately after the dispute between the two leaders, but in the course of time the Yugoslav communists tended to introduce changes in order to achieve two goals. Their first goal was to spread propaganda in the West that the political system in Yugoslavia was more liberal than in Soviet-dominated countries. The second goal was similar. The Yugoslav communists wanted to prove that there were profound differences between the two versions of communist rule in terms of Marxist ideology. The latter idea led to a change concerning the rigid system of planned economy, which was abandoned. Workers' management was introduced instead, albeit efficiently supervised by the ruling party.

In 1953 the constitutional settlement was altered, by way of adopting a special Constitutional Act. The 1953 Constitutional Act altered exclusively the provisions on the organisation of power found in the 1946 Constitution which was then in force. Self-management had already been introduced by way of legislation, and the decision makers must have considered the existing provisions

39 D. Popović, 'Le fédéralisme de l'ancienne', 43.

on individual rights in the 1946 Constitution to be quite sufficient. That is why only the organisation of power was reshaped by the introduction of considerable alterations. The collective head of state of the 1946 Constitution was abolished. A two-house representative body at the federal level of government was empowered by virtue of Article 15 of the Constitutional Act to elect the President of the Republic for a term of office equal to the one of the representative body itself. Articles 71 and 72 provided that the President of the Republic was the head of state and at the same time head of government, which was renamed the Federal Executive Council. Needless to say, Tito was elected President of the Republic, thus making his position within the constitutional system fairly transparent. He was secretary general of the Communist Party, the head of state and the prime minister. The form of government introduced by the 1953 Constitutional Act concluded the earlier phase of developments in socialist Yugoslavia. It was followed by another in which Tito's position within the constitutional settlement was the crucial issue; this was accompanied by the problem of his succession in power.

Developments – Crucial Issue

Throughout the constitutional history of socialist Yugoslavia, the official doctrine treated constitutional changes and developments from the ideological standpoint of an allegedly progressive evolution of the socialist system of self-management introduced in the 1950s. That was, however, only one facet of the coin, notably the official one. Its purpose was to obscure the real process of constitutional developments, consisting in the power struggle behind the scenes. Within the power struggle, the crucial issue was Tito's place in the constitutional and political settlement. Each constitutional change concerned that issue, as well as the one of the competence of the federation and federated republics. The two issues were connected. Tito's personal position was prevalent in the beginning of the second phase of developments. That phase started with the adoption of the 1963 Constitution, in which once again Tito's position was altered if compared to the previous constitutional settlement. In brief, the office of the head of state was separated from the one of prime minister. Tito was seventy years of age at the moment of adopting the 1963 Constitution, so that he remained the head of state and the chief of the only party existing in the country. He was no longer prime minister, having thus left the conduct of day-to-day government business to others, yet he retained the position of undisputed leader and was by far the most powerful politician in the country.[40]

40 D. Popović, 'Le fédéralisme de l'ancienne', 45; T. Marinković, *Serbia*, 65–67.

With an elderly leader in the situation in which the power was practically concentrated in one decision maker only, the question of succession inevitably appeared. The constitutional system as such seemed to have envisaged the leader's succession in power by way of introducing the office of vice President at the federal level of government. The provisions concerning terms of office of the President and vice President were peculiar. Notably, Article 220 of the 1963 Constitution provided for a presidential term of office of four years. The same person could be elected for another consecutive term, but the same provision excluded *expressis verbis* any limitation of tenure of office for Josip Broz Tito. In principle, any person could hold presidential office for two consecutive terms. It was, nevertheless, different for the office of vice President. Article 223 of the Constitution provided that the same person holding the office 'shall not be re-elected for a consecutive term'. Apparently the system was more rigid for the vice presidential office than for the head of state. This becomes understandable if some political facts are taken into account.

The Vice President of the Federal Republic became a Serb, Aleksandar Ranković (1909–83) – a fact which somehow created the impression that the successor to the country leadership would come from that ethnic group. Tito himself was a Croat. The presumed successor in power was a hardline communist, former minister of the interior and one of Tito's closest and most faithful collaborators, who controlled the secret service. These facts, in addition to the informal public opinion at the time of events, would have suggested that the elected vice President would be Tito's designated successor. However, neither the particular solution of the problem, nor the mode of political succession in general could hold water. The whole scheme only lasted for a little more than three years.[41]

Ranković was to remain in office until spring 1967, but he was politically eliminated in summer 1966 and had to resign. In finding a replacement for Ranković, it was clear that ethnicity played a role in the whole issue of Tito's succession. Another Serb took the office of vice President. It was Koča Popović (1908–92), former minister of foreign affairs, considerably different as a person from the man he replaced. Having spent twelve years in office as foreign minister, he was without proper political ambitions and heading for retirement. Popović belonged to a group of so-called Serbian liberals among the communists. The fall of Ranković, as Tito's presumed successor, could therefore be considered an achievement of the liberal tendency in Yugoslav politics under the communist regime. This was only partly true, however. Ranković was viewed as a communist hardliner and a supporter of the idea of a rather centralised

41 D. Popović, 'Le fédéralisme de l'ancienne', 45–46.

form of government. His main opponent in the communist nomenclature was Edvard Kardelj (1910–79), a Slovene politician who favoured decentralisation trends and was a sort of official theorist of Yugoslav socialism. Allegedly, Tito did not support Kardelj against Ranković wholeheartedly. There was a power struggle behind it. It has been remarked that a younger generation of communist elites rooted in the government structures of federated republics strove for more competence at that level of government. They perceived the hardliner as a threat to their careers.[42]

The struggle for Tito's succession went on, and the political crash of a strong man among the Serbs brought new issues to the agenda. The communist elites in the federated republics became more powerful than ever before, and in many aspects embraced nationalist stances. Although the nationalism of the elites in federated republics was in conflict with the leading idea of 'brotherhood and unity', it came to the surface little by little, so as to eventually dilute yugoslavism and the whole concept of the Yugoslav state.

Some scholars expressed the view that the concept of Yugoslavia as a federation of five constituent peoples and six federated republics was at the beginning grounded in the idea labelled as 'partisan yugoslavism'. It relied on the concept of brotherhood and unity and rooted its legitimacy in the Yugoslav socialist revolution. That kind of legitimacy was slowly replaced by 'socialist yugoslavism', which was identified with loyalty towards the self-management system. However, both concepts were attempts to create new sentiments of community at the level of Yugoslavia that would overcome ethnic tensions. They were performed in the one-party political system, under the rule of a centralised Communist Party.[43] Standpoints on Yugoslav identity were called into question already in the time of drafting a new constitution, which was adopted in February 1974.

The 1974 Constitution was the last one adopted in communist Yugoslavia. Some scholars labelled it as the gravedigger of Yugoslavia.[44] Instead of a federation, the 1974 Constitution introduced a confederal political settlement, despite the fact that such a transformation was not recognised in the official doctrine. It was evident in the Founding Principles of the Constitution,

42 T. Marinković, *Serbia*, 68; Tito's widow, Jovanka Broz, confirmed the idea of Ranković as Tito's successor in an interview given years ago, and published recently: cf. the Belgrade daily, *Danas*, 10 June 2020. She also revealed intrigues regarding communist elites.

43 J. Dragović-Soso, *Saviours of the Nation – Serbia's Intellectual Opposition and the Revival of Nationalism*, London 2002, 22–46; cf. also S. Malešević, 'Ethnicity and Federalism in Communist Yugoslavia and its Successor States', in: Y. Ghai (ed.), *Autonomy and Ethnicity*, Cambridge 2000, 154–56, 167–68.

44 cf. R. Marković, *Ustavno pravo*, Belgrade 2020, 139.

especially in determining the mode of decision making at the level of Yugoslavia, based on consensus of its constituent parts.[45] The background of the 1974 Constitution lies in the failure of the political system introduced in 1963. The latter was based on the concept of appointing a successor to Tito. It was replaced by the idea that the strong man of the regime was irreplaceable. To provide continuation of the socialist system of governance, the introduction of collective leadership seemed to be necessary. That is exactly what the 1974 Constitution provided for.

As regards the organisation of power, three aspects are of the greatest interest. Firstly, Tito's personal position was regulated. He became President for life. Secondly, the 1974 Constitution resolved the question of Tito's political succession. Thirdly the whole system was laid down on the concepts of parity of constituent units and their consensus in decision making. Article 333 of the 1974 Constitution contained praise of Tito, mentioning his merits, and among those especially the 'achievement of brotherhood and unity'. That was the provision's first section; in the second, the federal representative body was empowered to elect Tito to the office of President 'for an unlimited term of office'. Needless to say that the representative body made use of the provision.

The question of political succession to the President for life had indeed been resolved even before the adoption of the 1974 Constitution. The office of vice President existing in the 1963 Constitution was abolished by one of the constitutional amendments. The model with a presumed successor was replaced by one of collective leadership after Tito. That was canonised in the 1974 Constitution. Its Article 321 provided for Presidency of Yugoslavia. It was composed of one member from each of the constituent units, as well as of the chief of the only exisiting party. The latter was to sit 'by virtue of his office'. The participation of the party chief in the State Presidency did not play a significant role in the course of events to come. This was due to the fact that the situation in the unique party was similar to the one of the state. The ruling party was also crashing into pieces. However, giving the chief of the party a constitutional position was significant. Some of the processes of political developments reached their peak, or at least the institutions became transparent. The strong man of the regime became President for life, and the ruling party found its place in a constitutional provision on the organisation of power.

The parity of constituent units and consensus in the decision-making process were from a constitutional point of view the outstanding features of the 1974 Constitution. Its provisions proclaimed that six federated republics, as well as two autonomous provinces, which were parts of Serbia, were constituent

45 T. Marinković, *Serbia*, 68–69; R. Marković, *Ustavno pravo*, 139–40.

units of Yugoslavia. The autonomous provinces were given prerogatives matching those of the federated republics. At a first glance, this may have seemed to favour Serbia, because of the three votes it had in the decision-making bodies, instead of one. To understand the constitutional provisions, one needs to learn the context and take care of political facts. The governments in the two autonomous provinces were by no means under the impact of the government of Serbia. There were no constitutional instruments to enable the functioning of the Republic of Serbia as a whole. The original system of six started functioning as a system of eight players, although this was never fully admitted. At this point, one should bear in mind the fact that the government system of socialist Yugoslavia had always been illegitimate. Elections were not free, and there was no proper representation of the people. However, the concept of legitimacy overshadowed the foundations of government in Yugoslavia. Politicians striving for power and struggling behind the scenes in an illegitimate way tended to ground their claims on the alleged requirements of certain ethnicities. Thus, for instance, the fall of Ranković was perceived by many as a loss on the side of Serbian interests, despite the fact that he did not have a right to represent anyone because he had never been elected to any office in a democratic manner. At the level of the federated republics, nationalism prevailed in the 1970s. Its most fervent protagonists in some of the republics started requiring transformation of those republics into independent nation-states.

The decision-making mechanism at the level of Yugoslavia was construed in such a way that it could function only in the presence of an informal political arbiter. It is indeed a miracle that the whole constitutional settlement survived for a decade after Tito passed away. The parity system in the composition of the state organs that has been mentioned for the Presidency applied to the federal representative body, which was given the name of the Federal Assembly. It was a two-house body. Its houses were called the Federal Chamber and the Chamber of Republics and Provinces. In the latter, constituent units of Yugoslavia were represented, whereas the former, as provided for by Article 291 of the Constitution, was the representation of 'self-managing organisations and communities and socio-political organisations'. The official doctrine was hostile to the concept of the citizen. The formula 'working people and citizens' was used in the 1974 Constitution text, and remained interpreted exclusively in an ideological way, i.e. without any critical stance, let alone contestation. Lawyers mocked the formula in private by stating that the only citizens in the country were retired persons, since they could not fall within the first element in the formula. Each of the republics had thirty and each of the autonomous provinces had twenty delegates in one chamber, and twelve and eight respectively in the other. The delegates were not directly elected; instead, they were appointed by the representative bodies in the federated republics and autonomous provinces. Direct elections were indeed abolished. A system of indirect elections was introduced under the name of the delegates' system. A delegate was a deputy sent to a body by a delegation, which was itself composed of deputies sent by delegations of an inferior level. In brief, there were multiple indirect elections.[46] An illegitimate political settlement was on bad terms with direct elections. A wide range of works published in the line of thought of the official doctrine praised the delegates' system as the most democratic of all political systems. That whole area of literature can hardly be worthy of attention, although some of the works served the purpose of promotion in university careers in those times. The Presidency composed on the concept of parity was to take decisions by consensus. It led to insurmountable difficulties in an atmosphere of crisis and social decay impregnated by nationalism. The system was not able to face the challenge. Its institutional mechanism could not respond to the situation. With such institutions in place, Yugoslavia was bound to fall apart.[47]

10.3 Dismantling of the Country and Rump-Yugoslavia

The break-up of Yugoslavia came in 1991–92 as a result of the influence of different factors in a set of circumstances marked by the end of the Cold War. At a time when communist rule was over in many European countries, Yugoslavia was already deep in crisis. The form of government in the 1974 Constitution relied on a complicated mechanism. The political leaders were mostly conservative communists, and above all the country was indebted, suffering from economic crisis and remained outside European integration. The prerogatives of government of the federated republics undermined the central government, which was in many ways deprived of the competence to act. Such a distribution of powers fuelled the nationalism of the communist elites in the federated republics. There were two different attitudes as regards Yugoslavia and its identity. On the one hand the Serbs, living almost all over Yugoslavia, feared dissolution of the country, which would put them in a situation of living in several states instead of one. On the other hand, Slovenia and Croatia expressed wishes to secede from Yugoslavia and continue as independent states.

46 T. Marinković, *Serbia*, 68–69; on the delegates' system, cf. R. Marković, *Ustavno pravo*, 140–41.

47 cf. T. Marinković, *Serbia*, 70, with reference to Th. Fleiner and L. Basta-Fleiner.

This was accompanied by political developments in Serbia which materialised in a sort of separation among the communists. Two tendencies showed up, and the point over which they disagreed was the issue of Kosovo. This autonomous province was a part of Serbia with a strong majority of Albanians who represented some 80% of the population in the 1980s. In the other Serbian autonomous province, the ethnic situation was different: Vojvodina had a Serbian majority of 65%. However, the autonomous provinces of Serbia were given a huge amount of autonomy under the 1974 Constitution, so that they almost attained the status of federated republics. The government in Kosovo was controlled by Kosovo Albanians who claimed the status of a federated republic for the territory. This was unacceptable for the Serbs and fuelled their nationalism. Notably, the whole system was illegitimate, and there was no possibility of resolving any problem in a democratic manner, by way of debate and free elections. The social and political crisis was going on within the framework of the existing illegitimate communist regime. In such circumstances, a communist faction prevailed in Serbia, basing its stance on opposing the secessionist republics in the west and the Albanian nationalist provincial government in Kosovo. The leader of that faction was a hardline communist, an *apparatchik* accustomed to the power games in Communist Party committees. His name was Slobodan Milošević (1941–2006). He abandoned the communist ideology at least in form, so as to adopt a nationalist stance, thus creating a hybrid mixture of outdated hardline communism with a new, rather perverted nationalism.

The tensions between the federated republics of Yugoslavia grew, so as to produce an armed conflict. At its very beginning, while the institutions of the 1974 Constitution were still functioning to some extent, the conflict appeared to be between secessionists and the central government. As the institutions of central government, in the absence of consensus, were unable to act, the events turned into an ethnic conflict which concerned the reshaping of frontiers of the republics of former Yugoslavia. It was indeed a tragic fratricide war which led to bloodshed, numerous war crimes and crimes against humanity. The theatre of this warfare comprised parts of Croatia and the whole of Bosnia and Herzegovina.

The international community intervened in many ways, favouring ceasefire, negotiations and protection of minorities. It nevertheless took years before the efforts of the international community became fruitful. The conflict was only over in 1995. It had begun in 1991, with the secession of some of the federated republics. They all seceded in a similar way, by holding referenda on the issue of proclaiming independence. The most complicated case of all was Bosnia and Herzegovina, the only multi-ethnic republic in the Yugoslav federation.

Three constituent ethnic groups inhabiting that federated republic could not agree on holding a referendum to resolve the issue of secession and independence. Eventually, after years of warfare, the international community brokered an agreement that was accepted by all parties involved in the conflict. It provided for a constitution of Bosnia and Herzegovina based on ethnic power sharing. After the secessions of four federated republics, the remaining two, i.e. Montenegro and Serbia, formed a federation which was unofficially labelled as rump-Yugoslavia.[48]

Rump-Yugoslavia, which had the official name of the Federal Republic of Yugoslavia, adopted a constitution in April 1992. The political situations in the two republics remaining in Yugoslavia had traits in common. The traits that stood out among these consisted in the fact that former communist apparatchiks managed to get hold of power. Two leaders, Đukanović in Montenegro and Milošević in Serbia, renamed their respective parties, albeit they both inherited the structure and resources of the former communists. The new names were the Democratic Socialist Party of Montenegro and the Socialist Party of Serbia. The 1992 Constitution was an outcome of the basic agreement of the political elites in Serbia and Montenegro to preserve some form of Yugoslavia. The Constitution provided for a parliamentary form of government in a bicommunal federation. The Federal Assembly was a two-house parliament. In its upper house the two federated republics were equally represented, whereas the lower house was the representation of the people, however with positive discrimination in favour of Montenegro. This was necessary because of the sizes of the two republics and the disproportion in population. Serbia had a territory more than six times larger than Montenegro. In terms of population, Montenegro was considerably smaller, with some 600,000 inhabitants, compared to more than nine million in Serbia. The federal government was accountable to the Federal Assembly. The latter also had the right to elect the President of the Federal Republic. The whole constitutional settlement of 1992 was created in haste, in times of trouble. Its implementation suffered from political tensions in a turbulent atmosphere of conflicts, first caused by the war and later based within the country, because the leaders of the two republics disagreed on many issues.[49]

An important amendment was introduced to the 1992 Constitution, providing for direct presidential election. The amendment was to meet the wish of the strong man of Serbia to move to the Yugoslav level. Milošević became the President of the federation in 1997. However, this particular amendment served

---

48 R. Marković, *Ustavno pravo*, 142–45; D. Popović, *Osnovi*, 150–51.

49 R. Marković, *Ustavno pravo*, 144–48.

as a lever against its initiator. The opposition candidate, Vojislav Koštunica won the presidential election against Milošević in the year 2000. The latter was no longer in power, and was later indicted for war crimes and crimes against humanity. He was arrested, and sent to the International Criminal Tribunal for the former Yugoslavia, with its seat in The Hague for trial. The Milošević era was over in 2000, but the institutions remained the same. A new constitutional settlement was introduced some years later.

The federation of rump-Yugoslavia was reorganised by the Constitutional Charter of the State Union of Serbia and Montenegro, adopted in 2003. Disputes between Montenegrin and Serbian politicians on the political and constitutional settlement of rump-Yugoslavia were put to an end due to the mediation of the European Union in March 2002. In February 2003 the Constitutional Charter was adopted. It fundamentally reorganised rump-Yugoslavia and changed its name into the State Union of Serbia and Montenegro.[50]

The 2003 Constitutional Charter was a relatively short document of sixty-seven articles, most of which covered the organisation of power. It was accompanied by another charter on human and minority rights, passed the same month. The legislative power in the State Union was vested in a one-chamber parliament of 126 representatives, ninety-one from Serbia and thirty-five from Montenegro. The executive power was vested in the Council of Ministers, composed of five ministers. There was also a President of Serbia and Montenegro, appointed by the parliament, who was head of state. The President was indeed a part of collegial government; he presided over the Council of Ministers and could not act alone. A court with jurisdiction over the State Union as a whole was envisaged, with a seat in Podgorica, but it never came to fruition. The 2003 Constitutional Charter was the last stage in the deconstruction of Yugoslavia. It provided the possibility of both constituent parts organising referenda and leaving the Union, which Montenegro did in 2006. At the end of the long Yugoslav episode in its constitutional history, Serbia returned to its original form of nation-state.

50 On the 2003 Constitutional Charter in detail, cf. D. Popović, *Osnovi*, 154–80.

CHAPTER 11

Transition to Democracy: The Two Constitutions of Serbia

11.1 Introduction

Serbia's transition to democracy began in the 1990s, while the country was still a sub-national unit of former Yugoslavia, i.e. one of its federated republics. The process of transition to democracy in Serbia mirrored similar developments in other former communist countries in Europe, but with some specific features of importance. The most striking among these consisted of the fact that former communists remained in power in Serbia, merely altering their party's name. The communists were renamed socialists so as to remain the same, and avoid negotiating political transition with their opponents. The whole class of communist apparatchiks at various levels of government maintained their positions. The economy was not properly transformed into a free market form, and preserved many traces of the previous organisation of economic life. Avoiding economic changes was rendered easier in the presence of the self-management system of former Yugoslavia, which in some aspects imitated free market competition. However, one of the worst features in the Serbian transition to democracy was the embracing of nationalism by the communists in power. The fact that it was to some extent a response to the nationalism in Croatia does not provide an excuse. The two nationalisms nourished each other and used similar techniques of mass manipulation.[1]

The newly introduced nationalism in Serbia was peculiar. It was created and put forward by hardline communists. Their crucial policy line was to stay in power at any cost, and if possible in a form of government that would rely on the authoritarian regime of a one-party state. In the beginning they were openly hostile to liberal democracy and a multi-party political system. The politicians in power accepted the introduction of multi-partism with a heavy heart, and never perceived it as a competitive political system. Their idea was to preserve the levers of power by manipulation, even in the surroundings of a multi-party system. Therefore, and in order to legitimise their rule, the communist hardliners invoked the national interests of the Serbian people,

1 Cf. J. Glover, *Humanity – A Moral History of the 20th Century*, New Haven–London 2012, 129 for the stances of Serbian and Croatian nationalisms.

© BRILL SCHÖNINGH, 2021 | DOI:10.30965/9783657791026_012

understood in their own way, and proclaimed themselves to be protectors of those interests. Such a stance only had the purpose of serving the goal of remaining in power. Perceptions of national interests created in that way were fundamentally catastrophic and had nothing to do with the proper notion of national interest. One should bear in mind that the new nationalism came after decades of mostly informal, but nevertheless effective, suppression of religion and religious rights in former Yugoslavia. When the hardliners in power started tolerating and in some aspects even encouraging religion, it was a surprise. They were atheists whose new stance on the issue had indeed little to do with the Christian Orthodox religion prevailing in Serbia. The hardliners' new attitude and practice mostly consisted of arrogantly displaying national symbols, which, by the way, were not necessarily religious. This was accompanied by the spreading of anti-Western political attitudes in politics which were just remnants of communism, or allowing previously forbidden books to be published, etc. Above all, the essence of the ruling ex-communist hardliners' political opinion was their hostility towards liberal democracy. The new nationalism was designed to obscure the lack of legitimacy of the form of government at the end of the socialist era. The decision makers in Serbia refused to convoke a Constitutional Convention, preferring instead to adopt a new constitution in the one-party assembly of their regime. That was the birthplace of the 1990 Constitution of Serbia.

11.2 The 1990 Constitution

Background

The 1990 Constitution of Serbia was adopted in September that year, following the refusal of the Milošević regime government to organise elections for the Constitutional Convention, required by the opposition, which had meanwhile showed up in the country. After the fall of the Berlin Wall, transformation of communist systems was launched in East and Central Europe, and it was difficult for the ruling communists in Serbia to make an exception. The 1990 Constitution was therefore given a hybrid shape. It introduced modern institutions in a somewhat clumsy way, while nevertheless preserving many remnants of the previous communist form of government. To borrow the expression from Tanasije Marinković, the 1990 Constitution 'was formally embracing the values of liberal-democratic constitutionalism'.[2] Some of the features of the 1990 Constitution, however, brought innovations, as we shall see later in this

2 T. Marinković, *Serbia*, 70.

chapter. Even the organisation of power was modernised, despite the fact that the whole constitutional settlement was tailored to match the strong man in power.

Institutions

The 1990 Constitution provided for a semi-presidential form of government. The legislative power was vested in the one-chamber National Assembly composed of 250 deputies, directly elected in a secret ballot. Their term of office was four years. The first parliamentary elections under this Constitution were held using the system of majority voting and a run-off in the second round. The Socialist Party of Serbia, led by Milošević, won by a large margin, but nevertheless altered the system afterwards, so as to introduce a proportional one. First it applied in nine electoral districts, then in twenty-nine, and the distribution of seats was subject to the D'Hondt system. Some time later, after another reform of electoral legislation, the proportional system took its extreme form. The whole of Serbia became one constituency, and the same mode of distribution of seats applied, as had previously been in use for the electoral districts.[3]

The 1990 Constitution vested executive power in the President of the Republic and the government. The President of the Republic was directly elected by the people for a five-year term of office, as provided by Article 86 of the Constitution. He was vested with a suspensive veto (Article 84), but he was not limited by ministerial countersignature. That crucial institution of a parliamentary form of government did not exist in the 1990 Constitution. On the other hand, the President of the Republic was vested with the power to introduce a state of emergency and govern by issuing decrees during that time (Article 83).

The government was composed of a prime minister, deputy prime minister and ministers (Article 91). They were all accountable to the National Assembly, and the government as a whole had to rely on the confidence of that body. The government was empowered to conduct the policy of the Republic of Serbia (Article 90). In practice it never assumed the role a cabinet usually has in a parliamentary form of government, because the strong man of the regime has never been prime minister under the 1990 Constitution.

The judiciary was not fully subject to constitutional regulation and mostly preserved the organisation it had already had under the previous communist regime, which was desperately in need of reform. However, Article 101 of the 1990 Constitution made a step forward as regards independence of the judiciary. Its provision introduced judges' tenure of office for life, instead of

3 D. Popović, *Osnovi*, 184; T. Marinković, *Serbia*, 112.

the previous Yugoslav regulation in which judges had an eight-year tenure of office. The Constitution provided for the Supreme Court, and also for the Constitutional Court, which was not considered to be a part of the judicial system of the country. The Constitutional Court was given anachronic organisation and procedure. There was no possibility of individual constitutional complaint.

Wording and Language Style

The wording and language style of the 1990 Constitution was a considerable innovation, worthy of remark. It was indeed the language of the Constitution text that made an impression on both the public at large and the legal experts. To understand this issue, a small introduction is necessary. Notably, the quality of language of the constitutional texts had been deteriorating throughout the period of existence of socialist Yugoslavia. At first, the expressions that were in use corresponded with those in comparative law, so that legal provisions were easily understood. In a slow evolution, Yugoslav constitutional texts of the socialist era were becoming less and less comprehensible. This was due to the attempt by the text drafters to differentiate Yugoslavia from other communist regimes, but also to cover up and conceal the real political process of power struggle between communist elites in a form of government which was not based on free elections and therefore lacked legitimacy.

The language of constitutional texts in socialist Yugoslavia was reminiscent of the one used in the late Roman Empire. For instance, the old Roman scribe could not simply write down *Justinian the Emperor*. He had to use a formula instead: *Divus Pius Iustinianus, Victor ac Triumphator, semper Augustus*. Interestingly enough, the situation was similar in former Yugoslav constitutional law. An example can be illustrative in this regard. Article 1 of the 1974 Constitution of Yugoslavia defined the federation of Yugoslavia in the following way: 'The Socialist Federal Republic of Yugoslavia is a federal state having the form of a state community of voluntarily united nations and their Socialist Republics, and of the Socialist Autonomous Provinces of Vojvodina and Kosovo, which are constituent parts of the Socialist Republic of Serbia, based on the power of and self-management by the working class and all working people; it is at the same time a socialist self-management democratic community of working people and citizens and of nations and nationalities having equal rights.'[4]

4 https://www.worldstatesmen.org/Yugoslavia-Constitution 1974. Translated by M. Pavičić, Dr Jur.

Since the provision just quoted was supposed to determine the sovereign, those among readers of this text who have formal training in law are kindly invited to answer a simple question: who was the sovereign in Yugoslavia according to the 1974 Constitution? In brief, the purpose of deterioration of the language was primarily to deprive the texts of clarity and transparency. An illegitimate government tended to put out of sight the real relations of power. That is why the language of constitutional texts reflected bitter controversies, painfully burdened with tensions, in which drafts were debated and provisions formulated. The depths of the power struggle between communist elites in the federated units of Yugoslavia could not be displayed better than in reading constitutional texts. That, however, requires nerves and enormous patience.

In such a situation, the change of language in the 1990 Constitution was really an innovation which made a considerable step forward in the direction of transparency. It suffices to compare the provision just quoted to the text of Article 1 of the 1990 Constitution of Serbia, which read, 'The Republic of Serbia is a democratic state of all citizens living within it, founded upon the freedoms and rights of man and citizen, the rule of law, and social justice.' The whole gloomy atmosphere of the 1974 text simply disappeared in this provision. Credit for the alteration of wording and language goes to Professor Ratko Marković, who drafted the 1990 Constitution. However, Ratko Marković himself pointed to the contribution of a language expert, Professor Mihailo Stevanović, in this regard.[5] The improvement in wording was by no means sufficient to decisively influence the evaluation of the 1990 Constitution from a legal and constitutional standpoint. It contained a good number of deficiencies and weak points. Many of them were evident in the Constitution text itself, while others showed up in the course of its implementation.

Implementation

The implementation of the 1990 Constitution deserves special attention. Some of the evident shortcomings of the Constitution have already been mentioned above. For instance, the allegedly parliamentary form of government lacked countersignature. Another example of this kind was the absence of constitutional complaint, which rendered protection of human rights inefficient, etc. Those were institutions lacking in the 1990 Constitution text. Some other institutions created problems through their presence in the Constitution. Thus Article 55 of the Constitution proclaimed that the social and economic order was 'based on a free market economy with all forms of ownership'. The next

5 R. Marković, 'Ustav Republike Srbije iz 2006 – kritički pogled' [The Constitution of the Republic of Serbia from 2006 – a critical view], *Anali PFB* 2/2006, 40.

provision, Article 56, guaranteed the forms of ownership or property, by way of enumeration. They were 'social, state, private and cooperative property'. The fact that the constitutional provision guaranteed state property renders the provision hard to interpret, because the question will inevitably arise on the purpose of such a guarantee. Was the State supposed to interfere with its own property by way of deprivation, i.e. to expropriate itself? Such absurd provisions existed here and there in the text. Nevertheless, the main problem was the mention of social property in Article 56 of the Constitution.

The notion of social property was a specific construction of Yugoslav socialist law and its self-management system. It lacked legal definition, and could not be properly understood. Essentially, the system of enjoying social property was reminiscent of feudalism to some extent, with different tenures belonging to different levels of government. To provide an example, all possessions of what were called socially owned enterprises were assets in social property. An enterprise was entitled to use its possessions and had a specific entitlement called the 'right to dispose of the assets', so as to participate in the market. Such an enterprise was efficiently supervised at the municipal level of government, because the power holders at that level were competent to interfere with appointing its managerial staff. The same applied to the local branch of the only trade union existing in the country. That type of property provided possibilities for the rise of communist bureaucracy at various levels and represented the solid grounds of their social position. Therefore, maintenance of social ownership (or property) in the Constitution ran counter to the transition to the market economy officially proclaimed by the same act. Apart from this, the whole composition of the 1990 Constitution was old fashioned and followed a scheme developed in the constitutional evolution of Yugoslavia under communism.

Besides these evident deficiencies of the 1990 Constitution, there were others which appeared on the surface in the course of its implementation. Illustrations of these concern several Constitution provisions. For example, by virtue of Article 84 of the Constitution, the President of the Republic was in charge of promulgating an act adopted in the National Assembly. The same provision empowered the President to demand another vote of the same act. The President of the Republic was bound to promulgate the act passed for a second time in the National Assembly. This was a mechanism of suspensive veto. In practice, however, the provision was somewhat twisted. Notably, on some occasions the President in office required another vote, but the National Assembly never put the act to a second vote. This was due to the fact that the majority in the National Assembly was controlled by the presidential political party. If the strong man of the regime, who was the President, changed his mind, the legislators followed his view. To say the least, the system functioned as a presidential one, and the presidential suspensive veto turned into an absolute veto.[6] The transformation of the presidential veto evidenced the authoritarian character of the whole political settlement in Serbia under the 1990 Constitution.

Another example has already been mentioned in this chapter. It concerns the alteration of the electoral law. The 1990 Constitution was designed for elections in constituencies electing one representative each. Article 76 of the Constitution was clear in this respect, providing that 'a representative represents the citizens of the constituency he has been elected in'. When the reformed electoral system created only one constituency in the whole country it was a violation of the spirit of the Constitution, as well as of its Article 76. The fact that the opposition was striving for the introduction of a proportional electoral system does not change a lot. It explains why there was no contestation of the electoral reform, but doesn't make the latter conformant with the Constitution.[7] This example displays the attitude of the ruling party towards the form of government and the Constitution in general. The power holders' fundamental view has always been that the constitution as such was merely a tool and instrument of government. Properly speaking, under the 1990 Constitution there had never been an alteration in power. The alteration did not come until the year 2000, when the opposition leader won a direct presidential election against Milošević, who at that time was the President of rump-Yugoslavia. When the democratic opposition went on to win the parliamentary elections in Serbia later that year, i.e. after Milošević's defeat in the presidential election in rump-Yugoslavia in September, the opposition was perceived by voters as being *almost* in power. Once in power, the former Serbian opposition did not change the 1990 Constitution. This happened only when Montenegro left the bicommunal federation.

11.3 The 2006 Constitution

Background

The 2006 Constitution is in force in Serbia at the moment of writing this book. This Constitution was adopted according to the procedure provided for by the previous 1990 Constitution.[8] It was based on two drafts, one of which was

6 D. Popović, *Osnovi*, 186.

7 ibid. 184.

8 R. Marković, 'Ustav Republike Srbije iz 2006', 150; T. Marinković, *Serbia*, 72.

prepared by the government and the other by the President of the Republic at the time. The prime minister and the President belonged to two factions of the once-unified Democratic party. The two drafts were similar in many aspects and indeed represented different versions of the same set of ideas. It was therefore easy to merge the drafts at an advanced stage and produce a text submitted to the legislators and citizens for debate and approval. Since there are many deficiencies of the Constitution, which are to be discussed later on in this chapter, the author of this book has to confess his participation in the first stage of its drafting. He was one of those who produced the presidential draft, and bears his share of responsibility for its shortcomings.

The reasons for adopting the 2006 Constitution were twofold; at least, that was the opinion expressed by Ratko Marković, the drafter of the previous 1990 Constitution.[9] The first reason for passing a new constitution in 2006, according to Marković, was the wish to remove the political heritage of Slobodan Milošević in Serbia. The second reason was more peculiar, and consisted in the fact that the democrats then in power wanted to preserve Kosovo within the boundaries of Serbia. This needs a short explanation. Notably, after the NATO armed intervention in 1999 against Serbia and Montenegro, forming rump-Yugoslavia at that time, international forces were installed in Kosovo. This was done on the grounds of the 1244 Resolution of the UN Security Council. Serbia lost effective control over its autonomous province, and the status of the latter would be determined by way of negotiations. Serbian authorities feared the possibility of losing the autonomous province for good. That is why a preamble was introduced in the 2006 Constitution.

Ratko Marković was basically right in stating reasons for adopting the Constitution, which is still in force. He disapproved of both, but nevertheless fairly displayed them in his article of 2006, commenting on the new constitution. The first reason, i.e. removing the authoritarian heritage, is quite clear, whereas the second materialised in introducing a preamble to the Constitution. The preamble is relatively short and places the foundations of the Constitution in the state tradition of the Serbian people, as well as in the equality of citizens and ethnic communities in Serbia. This is the substance of the first phrase of the preamble. Its second phrase is longer and states that Kosovo and Metohija, which is the official name of Kosovo in Serbian law, is an integral part of the territory of Serbia. As such, it enjoys substantial autonomy. All authorities of sovereign Serbia are under obligation to protect the autonomous status of the province. This particular text represents the most general stance of Serbia on

9 R. Marković, 'Ustav Republike Srbije iz 2006', 6–7.

what may be labelled as the Kosovo issue, which remains unresolved at the time of writing this book in spring 2020.

Institutions

The 2006 Constitution maintained the semi-presidential form of government of the previous constitution. The legislative power is vested in the National Assembly, which is a one-chamber body composed of 250 members, as provided by Article 100 of the Constitution. The term of office of the members of the National Assembly is four years (Article 102). During the implementation of the 1990 Constitution, after the shift of power to democrats, a problem occurred in respect of the legal status of deputies to the National Assembly. There was a dispute over the issue of whether the mandate to represent voters in the National Assembly belonged to the deputy himself, or to a party or coalition of parties that presented the ticket on which the deputy was elected? The latter possibility originated in the proportional system for parliamentary elections, which has been maintained to date. The Constitutional Court entrenched the issue by ruling in favour of a single deputy being the master of the mandate. The ruling was given on the grounds of the 1990 Constitution.[10] The 2006 Constitution altered the stance on the issue. Its Article 102 provides that a deputy to the National Assembly is entitled to allow the political party that puts him or her on the ticket to dispose of the mandate. In other words, although master of the mandate to sit in the National Assembly, a deputy is entitled to make his party master of his parliamentary seat. This turned out to be important in parliamentary practice, in which party defections are relatively frequent. Notably, the ruling party at the moment of writing this book started as a fraction of another party, while in opposition. The party system in Serbia is still relatively unstable and suffers from corruption. Implementation of electoral legislation creates problems and disputes.[11] It should be reformed, so as to introduce stability into the whole political settlement.

Like the legislative, in 2006 the executive branch of government maintained the form it had under the previous constitution. There are two constitutional factors vested with executive power: the President of the Republic and the government. By virtue of Article 111 of the Constitution, the President of the Republic embodies 'the state unity of the Republic of Serbia'. Article 112 empowers the President *inter alia* to represent the Republic, promulgate laws, appoint the prime minister and Serbian ambassadors, all upon the government's proposal. Article 113 outlines the presidential suspensive veto. The

---

10 D. Popović, *Osnovi*, 184–85.

11 T. Marinković, *Serbia*, 114–20.

President of the Republic is directly elected by the people for a five-year term of office (articles 114 and 116). Article 115 of the 2006 Constitution provides on incompatibility, stating that the 'President of the Republic may not perform any other public office or involve into a professional activity'. Notably, out of three persons holding office under the Constitution currently in force, including the President in office at the moment of writing this book, only one was not in breach of this provision. It was Tomislav Nikolić; the other two remained leaders of their respective political parties, while in office.

According to Article 122 of the 2006 Constitution, the executive power is vested in the government. The government is composed of the prime minister, deputy prime ministers and ministers. By virtue of Article 125 they are all accountable to the National Assembly. The government must enjoy the confidence of the national representative body (articles 130 and 131). The President of the Republic, after consultations with parties represented in parliament, appoints the prime minister, who presents the programme of the government and its composition at the session of the National Assembly. The government acquires office if the majority of all deputies in the National Assembly approve this by a vote (Article 127).

Article 124 of the Constitution provides that the government is accountable before the National Assembly 'for the policy of the Republic of Serbia, for the execution of laws and other acts of the National Assembly, as well as for the activity of state administration'. Marinković seems inclined to interpret this provision in the sense of construing the notion of countersignature, although tacitly, because he does not say that foreign policy falls within the scope of presidential competence. This somehow transpires from his text. Marković for his part resolutely states that foreign policy is within the remit of the government.[12] Neither of the two attitudes appears to be justified. Marković's opinion runs counter to reality. It is the President of the Republic that usually conducts the country's foreign policy. Marinković somehow implies countersignature, which does not exist. The only true conclusion is that the 2006 Constitution did not overcome the weak point of the 1990 Constitution. Both texts lack the notion of countersignature, and the drafters of the Constitution currently in force, including the author of this book, are to blame for such a state of affairs. The lack of countersignature in the Constitution text brings evidence of the remnants of authoritarianism that are still present in Serbia.

Articles 142 to 155 of the 2006 Constitution are devoted to the judiciary. There is a provision on judicial independence (Article 149). As to the appointment of judges, the weak point of the system is the implication of the National

12 T. Marinković, *Serbia*, 132; R. Marković, 'Ustav Republike Srbije iz 2006', 346.

Assembly in the procedure. Article 147 provides that the National Assembly appoints a judge to the office for the first time, on the proposal of the High Judiciary Council. That body is composed of eleven members. Eight of them are elected to sit for five years. Six of these members are judges, and two are renowned lawyers. They are elected by the National Assembly. Three other members of the High Judiciary Council are the chief justice of the highest court in the country, the minister of justice and the chair of the standing committee competent for the judiciary in the National Assembly (Article 153). By virtue of Article 147 of the Constitution, it is the High Judiciary Council that is competent for the appointment of judges, with one exception, which has been mentioned.[13] When entering the judicial corps, a judge is appointed by the National Assembly. His further career is decided by the High Judiciary Council.

Article 143 of the Constitution provides on the court system in Serbia in a general way. It has altered the name of the highest court in the country to the Supreme Court of Cassation. Serbia nevertheless remains among those countries in which the highest court is entitled to decide a case by a judgment on its merits, and not only exercise the so-called cassation power, by merely quashing a decision rendered in the second instance.

Although already planned and drafted under the previous Constitution, it was under the 2006 Constitution that judicial reform took place in Serbia. The whole process was complicated and led to disputes.[14] Its outcome was nevertheless the modernisation of the Serbian judiciary, at least to a certain degree, which is by no means sufficient from the standpoint of the values required by rule of law in a liberal democracy. However, the old communist court system, with more than thirty courts of appeal in a small country, was abandoned. In a three-tier system of courts, there are now five appelate courts of general jurisdiction.

One of the significant improvements of the previous constitutional settlement achieved by the 2006 Constitution concerns the composition and competence of the Constitutional Court. It is composed of fifteen justices whose term of office is nine years. Article 172 of the Constitution provides that five justices are appointed by the National Assembly, five by the President of the Republic and five by the plenary session of the Supreme Court of Cassation. By virtue of the same provision, the National Assembly is entitled to appoint five persons from a list of ten candidates presented by the President of the

13 On judiciary in general, cf. T. Marinković, *Serbia*, 138–40; on the appointment of judges and the High Judiciary Council, R. Marković, 'Ustav Republike Srbije iz 2006', 525–30.

14 T. Marinković, *Serbia*, 141–43.

Republic. In the same way, the President of the Republic is entitled to appoint five persons from a list of ten candidates presented by the National Assembly.[15]

The greatest innovation as regards the Constitutional Court is contained in Article 170 of the 2006 Constitution, which provides for individual constitutional complaint. The Constitutional Court developed its own jurisprudence at the beginning, before becoming submerged by pending cases.[16] This is a problem worthy of attention and calls for a thorough reform which does not concern that body exclusively, but rather the whole legal system of Serbia and its constitutional settlement.

An Overview

If at the end of this chapter one wants to make an overview of the 2006 Constitution, several considerations appear to be necessary. The most important circumstance has already been pointed to. Ratko Marković, the drafter of the 1990 Constitution was right when assessing the 2006 Constitution in general. That Constitution is indeed only a revisited text of the 1990 Constitution.[17] This statement portrays the 2006 Constitution drafters poorly, including the author of this book. However, revisiting a previous text would not have been an enormous failure, had that text been of a high value. Regretfully, that was not the case.

An additional issue for the 2006 Constitution is that it included, via the intermediary of its 1990 role model, some traits and features that render the 2006 Constitution out of date. There are remnants of the old, communist approach to certain issues and institutions, but above all that is true for the structure of the text and its normative technique. One example can be illustrative in this regard. The 2006 Constitution consists of ten sections, the last containing just one provision regulating the entry of the Constitution into force. However, Section IV has only one article (97), which regulates the jurisdiction of the Republic of Serbia. Ratko Marković, in his critical stance, put forward the statement that this particular article was superfluous.[18] This is true, but not for the reasons stated by Marković, which consisted in the fact that Serbia in 2006 was no longer a sub-national unit, but indeed an independent nation-state. To refer to the jurisdiction of either a sub-national unit or a nation-state in the way applied in Article 97 of the 2006 Constitution was to speak in the style of

---

15 ibid. 143–46.

16 T. Marinković, *Serbia*, 146–49. R. Marković 'Ustav Republike Srbije iz 2006', 556–77 merges the text on the Constitutional Court of Serbia with comparative law considerations, and only marginally refers to the Serbian law.

17 R. Marković, 'Ustav Republike Srbije iz 2006', 6.

18 ibid. 11.

the communist constitutions of former Yugoslavia. It is by no means a rule in comparative law, but rather an exception created in times of the authoritarian regime, which the drafters could not get rid of. The problem is more deeply rooted than Marković wished to admit.

Another remnant of the socialist past penetrated the 2006 Constitution, via the intermediate 1990 Constitution. Notably, the old socialist constitutions in former Yugoslavia relied on the Marxist doctrine on property. Private property was not properly protected by the constitutional provisions. An illustrative example can be seen in Article 23 of the 1963 Constitution of Yugoslavia. It provided that the 'right to property' was guaranteed on goods for personal use; however, it also mentioned, *expressis verbis*, that it was apartments and houses that were considered exclusively for personal use. The 1990 Constitution, departing from such ideas, wanted to make a step forward, but only introduced a hybrid system. Its Article 34 proclaimed that the 'right to property' was guaranteed. However, Article 56 guaranteed 'social, state, private and cooperative as well as other types of property'. The problem of proper interpretation of this provision has already been pointed out in this chapter. The 1990 Constitution did not take a liberal standpoint, but mixed it with authoritarianism. This fact becomes evident in the presence of the articles mentioned. Protection of private property was timidly introduced in the 1990 Constitution.[19] In comparison to the articles just mentioned of the 1990 Constitution, the corresponding Article 58 of the 2006 Constitution does not seem to be superior in wording; quite the contrary. Article 58 imitates the approach of the provisions of the 1990 Constitution. The introduction of the language of the European Convention on Human Rights does not bring a substantial change. Article 58 speaks of 'peaceful enjoyment of property', and the expression stems from the Convention for the Protection of Human Rights and Fundamental Freedoms, ratified by Serbia. Article 58 of the 2006 Constitution avoids mentioning private property. It introduces the formula 'property and other property rights' without any definition, let alone precise, of these rights. It regulates the 'right to property' instead of protecting private property, thus remaining in the socialist tradition, without any plausible reason. Authoritarian roots lie deep in our minds. They are not easy to overcome.

---

19 On the deficiencies and remnants of the past in the 2006 Constitution, cf. D. Popović, 'Ustav Republike Srbije od 2006.g. u istorijskoj perspektivi' [The Constitution of the Republic of Serbia from 2006 in a Historical Perspective], in: T. Ilić and M. Božić (eds), *NOMOPHYLAX: Zbornik radova u čast Srđana Šarkića (Collection of Papers in Honour of Srđan Šarkić)*, Belgrade 2020, 603-619.

There is, however, something worse than the deficiencies of the 2006 Constitution, which penetrated its text through the intermediary of the 1990 Constitution. Notably, in some aspects the Constitution text of 2006 made a step back in comparison to the one of 1990. An example of this is the determination of the sovereign in the 2006 Constitution. We have seen above that after decades of painful determinations of sovereign in Yugoslav socialist constitutions, the 1990 Constitution introduced a transparent provision on the issue. Its Article 1 read, 'The Republic of Serbia is a democratic state of all citizens living within it, founded upon the freedoms and rights of man and citizen, the rule of law, and social justice.' The 2006 Constitution altered this stance, and its Article 1 reads: 'The Republic of Serbia is the state of the Serbian people and all citizens living in it, founded on the rule of law and social justice, principles of civic democracy, human and minority rights and freedoms and adherence to European principles and values.' Introducing European values into the text of this provision is welcome, but the whole provision is nevertheless a step back towards the old socialist Yugoslav definitions of federated republics as sub-national units. It was important then, as it appeared to be in 2006 as well, to put forward ethnicity and add all citizens as a kind of decoration. The 2006 Constitution in this particular respect seems retrograde if compared to the 1990 Constitution, which if considered in its entirety was only a hybrid of authoritarinism and liberalism.

To sum up, the 2006 Constitution of Serbia does not properly meet the standards of modern constitutional settlements. It suffers its deeply rooted authoritarian heritage. To be able to understand the phenomenon, one needs to launch oneself into a study of constitutional history.

Concluding Remarks

What is the message, if any, of more than two centuries of constitutional history in Serbia? Constitutional developments were not rectilinear, they had ups and downs. There were noble attempts to modernise the country and conservative forces trying to avoid alterations of the social structure and respective constitutional settlements. However, above all controversies and doubts, and in spite of deviations made here and there, an ideal seems to have been triumphant in the constitutional history of Serbia. That ideal is Europe. It is probably not by chance that Europe was referred to at the beginning of Serbian constitutional developments and again 200 years later in almost the same way and in a comparable context.

It was in 1804 that Dositej Obradović published a poem in Vienna dedicated to Serbia, glorifying 'her brave warriors and sons' at the beginning of the First Serbian Uprising against the Ottoman rule. The poem became well known under the title *Arise Serbia* (*Vostani Serbije*), but in addition to its dedication to warriors and celebrating their efforts it had another leading idea, quite remote from the notions of armed conflicts and warfare. In its first stanza the poet invited Serbia, personifying the country as the mother of her children, to arise so as to let the children see her face. In the third stanza the poet addressed Serbia, the mother of her children, asking her to rise in order to show her delightful face to Europe.

The poet's idea was clear. Serbia should be a nation among nations in Europe, and to achieve that goal she had to reveal her delightful face not only to her children, as a mother usually does, but to the whole of the continent. Notably, in the poet's view Serbia's place was in Europe, but to be able to accede to her place the country stood before the efforts to deserve it, i.e. to improve and be able to compete with other nations in spirit and virtue. Dositej Obradović was aware of the fact that Serbia's homecoming to Europe meant the adoption of many values that featured European civilisation. Accepting those values and attaining virtues was the path to Europe.

Two centuries later, the drafters of the 2006 Constitution of Serbia took almost the same stand in Article 1 of the Constitution. The text reads that the Republic of Serbia is founded *inter alia* on the 'adherence to European principles and values'. An intermittent line of arduous developments stands between these two mentions of Europe and its values, providing a link. On one hand, this proves that Serbia remained faithful to the call of her destiny as well as to the path she chose to follow a long time ago. On the other hand, however, the somewhat programmatic character of Article 1 of the 2006 Constitution

© BRILL SCHÖNINGH, 2021 | DOI:10.30965/9783657791026_013

brings evidence to the fact that Serbia has not achieved this goal so far. Serbia is still on her way towards Europe. There is a determination to adopt European values, but these values have not fully materialised in the everyday life of the citizens. They still strive for virtue, especially in the field of constitutional law, which has been the subject of this study. It is therefore legitimate to raise the possibility, no matter how naive it may sound, of finding some inspiration in history. Is there anything in the treasury we have inherited from our past that we could try to adopt or revive, or at least use as a source of inspiration? The answer of the author of this book to such questions is in the affirmative.

Yes, there are lessons of the past to which we should pay attention. One of these stems from the depths of Serbia's constitutional history and brings us back to the nation's origins. Due to the complicated set of circumstances, the advice which the Serbs received from a learned lawyer in 1805 was neglected, probably because of being misunderstood in the course of turbulent events. The author of the advice passed away young and could not advocate his opinion, explain it and make it acceptable to his fellow countrymen. The author of the advice was Božidar Grujović, and his stance was put forward in the only text he left to posterity by way of an intermediary, since the original document was lost. In his 'A Word on Freedom', Grujović expressed a view which regretfully hasn't found many followers. It concerns the role of Constitution in the very foundation of society. His text read, 'Therefore is the law the overlord and judge in the country. The lords, the masters and the government, the clergy and the military, as well as the people as a whole, must be under the law, notably under the one and the same law.' That 'one and the same law' was for Grujović the Constitution, for he stated later in his text, 'Where there is a good constitution, that is where the law is well established, and the authority is well set up under the law, there is freedom'.

Grujović advocated a concept which has not found a proper echo in the constitutional history of Serbia, except in the words of Vuk Karadžić in 1832. Even that was not an echo in the right sense of the term, because it cannot be established that Vuk Karadžić was directly influenced by Grujović. The concept that Grujović advocated was *constitutional supremacy*. It would take a lot of effort (and maybe another book!) to explain the concept in all its relevant aspects. At this point it seems sufficient to put forward some of its main features. The most important of these is the requirement of conformity of all laws and legal acts of whatever kind with the Constitution. A lawyer may remark on this that such an attitude is widely spread in Serbia and consequently does not pose a problem. The attitude is indeed widely spread, for there is no controversy among lawyers and citizens over the conformity of laws, decrees and all other acts with the Constitution. The problem concerns the materialisation of the stance just expressed. Notably, the constitutional conformity of laws can be carried out only if the Constitution is applied directly, to the letter, by the courts of law. In other words, it is the justiciability of the Constitution that lays the foundations of constitutional supremacy. This is indeed an indispensable trait of constitutional supremacy. The latter does not exist in Serbia at the moment, because there is no direct application of Constitution provisions by the judiciary. The courts in Serbia are reluctant to adopt such a practice, despite the fact that there are no legal impediments for its adoption.

The author of this book is fully aware of the fact that introducing such a system into the constitutional law of Serbia would require a considerable amount of effort in the field of education. This concerns the teaching of law in general, and especially teaching constitutional law. That is why the academic community is in the position to assume the role of vanguard in constitutional developments. The academics and universities should take a bold stand in the further evolution of the constitutional law of Serbia. Others will then be ready to follow. The citizens would certainly be sympathetic to such developments and willing to embrace improvements, bringing more efficient protection of their rights. By seconding such an enterprise, the citizens will fulfil their task of attaining virtue in the constitutional sense of the term. While we are still waiting for developments to come, and expecting the future to be bright, the message of constitutional history remains the same as it used to be at its beginning two centuries ago: *Arise Serbia …* to stand upright in virtue.

A Word on Freedom

The law is the will of the country, which commands to the whole of the country and to everyone to perform good and to prevent evil. Therefore is the law the overlord and judge in the country. The lords, the masters and the government, the clergy and the military, as well as the people as a whole, must be under the law, notably under the one and the same law. The law should reward the good who merit, and punish the evil, disobedient and the lazy in performing their duties. That is why the law must be rational and just.

The law is to the country what the food is to a man, or the drink, air, clothes and home; that is as a man without food and drink must die, in the same way a country without law must collapse, return to slavery, become totally torn apart and perish. However, the law must be as good as the food. Then how are we going to create such a good law, under which the country will be honest and happy, stand bold and solid, and become more glorious and upright through generations to come? That is the first question that we shall answer prudently, for the people's happiness or disaster depends on the answer.

This is what our heart and soul can best teach us. What is it that each and every rational, honourable and honest man is obedient to and to what he remains faithful until his very last hour? Everyone will say, I am obedient to reason and justice. I shall faithfully comply with these until I die even if I were hungry or thirsty, unclothed or barefooted. Each and every man and woman and child says so deep from the bottom of the heart: command me reasonably, and do me justice, and if need be, I shall shed my blood for you. Is there in the world anything nicer, sweeter or more likeable than a convict saying to his judge: thou hast sentenced me reasonably and justly, and I shall willingly sustain thy punishment.

That is why the reason and justice are two halves of welfare. Where there is no reason and justice there is no law.

Let us raise and establish in Serbia these two – reason and justice, and make them bold with all our strength so that each force and power shall be subjugated to them. And let this wise and righteous law be our overlord and commander. Let that law command the masters, the dukes, the council, the clergy, the bishops and everyone, little or great. It will protect us and preserve the freedom and the willingness.

Where there is a good constitution, that is where the law is well established, and the authority is well set up under the law, there is freedom, there is

 | DOI:10.30965/9783657791026_014

willingness. And where one or few command at their own will, and disobeying the law do what pleases them, there the country has perished, there is no freedom, no security, and no well-being. There is only banditism and renegade under a different name.

No one of the people may be empowered to do evil even to the poorest of men, and that is especially the case with the one whom people chose to be judge and commander, that one must not only be forbidden to do evil, but he must under all circumstances do good for otherwise he would by no means merit to be the judge and the chief.

The first duty of the head of the country is to take care that each and everyone be secured for himself, for his life, his children and wife, for his home, estate and dignity. The security of 1) life, 2) estate and 3) dignity is what everyone, including a child that has not been born yet, claims from the commander, and if the head of the country refuses or fails to secure them life, estate and dignity, then he does not merit to be the head of the country anymore.

The second duty of the head of the country is to liberate those who are not free, because in freedom is our life twice as much dearer and sweeter. Freedom is what makes us different from a beast; what a slave is deprived of is what makes him a man. It is better to die than to live in obnoxious slavery.

It is freedom, freedom that makes us men; freedom and willingness provide strength to a soldier and to dukes and commanders the wisdom and fairness. Freedom provides a kind heart to the superiors towards the younger, freedom enlightens the priestendom to raise their hands to bless their free herd. Freedom brings wisdom to the people's council, freedom enriches everyone, be it a shepherd with his herd, a traveller on the road, a soldier in the troops, or a housefather at home, freedom enjoys or consoles him, and renders his life precious. In a free land one works better in the field, more fruitful is the cattle, one eats fine bread and drinks good wine. In one word, where there is no freedom, there is no life.

(translation Dragoljub Popović)

Bibliography

Books and Articles

Anonymous, *Porota*, I–III, September 1881 (review of the book of K. J. Schmidt, *Die Grundlagen der Verwaltuntungspflege im konstitutionell-monarchischen Staate*, Stuttgart 1878).

Antić, A., *Beleške*, Zaječar 2010.

Avramović, D., 'Vladavina prava i pravna država – istost ili različitost', *Zbornik radova Pravnog fakulteta u Novom Sadu* 3/2010.

Avramović, S., 'The Serbian Civil Code of 1844: A Battleground of Legal Traditions', in: Th. Simon (ed.), *Konflikt und Koexistenz, Die Rechtsordnungen Südosteuropas im 19. Und 20. Jahrhundert*, Frankfurt am Main 2017.

Balkovec, B., 'Izborno zakonodavtsvo prve jugoslavenske države (1918–1941)', *Časopis za suvremenu povijest*, 1/2016.

Basta, D., 'Životni put Božidara Grujovića (Teodora Filipovića)', in: J. Trkulja and D. Popović (eds), *Liberalna misao u Srbiji - Prilozi istoriji liberalizma od kraja 18. do sredine 20. veka*, Belgrade 2001.

Bataković, D., 'On Parliamentary Democracy in Serbia 1903–1914: Political Parties, Elections, Political Freedoms', *Balcanica XLVIII* (2017).

Bujuklić, Ž., 'Nation-building and the Emergence of Serbian Legal Studies', in: Th. Simon (ed.), *Konflikt und Koexistenz, Die Rechtsordnungen Südosteuropas im 19. Und 20. Jahrhundert*, Frankfurt am Main 2017.

Constant, B., *Cours de la politique constitutionnelle*, Paris 1861.

Cunibert, B., *Srpski ustanak i prva vladavina Miloša Obrenovića 1804–1850*, Belgrade 1901.

Dimić, Lj., 'Uzroci Velikog rata, Srbija i jugoslovensko ujedinjenje', in: B. Begović-Z. Mirković (eds), *Sto godina od ujedinjenja: stvaranje države i prava*, Belgrade 2020.

Gavrilović, A., *Beogradska Velika škola 1808–1813*, Belgrade 2013.

Gavrilović, M., *Miloš Obrenović, knj. III*, Belgrade 1908.

Gavrilović, M., 'Suspendovanje Sretenjskog ustava', *Iz nove srpske istorije*, Belgrade 1926.

Geršić, G., *Enciklopedija prava*, Belgrade 2012.

Glover, J., *Humanity – A Moral History of the 20th Century*, New Haven–London 2012.

Grol, V., *Pravna misao Milovana Milovanovića*, Belgrade 1989.

Dimitrijević, V., (ed.), *Human Rights in Yugoslavia – Belgrade Centre for Human Rights Report*, Belgrade 1999.

Dippel, H., 'Human Rights - From Societal Rights to Individual Rights', *Universidade de Coimbra, Boletim da Faculdade de Direito*, Vol. LXXXIV (2008).

Dragnich, A., *The Development of Parliamentary Government in Serbia*, New York 1978.

Dragović-Soso, J., *'Saviours of the Nation' – Serbia's Intellectual Opposition and the Revival of Nationalism*, London 2002.

Ivić, P. and J. Kašić, 'O jeziku kod Srba u razdoblju od 1804. do 1878. godine', *Istorija srpskog naroda V-2*, Belgrade 1981.

Janković, D., *Srpska država Prvog ustanka*, Belgrade 1984.

Janković, D. and M. Mirković, *Državnopravna istorija Jugoslavije*, Belgrade 1989.

Janković, D. and M. Mirković, *Državnopravna istorija Jugoslavije*, Belgrade 1997.

Jellinek, G., *Allgemeine Staatslehre*, Berlin 1914.

Jevtić, D. and D. Popović, *Narodna pravna istorija*, Belgrade 2012.

Jovanović, A., 'Rad na "Toržestvenim zakonima" II, Doterivanje prevoda', *Arhiv za pravne i društvene nauke*, XI/1/1911.

Jovanović, S., *Ustavno pravo*, Belgrade 1907.

Jovanović, S., *O državi – osnovi jedne pravne teorije*, Belgrade 1922.

Jovanović, S., *Vlada Milana Obrenovića, knjiga druga 1878–1889*, Belgrade 1927.

Jovanović, S., *Vlada Aleksandra Obrenovića, knjiga prva*, Belgrade 1929.

Jovanović, S., *Vlada Aleksandra Obrenovića, druga knjiga*, Belgrade 1931.

Jovanović, S., *Ustavobranitelji i njihova vlada, Sabrana dela, tom 3*, Belgrade 1990.

Jovanović, S., *Druga vlada Miloša i Mihaila, Sabrana dela 3*, Belgrade 1990.

Jovanović, S., *Ustavno pravo Kraljevine Srba, Hrvata i Slovenaca*, Belgrade 1995.

Jovičić, M. (ed.), *Ustavi Kneževine i Kraljevine Srbije 1835-1903*, Belgrade 1988.

Kandić, Lj., 'Ustav of 1838. godine –"Turski ustav"', in: M. Jovičić (ed.), *Ustavi Kneževine i Kraljevine Srbije 1835-1903*, Belgrade 1988.

Karadžić, V. S., *Istorijski spisi*, Belgrade 1985.

Karadžić, V. S., *Srpske narodne pjesme IV*, Belgrade 1985.

Kelly, J. M., *A Short History of Western Legal Theory*, Oxford 1999.

Kleynheyer, G. and J. Schröder, *Deutsche Juristen aus fünf Jahrhunderten*, Heidelberg 1989.

Konstantinović, M., *Politika sporazuma – dnevničke beleške 1939–1941; londonske beleške 1944–1945*, Novi Sad 1998.

Krkljuš, Lj. 'Proekt Ustava za Vojvodovinu Srbsku Stefana Radičevića', in: SANU, *Ustavni razvitak Srbije u XIX i početkom XX veka*, Belgrade 1990.

Lešjanin, M., *Državna služba i državne sluge*, Beč 1859.

Lukić, R., 'Jovan Sterija Popović – professor prirodnog prava na Liceju', *Anali Pravnog fakulteta u Beogradu*, V/1957.

Ljušić, R., *Kneževina Srbija (1830–1839)*, Belgrade 1986.

Ljušić, R., *Orijentalni novinar, evropski političar – Dimitrije Davidović (1789–1838)*, Belgrade 2006.

Malešević, S., 'Ethnicity and Federalism in Communist Yugoslavia and its Successor States', in: Y. Ghai (ed.), *Autonomy and Ethnicity*, Cambridge 2000.

Marinković, T., 'Serbia', in: *International Encyclopedia of Laws: Constitutional Law*, Alphen aan den Rijn 2019.

Marinković, T., 'Ustavni identitet vidovdanske Jugoslavije', in: B. Begović and Z. Mirković, *Sto godina*, Belgrade 2020.

Marković, B. S., *Dimitrije Matić – lik jednog pravnika*, Belgrade 1977.

Marković, B. S., 'Foreword', in D. Matić, *Načela umnog državnog prava, Kratki pregled istorijskog razvitka načela prava, morala i države od najstarijih vremena do naših dana*, Belgrade 1995.

Marković, M., *Pravna država*, Belgrade 1939.

Marković, R., 'Ustav Republike Srbije iz 2006 – kritički pogled', *Anali PFB* 2/2006.

Marković, R., *Ustavno pravo*, Belgrade 2020.

Marković, S., 'Patterns of National Identity Development among the Balkan Orthodox Christians during the Nineteenth Century', *Balcanica* XLIV (2013).

Matić, D., *Načela umnog državnog prava, Kratki pregled istorijskog razvitka načela prava, morala i države od najstarijih vremena do naših dana*, Belgrade 1995.

Matić, D., *Javno pravo Knjažestva Srbije*, Belgrade 1851.

Matić, D., *Đački dnevnik* (1845–1848), Belgrade 1974.

Menger, C. F., *Deutsche Verfassungsgeschichte der Neuzeit, 7. Auflage*, Heidelberg 1990.

Milićević, M. Đ., *Pomenik*, Belgrade 1888.

Milićević, M. Đ., *Pomenik znamenitih ljudi u srpskom narodu*, Belgrade 1959.

Milosavljević, B., 'Dimitrije Matić. Navodni prelaz s hegelovstva na naturalizam', *Theoria* 1 (2015).

Milovanović, M., *Državno pravo i Načela spoljne politike*, Belgrade 1997, Radoslav and Dubravka Stojanović, editors.

Milovanović, M. Đ., *Državno pravo i druge ustavnopravne studije*, Belgrade 1997, Ratko Marković, editor.

Mirković, M., 'Ustav od 1903. godine' in: M. Jovičić (ed.), *Ustavi Kneževine i Kraljevine Srbije 1835–1903*, Belgrade 1988.

Mirković, Z., 'Die Anfänge des Rechtsstudiums im Serbien der Neuzeit und die Juristenausbildung in der Habsburger Monarchie (Ein Beispiel des Rechtstransfers)', *Annals FLB, Belgrade Law Review LVIII*, 3/2010.

Mirković, Z., *Srpska pravna istorija*, Belgrade 2017.

Mrđenović, D., *Ustavi i vlade*, Belgrade 1988.

Naumović, S., 'Ustaj seljo, ustaj rode: Simbolika seljaštva i politička komunikacija u novijoj istoriji Srbije', *Godišnjak za društvenu istoriju* II/1 1995.

Nenadović, J., 'O zadatku države', *Pravnik* 3 (1893).

Nenadović, M., *Memoari*, Novi Sad–Belgrade 1969.

Nikolić, D., 'Prvi pokušaj izrade građanskih zakona u Srbiji', *Zbornik radova Pravnog fakulteta u Nišu*, Niš 1981.

Nikolić, D., 'The 1860 Criminal Code of the Principality of Serbia', in: Th. Simon (ed.), *Konflikt und Koexistenz, Die Rechtsordnungen Südosteuropas im 19. Und 20. Jahrhundert*, Frankfurt am Main 2017.

Novaković, S., *Beseda*, Belgrade 1882.

Novaković, S., 'Srbija u 1834 – pisma grofa Boa-le-Konta De Rinji, ministru inostranih dela u Parizu o tadašnjem stanju u Srbiji', *Spomenik SKA* XXIV, Belgrade 1894.

Novaković, S., *Ustavno pitanje i zakoni Karađorđeva vremena*, Belgrade 1907,

Novine Srbske 1834–1835.

Obradović, D., *Izabrani spisi*, Novi Sad–Belgrade 1969.

Obradović, D., *Izabrana dela*, Belgrade 2005.

Obradović, D., *Etika*, Belgrade 2007.

Panić-Surep, M., *Filip Višnjić – život i delo*, Belgrade 1967.

Pavić, M., *Rađanje nove srpske književnosti*, Belgrade 1983.

Pavlović, M., *Preobraženski ustav – prvi srpski ustav*, Kragujevac 1997.

Pavlović, M., *Srpska pravna istorija*, Kragujevac 2005.

Pavlović, M., *Pravna evropeizacija Srbije*, Kragujevac 2008.

Popović, D., 'Dva oprečna shvatanja o vladavini prava u obnovljenoj Srbiji', in: V. Vasilijević (ed.), *Pravna država*, Belgrade 1991.

Popović, D., 'Begriff des Rechtsstaates nach den Auffassungen der Serbischen Rechtsprofessoren im XIX. Jahrhundert', *Rechtstheorie* 24 (1993).

Popović, D., *Prapočetak srpskoga parlamentarizma – klice i preuranjen plod*, Belgrade 1996.

Popović, D., 'Strani uticaji na našu udžbeničku književnost ustavnoga prava (Matić i Milovanović)', in: K. Čavoški (ed.), *Ustavnost i vladavina prava*, Belgrade 2000.

Popović, D., 'Dimitrije Davidović – od narodne k pojedinačnoj slobodi', in: J. Trkulja and D. Popović (eds), *Liberalna misao u Srbiji – prilozi istoriji liberalizma od kraja XVIII do sredine XX veka*, Belgrade 2001.

Popović, D., 'Le fédéralisme de l'ancienne Yougoslavie revisité; Qu'est-ce qui n'a pas fonctionné?' *Revue internationale de politique comparée* 10/2003.

Popović, D., *Osnovi ustavnog prava*, Belgrade 2004.

Popović, D., *Uvod u uporedno pravo*, Belgrade 2005.

Popović, D., *Misao o pravu u delima srpskih pisaca*, Belgrade 2011.

Popović, D., 'Les droits fondamentaux dans les deux premières constitutions serbes (1835 et 1838)', *Etudes balkaniques*, 19–20/2013–14.

Popović, D., 'The Dawn of Human Rights in Serbian Legal Thought', in: Th. Simon (ed.), *Konflikt und Koexistenz* (2017).

Popović, D., *Comparative Government*, Cheltenham, UK–Northampton MA, USA, 2019.

Popović, D., 'Arduous Path to Constitutionalism – Serbian constitutional developments in the first half of the nineteenth century', *Pravni zapisi* (The Union University of Belgrade Law Review), 1/2019.

Popović, D., 'Ustav Republike Srbije od 2006.g. u istorijskoj perspektivi', in: T. Ilić and M. Božić (eds), *NOMOPHYLAX: Collection of Papers in Honour of Srđan Šarkić*, Belgrade 2020.

Popović, J. S., *Prirodno pravo* (cf. M. Stojanov (ed.)).

Popović-Obradović, O., *The Parliamentary System in Serbia 1903-1914*, Belgrade 2013 (translated by B. Magaš).

Prodanović, J., *Ustavni razvitak i ustavne borbe u Srbiji*, Belgrade 1936.

Radičević, S., *Proekt ustava za Vojvodovinu Srbsku sa državoslovnim primetbama*, Zemun 1849.

Radović, R., 'Prirodnopravna teorija monarhiskog apsolutizma u političkoj filosofiji vojvođanskih Srba', *Arhiv za pravne i društvene nauke* 5/1939.

Ranke, L., *Die Serbische Revolution*, Hamburg 1829.

Ranke, L., *Srpska revolucija*, Belgrade 1991.

Savić, S., *Počeci teorije i filozofije prava u Srba*, Banja Luka 1998.

Simon, Th. (ed.), *Konflikt und Koexistenz. Die Rechtsordnungen Südosteuropas im 19. und 20. Jahrhundert, Band II*, Frankfurt am Main 2017.

Skerlić, J., 'Dositej Obradović' in: D. Obradović, *Izabrana dela*, Belgrade 2005.

Stefanovski, M., *Postanak Namesničkog ustava*, Belgrade 2016.

Stefanovski, M., *Srednjovekovna shvatanja uzorne vladavine*, Belgrade 2018.

Stojančević, V., 'Srpski narod pred prvi ustanak', *Istorija srpskog naroda V – 1*, Belgrade 1981.

Stojanov, M. (ed.), *Prirodno pravo Jovana Sterije Popovića*, Novi Sad 1995.

Stokes, G., *Politics as Development – The Emergence of Political Parties in Nineteenth-Century Serbia*, Durham and London 1990.

Szabadfalvi, J., 'Natural Law Tradition in Hungary from the End of the Middle Ages to 19th Century', http://L'ircocervo.it/ 1/2011.

Šarkić, S., 'The Beginning of Serbian Constitutionality', in: Th. Simon (ed.), *Konflikt und Koexistenz. Die Rechtsordnungen Südosteuropas im 19. und 20. Jahrhundert, Band II*, Frankfurt am Main 2017.

Thireau, J.-L., *Introduction historique au droit*, Paris 2009.

Ubicini, A., *Constitution de la Principauté de Serbie*, Paris 1871.

Veljković, V., *Odnos sudske i administrativne vlasti u državi*, Belgrade 1896.

Vračar, S., 'Prethodni pogled na ustavnopravni sistem Slobodana Jovanovića', Foreword to S. Jovanović, *Ustavno pravo Kraljevine Srba, Hrvata i Slovenaca*, Belgrade 1995.

Zdravković, M., 'Formiranje države bez konsenzusa', in: B. Begović and Z. Mirković, *Sto godina* ... Belgrade 2020.

Živanović, Ž., *Politička istorija Srbije u drugoj polovini devetnaestog veka, knjiga prva*, Belgrade 1923.

Personal Names Index